THE BUDGET DOCUMENTS

Budget of the United States Government, Fiscal Year 2017 contains the Budget Message of the President, information on the President's priorities, and summary tables.

Analytical Perspectives, Budget of the United States Government, Fiscal Year 2017 contains analyses that are designed to highlight specified subject areas or provide other significant presentations of budget data that place the budget in perspective. This volume includes economic and accounting analyses; information on Federal receipts and collections; analyses of Federal spending; information on Federal borrowing and debt; baseline or current services estimates; and other technical presentations.

The *Analytical Perspectives* volume also has supplemental materials that are available on the internet at *www.budget.gov/budget/Analytical_Perspectives* and on the Budget CD-ROM. These supplemental materials include tables showing the budget by agency and account and by function, subfunction, and program.

Appendix, Budget of the United States Government, Fiscal Year 2017 contains detailed information on the various appropriations and funds that constitute the budget and is designed primarily for the use of the Appropriations Committees. The *Appendix* contains more detailed financial information on individual programs and appropriation accounts than any of the other budget documents. It includes for each agency: the proposed text of appropriations language; budget schedules for each account; legislative proposals; narrative explanations of each budget account; and proposed general provisions applicable to the appropriations of entire agencies or group of agencies. Information is also provided on certain activities whose transactions are not part of the budget totals.

ELECTRONIC SOURCES OF BUDGET INFORMATION

The information contained in these documents is available in electronic format from the following sources:

Internet. All budget documents, including documents that are released at a future date, spreadsheets of many of the budget tables, and a public use budget database are available for downloading in several formats from the internet at *www.budget.gov/budget*. Links to documents and materials from budgets of prior years are also provided.

Budget CD-ROM. The CD-ROM contains all of the printed budget documents in fully indexed PDF format along with the software required for viewing the documents.

The Internet and CD-ROM also include many of the budget tables in spreadsheet format, and supplemental materials that are part of the *Analytical Perspectives* volume. It also includes *Historical Tables* that provide data on budget receipts, outlays, surpluses or deficits, Federal debt, and Federal employment over an extended time period, generally from 1940 or earlier to 2017 or 2021.

For more information on access to electronic versions of the budget documents (except CD-ROMs), call (202) 512-1530 in the D.C. area or toll-free (888) 293-6498. To purchase the Budget CD-ROM or printed documents call (202) 512-1800.

I0447350

GENERAL NOTES

1. All years referenced for budget data are fiscal years unless otherwise noted. All years referenced for economic data are calendar years unless otherwise noted.

2. Detail in this document may not add to the totals due to rounding.

U.S. GOVERNMENT PRINTING OFFICE, WASHINGTON 2016

For sale by the Superintendent of Documents, U.S. Government Publishing Office
Internet: bookstore.gpo.gov   Phone: toll free (866) 512-1800;   DC area (202) 512-1800
Fax: (202) 512-2104 Mail: Stop IDCC, Washington, DC 20402-0001

Table of Contents

On the cover:
Denali National Park
Photo by Jacob Frank, National Park Service
Photograph has been reformatted from full color to monochrome

THE BUDGET MESSAGE OF THE PRESIDENT

To the Congress of the United States:

As I look back on the past seven years, I am inspired by America's progress—and I am more determined than ever to keep our country moving forward. When I took office, our Nation was in the midst of the worst recession since the Great Depression. The economy was shedding 800,000 jobs a month. The auto industry was on the brink of collapse and our manufacturing sector was in decline. Many families were struggling to pay their bills and make ends meet. Millions more saw their savings evaporate, even as retirement neared.

But thanks to the grit and determination of the American people, we rescued our economy from the depths of the recession, revitalized our auto industry, and laid down new rules to safeguard our economy from recklessness on Wall Street. We made the largest investment in clean energy in our history, and made health care reform a reality. And today, our economy is the strongest, most durable on Earth.

Our businesses have created more than 14 million jobs over 70 months, the longest streak of job growth on record. We have cut our unemployment rate in half. Our manufacturing sector has added nearly 900,000 jobs in the last six years—and our auto industry just had its best year of sales ever. We are less reliant on foreign oil than at any point in the previous four decades. Nearly 18 million people have gained health coverage under the Affordable Care Act (ACA), cutting the uninsured rate to a record low. Our children are graduating from high school at the highest rate ever. And we managed to accomplish all of this while dramatically cutting our deficits by almost three-quarters and setting our Nation on a more sustainable fiscal path. Together, we have brought America back.

Yet while it is important to take stock of our progress, this Budget is not about looking back at the road we have traveled. It is about looking forward. It is about making sure our economy works for everybody, not just those at the top. It is about choosing investments that not only make us stronger today, but also reflect the kind of country we aspire to be—the kind of country we want to pass on to our children and grandchildren. It is about answering the big questions that will define America and the world in the 21st Century.

My Budget makes critical investments while adhering to the bipartisan budget agreement I signed into law last fall, and it lifts sequestration in future years so that we continue to invest in our economic future and our national security. It also drives down deficits and maintains our fiscal progress through smart savings from health care, immigration, and tax reforms. And, it focuses on meeting our greatest challenges not only for the year ahead, but for decades to come.

First, by accelerating the pace of American innovation, we can create jobs and build the economy of the future while tackling our greatest challenges, including addressing climate change and finding new treatments—and cures—for devastating diseases.

1

The challenge of climate change will define the contours of this century more dramatically than any other. Last year was the hottest on record, surpassing the record set just a year before. Climate change is already causing damage, including longer, more severe droughts and dangerous floods, disruptions to our food and water supply, and threats to our health, our economy, and our security.

We have made great strides to foster a robust clean energy industry and move our economy away from energy sources that fuel climate change. In communities across the Nation, wind power is now cheaper than dirtier, conventional power, and solar power is saving Americans tens of millions of dollars a year on their energy bills. The solar industry employs more workers than the coal industry—in jobs that pay better than average.

Despite these advances, we can and must do more. Rather than shrinking from the challenge, America must foster the spirit of innovation to create jobs, build a climate-smart economy of the future, and protect the only planet we have. To speed our transition to an affordable, reliable, clean energy system, my Budget funds Mission Innovation, our landmark commitment to double clean energy research and development funding. It also calls for a 21st Century Clean Transportation initiative that would help to put hundreds of thousands of Americans to work modernizing our infrastructure to ease congestion and make it easier for businesses to bring goods to market through new technologies such as autonomous vehicles and high-speed rail, funded through a fee paid by oil companies. It proposes to modernize our business tax system to promote innovation and job creation. It invests in strategies to make our communities more resilient to floods, wildfires, and other effects of climate change. And, it protects and modernizes our water supply and preserves our natural landscapes. These investments, coupled with those in other cutting-edge technology sectors ranging from manufacturing to space exploration, will drive new jobs, new industries, and a new understanding of the world around us.

Just as a commitment to innovation can accelerate our efforts to protect our planet and create a sustainable economy, it can also drive critical medical breakthroughs. The Budget supports a new "moonshot" to finally cure cancer, an effort that will be led by the Vice President and will channel resources, technology, and our collective knowledge to save lives and end this deadly disease. It also supports the Precision Medicine Initiative to accelerate the development of customized treatments that take into account a patient's genes, environment, and lifestyle, as well as the BRAIN Initiative, which will dramatically increase our understanding of how the brain works.

Second, we must work to deliver a fair shot at opportunity for all, both because this reflects American values and because, in the 21st Century global economy, our competitiveness depends on tapping the full potential of every American. Even as we have rebounded from the worst economic crisis of our lifetimes, too many families struggle to reach the middle class and stay there, and too many kids face obstacles on the path to success.

Real opportunity begins with education. My Budget supports the ambitious goal that all children should have access to high-quality preschool, including kids from low-income families who too often enter kindergarten already behind. It also supports States and cities as they implement a new education law that will place all students on a path to graduate prepared for college and successful careers. The bipartisan Every Student Succeeds Act sets high standards for our schools and students, ensures that States are held accountable for the success of all students, including those in the lowest performing schools, spurs innovation in education, helps schools recruit and support great teachers, and encourages States to reduce unnecessary testing. And because jobs in science, technology, engineering, and mathematics are projected to grow faster than other jobs in the years ahead, the Budget makes critical investments in math and science. Through a new Computer Science for All initiative, the Budget will expand the teaching and learning of these important concepts across America's schools, better preparing our Nation's students for today's innovation economy.

Higher education is the clearest path to the middle class. By 2020, two-thirds of jobs will require some education beyond high school. For our students and for our economy, we must make a quality college education affordable for every American. To support that goal, the Budget strengthens Pell Grants to help families pay for college by increasing the scholarships available to students who take enough courses to stay on track for on-time graduation, allowing students making progress toward their degrees to get support for summer classes, and providing scholarships to help incarcerated Americans turn their lives around, get jobs, and support their families. It also offers two years of free community college to every responsible student and strengthens the American Opportunity Tax Credit.

In addition to preparing students for careers, we must help workers gain the skills they need to fill jobs in growing industries. My Budget builds on the progress we have made to improve the Nation's job training programs through implementation of the bipartisan Workforce Innovation and Opportunity Act. It funds innovative strategies to train more workers and young people for 21st Century jobs. And it doubles down on apprenticeships—a proven pathway to the middle class—and supports a robust set of protections for the health, safety, wages, working conditions, and retirement security of working Americans.

Even as we invest in better skills and education for our workforce, we must respond to dramatic changes in our economy and our workforce: more automation; increased global competition; corporations less rooted in their communities; frequent job changes throughout a worker's career; and a growing gap between the wealthiest and everyone else. These trends squeeze workers, even when they have jobs, even when the economy is growing. They make it harder to start a career, a family, a business, or retirement.

To address these changes and give Americans more economic security, we need to update several key benefit structures to make sure that workers can balance work and family, save for retirement, and get back on their feet if they lose a job. The Budget supports these priorities by funding high-quality child care, encouraging State paid leave policies, extending employer-based retirement plans to part-time workers, putting us on a path to more portable benefit models, and providing a new tax credit for two-earner families. It also modernizes the unemployment insurance system, so that more unemployed workers receive the unemployment benefits they need and an opportunity to retrain for their next job. And, if that new job does not pay as much initially, it offers a system of wage insurance to encourage workers to rejoin the workforce and help them pay their bills. The Budget includes tax cuts for middle-class and working families that will make paychecks go further in meeting the costs of child care, education, and saving for retirement. It builds upon the demonstrated success of the Earned Income Tax Credit by expanding it for workers without children and non-custodial parents.

Providing opportunity to all Americans means tackling poverty. Too many Americans live in communities with under-performing schools and few jobs. We know from groundbreaking new research that growing up in these communities can put lifelong limits on a child's opportunities. Over the past few years, we have made progress in supporting families that were falling behind. For example, working family tax credits keep more than 9 million people—including 5 million children—out of poverty each year, and the ACA provides access to quality, affordable health care to millions. Nevertheless, we need to do more to ensure that a child's zip code does not determine his or her destiny. Improving the opportunity and economic security of poor children and families is both a moral and an economic imperative.

The Budget funds innovative strategies to support this goal, including helping families move to safer neighborhoods with better schools and more jobs, revitalizing distressed communities to create more neighborhoods of opportunity, preventing families experiencing a financial crisis from becoming homeless, and ensuring that children have enough to eat when school is out for the summer. It also supports efforts to break the cycle of poverty and incarceration through criminal justice reform.

Finally, as we work to build a brighter future at home, we must also strengthen our national security and global leadership. The United States of America is the most powerful nation on Earth, blessed with the finest fighting force in the history of the world.

Still, this is a dangerous time. We face many threats, including the threat of terrorist attacks and violent extremism in many forms. My highest priority is keeping the American people safe and going after terrorist networks. That is why my Budget increases support for our comprehensive strategy to destroy the Islamic State of Iraq and the Levant (ISIL), in partnership with more than 60 other countries, by eliminating its leadership, cutting off its financing, disrupting its plots, stopping the flow of terrorist fighters, and stamping out its vicious ideology. If the Congress is serious about winning this war and wants to send a message to the troops and the world, it should specifically authorize the use of military force against ISIL.

The Budget also sustains and builds the strength of our unmatched military forces, making the investments and reforms that will maintain our Nation's superiority and ensure our advantage over any potential adversary. It also makes investments to ensure that our men and women in uniform, who sacrifice so much to defend our Nation and keep us safe, get the support they have earned to succeed and thrive when they return home.

Cybersecurity is one of our most important national security challenges. As our economy becomes increasingly digital, more sensitive information is vulnerable to malicious cyber activity. This challenge requires bold, aggressive action. My Budget significantly increases our investment in cybersecurity through a Cybersecurity National Action Plan. This Plan includes retiring outdated Federal information technology (IT) systems that were designed in a different age and increasingly are vulnerable to attack, reforming the way that the Federal Government manages and responds to cyber threats, and recruiting the best cyber talent. It will also help strengthen cybersecurity in the private sector and the digital ecosystem as a whole, enhancing cyber education and making sure companies and consumers have the tools they need to protect themselves. But many of our challenges in cybersecurity require bold, long-term commitments to change the way we operate in an increasingly digital world. That is why, to complement these steps, I am also creating a commission of experts to make recommendations for enhancing cybersecurity awareness and protections inside and outside of Government, protecting privacy, and empowering Americans to take better control of their digital security.

To ensure security at home, we must also demonstrate leadership around the world. Strong leadership means not only a wise application of military power, but also rallying other nations behind causes that are right. It means viewing our diplomacy and development efforts around the world as an essential instrument of our national security strategy, and mobilizing the private sector and other donors alongside our foreign assistance to help achieve our global development and climate priorities. The Budget supports this vision with funding for effective global health programs to fight HIV/AIDS, malaria, and other illnesses; assistance for displaced persons and refugees, including from Syria; and expanding educational opportunities for girls, among many other critical development initiatives.

As we make these investments to meet our greatest challenges, we are also working to build a 21st Century Government that delivers for the American people. The Budget supports efforts to make the Federal Government more efficient and effective, through smarter IT delivery and procurement, improving digital services, eliminating outdated regulations, and recruiting and retaining the best talent. It also invests in a new approach to working in local communities, one that disrupts an outdated, top-down approach, and makes our efforts more responsive to the ideas and concerns of local citizens. The Budget supports the use of data and evidence to drive policymaking, so the Federal Government can do more of what works and stop doing what does not.

The Budget is a roadmap to a future that embodies America's values and aspirations: a future of opportunity and security for all of our families; a rising standard of living; and a sustainable, peaceful planet for our kids. This future is within our reach. But just as it took the collective efforts of the American people to rise from the recession and rebuild an even stronger economy, so will it take all of us working together to meet the challenges that lie ahead.

It will not be easy. But I have never been more optimistic about America's future than I am today. Over the past seven years, I have seen the strength, resilience, and commitment of the American people. I know that when we are united in the face of challenges, our Nation emerges stronger and better than before. I know that when we work together, there are no limits to what we can achieve. Together, we will move forward to innovate, to expand opportunity and security, and to make our Nation safer and stronger than ever before.

BARACK OBAMA

THE WHITE HOUSE,
    FEBRUARY 9, 2016.

BUILDING ON OUR ECONOMIC AND FISCAL PROGRESS

A Record of Job Growth and Economic Expansion

When the President took office in January 2009, he faced an economy shrinking at its fastest rate in over 50 years. Nearly 800,000 Americans lost their jobs in that month alone. The President and the entire Administration acted quickly to jumpstart the economy and create jobs through the Recovery Act; rescue the auto industry from near collapse; fight for passage of the Affordable Care Act (ACA) to provide quality, affordable insurance coverage to millions of Americans and help slow the growth of health care costs; and secure the Dodd-Frank Wall Street Reform and Consumer Protection Act to help prevent future financial crises.

Under the President's leadership, the U.S. economy has become an engine of job growth and economic expansion, outpacing other advanced economies in recovery from the Great Recession. In 2015, the U.S. economy achieved a number of significant milestones. American businesses extended their record streak of consecutive months of job growth, adding more than 14 million new jobs over the past 70 months. The two-year period ending December 2015 marked the strongest two years of job creation since 2000. Significantly, all of the net employment gains since early 2010 have been in full-time positions.

Since October 2009, the unemployment rate has been cut in half, declining 0.6 percentage points in 2015 and falling below its pre-recession average. Unemployment has fallen five percentage points since its peak in early 2010, much faster than forecasted. Long-term unemployment has fallen by 70 percent from its peak,

More than 14 Million Jobs Added Over the Past 70 Months

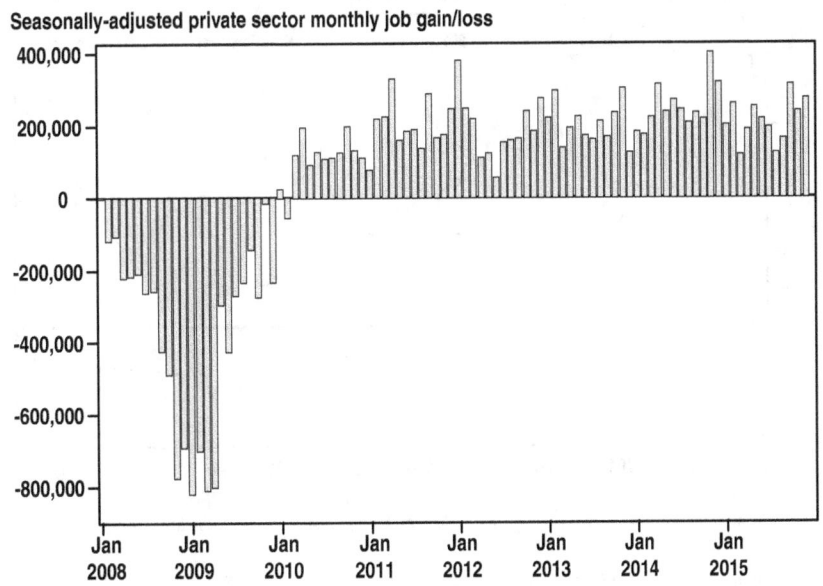

Seasonally-adjusted private sector monthly job gain/loss

Source: Bureau of Labor Statistics

declining at a faster rate than overall unemployment and reaching its lowest rate since 2008. While there is more work to do to boost wages as the economy continues to grow, there are encouraging signs that earnings are on the rise.

The manufacturing sector has made major gains over the course of the economic recovery. Since February 2010, the economy has added 878,000 new manufacturing jobs—the first sustained job growth in the sector since the 1990s.

The economy is not only recovering, it is evolving. The President has made the largest investments in clean energy in American history, and America is less reliant on foreign oil than at any point in the previous four decades. Wind production now provides clean electricity to power 17 million homes and supports tens of thousands of jobs across the Nation. Solar electricity generation has increased thirty-fold since 2008, and the solar industry is creating jobs 12 times faster than the rest of the economy.

American families are benefiting from a growing economy. Rising home prices have restored more than $6 trillion in home equity, while the number of seriously delinquent mortgages has reached an eight-year low. Under the Affordable Care Act (ACA), health care prices have risen at the slowest pace in 50 years, while the rate of uninsured Americans has dropped to the lowest level on record. In addition, the strong job market and safety net enhancements have made a dent in poverty. While child poverty remains too high, Census data show the past two years have seen the fastest decline in child poverty since 2000.

The United States right now has the strongest, most durable economy in the world. The determination and resilience of the American people, coupled with the President's decisive actions during the financial crisis, brought the economy back from the brink.

Reflecting on Our Fiscal Progress

Even as the Administration made critical investments to jumpstart the economy, it also succeeded in putting the Nation on a sound fiscal path. Since 2009, under the President's leadership, Federal deficits have fallen by nearly three-quarters—the most rapid sustained deficit

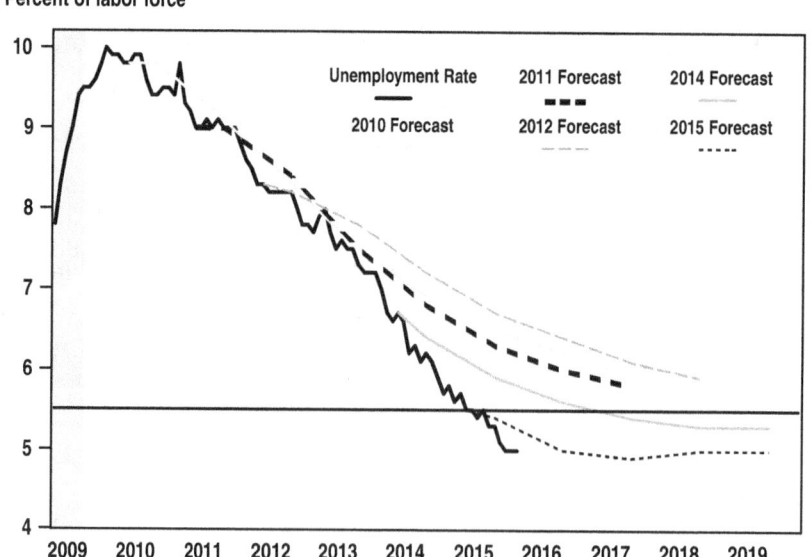

Unemployment Rate has Fallen Faster than Forecasted

Percent of labor force

Note: Annual forecasts are current as of March of the stated year. Shading denotes recession.

Source: Blue Chip Economic Indicators; Bureau of Labor Statistics, Current Population Survey

reduction since just after World War II. The annual deficit in 2015 fell to 2.5 percent of the Gross Domestic Product (GDP), the lowest level since 2007, and well below the average of the last 40 years. Over the past six years, actual and projected deficits have fallen due to three main factors.

First, economic growth has helped accelerate the pace of deficit reduction. Growth in recent years has increased revenues and reduced spending on "automatic stabilizer" programs, such as unemployment insurance, that automatically increase during economic downturns.

Second, since 2010, the President has worked on a bipartisan basis to put in place deficit reduction measures totaling $3.8 trillion from 2017 through 2026, not counting the hundreds of billions of dollars in additional savings achieved by winding down wars in Iraq and Afghanistan. These measures include restoring Clinton-era tax rates on the highest-income Americans. These restored rates in combination with other tax policies enacted under the President's leadership, have led to the top 0.1 percent of families contributing more than $500,000 in additional taxes each year on average, according to a Department of the Treasury analysis. At the

same time, tax cuts have increased the after-tax incomes of working families of modest means. Discretionary spending restraint has also played a role in deficit reduction, but sequestration cuts have contributed only a minority of the discretionary savings achieved since 2010, while shortchanging investment and cutting critical services.

Finally, deficits have fallen due to exceptionally slow health care cost growth. When the President took office, he immediately identified health care costs as one of the major drivers of the Nation's long-term fiscal challenges. In his Address to a Joint Session of the Congress in February 2009, he called for health reform as "a step we must take if we hope to bring down our deficit in the years to come." In the months that followed, the President fought to enact comprehensive health care reform even as the Administration took aggressive actions to bolster the economy and help Americans get back to work. Central to the ACA, which was signed into law in 2010, were a series of reforms designed to rein in health care cost growth by reducing excessive payments to private insurers and health care providers in Medicare, developing and deploying new payment models that reward high-quality efficient care, and implementing an

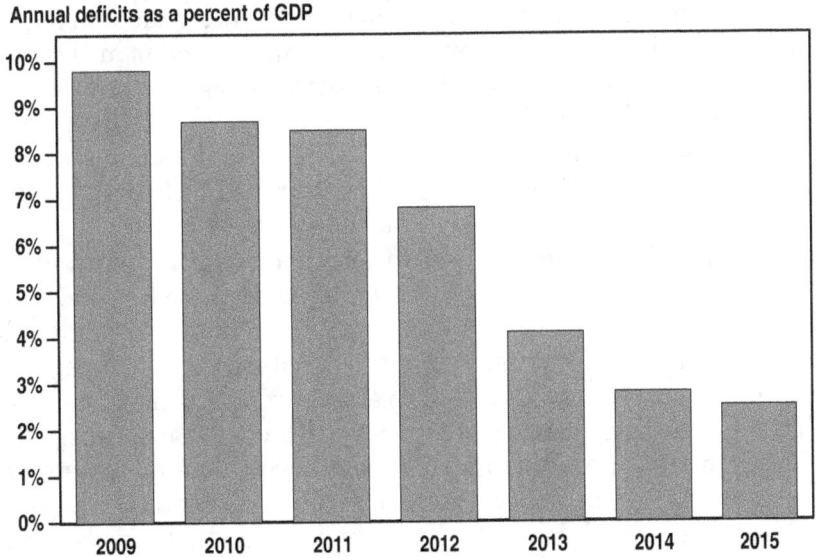

2009-2015 was the Fastest Period of Sustained Deficit Reduction Since WWII

Annual deficits as a percent of GDP

excise tax on the most costly health plans in the employer market. These reforms together create strong incentives for efficient and effective coverage, and have moved us toward paying for value, rather than volume, in health care services.

In the years since 2010, we have seen prolonged slow growth in per-beneficiary health care spending in both private insurance and public programs. In 2014, in both Medicare and private health insurance, per-enrollee spending grew by less than one-third the rate seen over the preceding decade, adjusting for inflation. While some of the slowdown can be attributed to the Great Recession and its aftermath, there is increasing evidence that much of it is the result of structural changes, including the reforms enacted in the ACA.

The health care cost slowdown is already yielding substantial fiscal dividends. Compared with the 2011 Mid-Session Review, aggregate projected Federal health care spending for 2020 has decreased by $185 billion based on current budget estimates, savings above and beyond the deficit reduction directly attributed to the ACA when it was passed.

Helping, Not Hurting, the Economy: The Bipartisan Budget Act of 2015

Sustained economic growth is a necessary pillar of fiscal health. As the American people work to continue our economic and fiscal progress, it is critical that the Federal Government support, rather than impede, economic growth. That means ending the harmful spending cuts known as sequestration, which limit the ability to invest in the building blocks of long-term economic growth, like research and development (R&D), infrastructure, job training, and education.

Early in the Administration, the President and the Congress worked together to enact measures to stabilize and restore growth to a faltering economy and to rebuild it on a stronger foundation for the long run. In addition to the Recovery Act, the ACA, and the Dodd-Frank Wall Street Reform and Consumer Protection Act, the Congress took bipartisan action in 2010 on a number of temporary measures to jumpstart the recovery.

Unfortunately, policies adopted in subsequent years hurt, rather than helped, the economy. Sequestration cuts that were never intended to take effect were implemented in March 2013, reducing GDP by 0.6 percentage points and costing 750,000 jobs, according to the Congressional Budget Office (CBO). In 2011, and again in 2013, congressional Republicans sought to use the Nation's full faith and credit as a bargaining chip, driving down consumer confidence and driving up uncertainty. The Federal Government shutdown in October 2013 created further uncertainty and reduced growth in the fourth quarter of 2013 by 0.3 percentage points.

Following the Government shutdown, policymakers started to move away from manufactured crises and austerity budgeting, helping to lay the groundwork for job market gains and stronger growth. The President worked with the Congress to secure a two-year budget agreement (the Bipartisan Budget Act of 2013) that replaced a portion of the harmful sequestration cuts and allowed for higher investment levels in 2014 and 2015. The Council of Economic Advisers estimated that the 2013 budget deal would create about 350,000 jobs over the course of 2014 and 2015, so it likely made a significant contribution to the improvement in the labor market over the past two years.

With harmful sequestration cuts scheduled to return in full in 2016, the President made clear that he would not accept a budget that locks in these short-sighted cuts and that the Congress would again have to take action to address them. The President's 2016 Budget laid out a path to do so: it replaced the sequestration cuts with smart reforms in areas like health care that would improve quality while controlling health care cost growth. It also proposed critical investments in economic growth and opportunity that could only be made by lifting sequestration.

In October 2015, the President worked with congressional leaders from both parties to secure another two-year budget agreement (the Bipartisan Budget Act of 2015 or BBA) that will create an estimated 340,000 jobs in 2016 alone, while supporting middle-class families, investing in long-term growth, protecting Social Security, and safeguarding national security. The BBA provided roughly 75 percent more sequestration relief over two years than the budget agreement reached in 2013, including nearly 90 percent of the discretionary sequestration relief the President requested in 2016. The sequestration relief was fully paid for, and employed a number of reforms the President put forward in the Budget. The BBA also included critically important provisions to bolster the financing of the Social Security Disability Insurance Program (SSDI), ensuring that the program can continue to provide workers with serious disabilities and their families the full benefits they have earned. Without congressional action, SSDI would have run short of funds in December 2016, resulting in large benefit cuts.

Some private forecasters have estimated that the measures in this agreement will lead to the first year with a net positive contribution from Federal fiscal policy to GDP growth since 2010. The agreement ended yet another period of brinksmanship and uncertainty and put us on a path to avoid more manufactured crises in the months ahead.

Because of the sequestration relief secured in the BBA, the President and congressional leaders were able to come together to invest in many of the key priorities from the President's 2016 Budget that will help the economy and middle-class families, including:

- *Job Training*. A $90 million landmark new effort to expand apprenticeships, creating more opportunities for hard-working Americans to acquire the skills they need to succeed in good jobs that are available now.

- *Research*. A seven percent increase in National Institutes of Health funding between 2015 and 2016 will go toward critical research priorities like Alzheimer's disease, addressing antibiotic resistance, cancer, and the Precision Medicine Initiative.

- *Early Learning*. A six percent increase in Head Start funding, including a new, nearly $300 million investment, to increase the number of Head Start programs that provide a full school day and a full school year, which research shows promotes better outcomes for children.

- *Clean Energy*. An eight percent increase in funding between 2015 and 2016 for clean energy projects supported by the Department of Energy's Office of Energy Efficiency and Renewable Energy in cooperation with industry, universities, and the national labs.

- *Advanced Manufacturing*. Resources for new manufacturing innovation institutes building toward the President's goal of 15 institutes by the end of his term, representing over $225 million of additional and continuing investments in 2016. Each of these manufacturing institutes brings together leading companies, universities, and non-profits to co-invest in the development of game-changing manufacturing technologies that make the U.S. more competitive for manufacturing jobs and investment.

The President and the Congress have now come together twice to avoid harmful sequestration cuts, replacing the savings with a smarter mix of revenues and spending reforms, and investing equally in the economy and national security. These actions further highlight that the President's proposal to fully offset the cost of ending sequestration is consistent with his vision to make necessary investments to support economic growth and opportunity, and to put the Nation on a more fiscally sustainable path.

Providing sequestration relief and investing in the economy through the BBA and subsequent year-end 2016 budget legislation (the 2016 Consolidated Appropriations Act or 2016 Omnibus) were only a part of the bipartisan budget-related accomplishments in 2015. In

April, the Congress passed legislation that permanently reforms the Medicare physician payment system and extends the critical Children's Health Insurance Program, which provides coverage to millions of American children. Nearly every year, for the past 13 years, physicians have faced the possibility of cuts in their payments from Medicare unless the Congress passed a so-called "doc fix." The 2016 Budget called for putting a permanent end to this annual crisis and reforming Medicare physician payments to promote high-quality efficient care. The enacted legislation achieved these aims, providing certainty for physicians and preserving patient access to care, while also encouraging delivery system reforms designed to improve quality and improve the sustainability of the Medicare program over the long term.

Also, as part of the 2016 Omnibus, the Congress reached a bipartisan agreement on expiring tax provisions that will extend critical tax relief to working families, incentivize private-sector innovation through support for R&D, and simplify and cut taxes for small businesses while putting dozens of corporate tax breaks on a real path to expiration. The legislation signed into law by President Obama permanently extends Recovery Act expansions of the Child Tax Credit and Earned Income Tax Credit that were scheduled to expire after 2017, which will provide a tax cut of about $900 on average for millions of working families a year. If the expansions had been allowed to expire, more than 16 million people—including eight million children—would have fallen into, or deeper into, poverty in 2018. The agreement also makes permanent the President's American Opportunity Tax Credit, first enacted in the Recovery Act, which helps families afford college with up to $10,000 in tax credits for tuition, fees, and books over four years. In addition, the agreement extends for five years wind and solar tax credits, boosting investments in these energies, which will significantly reduce carbon dioxide emissions. However, the tax agreement did not offset the cost of the business tax breaks it contained and did not take necessary steps to reform the business tax system. As the President has proposed, the Congress should pass business tax reform that closes loopholes, makes the tax system fairer, and pays for these tax cuts.

Building on Our Success for a Stronger Economy

The BBA provides a critical increase in discretionary funding for 2016 and 2017, including nearly two-thirds of the sequestration relief for 2017 that the President called for in the 2016 Budget. The 2017 Budget builds on the achievements secured for 2016 and adheres to the agreement's discretionary funding levels. Still, not fully replacing sequestration in 2017 has consequences, including hindering the ability to make needed investments that are critical to building durable economic growth in the future and maintaining America's edge as the leader in innovation and cutting-edge science.

For that reason, the Budget includes a series of investments using mandatory funding that will help maintain preeminence in science and engineering, support jobs and economic growth, expand opportunity, and ensure that we continue to demonstrate economic leadership for decades to come.

These critical investments include a range of R&D efforts, from basic science research in the physical, environmental, and agricultural sciences, to launching a cancer "moonshot" through investments in biomedical research, to supporting earth science, space science, aeronautics, and exploration missions at the National Aeronautics and Space Administration—all with the potential to fundamentally change what America is capable of achieving.

The investments also support early learning, which provides a strong foundation for children's future success in school and in life, including the President's Preschool for All initiative to ensure four-year-olds across the Nation have access to high-quality preschool programs. They also fund a historic investment to ensure that all low- and moderate-income families with young children have access to high-quality child care that supports children's development and helps parents work.

In addition, the investments fund computer science opportunities for K-12 students, strengthen community colleges, which expand students' opportunities to pursue the knowledge and skills they need for well-paying jobs, and criminal justice reform, to break the cycle of poverty and incarceration that traps too many Americans and ultimately detracts from communities, the workforce, and economic growth. These investments also support expanded access to treatment for opioid use disorders, with a goal of ensuring that all who seek treatment can access it by the end of 2018; and funding to help more Americans receive needed mental health care, especially for serious mental illnesses.

These investments also build on the success in sharply reducing veteran homelessness and set a path for ending homelessness among all of America's families; they enable partnerships with State and local governments to help families get through a financial crisis and remain self-sufficient and thrive. The investments fund a robust effort to enhance national and economic security through an intensive effort to strengthen cybersecurity across the Federal Government.

The Budget also recognizes that without further congressional action, sequestration will return in full in 2018, threatening the economy. That is why the Budget once again proposes to end sequestration and replace the savings by cutting inefficient spending and closing tax loopholes. Reversing sequestration would allow domestic and security investments needed to help move the Nation forward. These include investments to strengthen the economy and drive growth and opportunity by improving the education and skills of the U.S. workforce, accelerating scientific discovery, and creating jobs through pro-work, pro-family initiatives. Ending sequestration is also necessary to address critical national security priorities and fund national defense in a fiscally responsible manner. Ending this destructive policy would enable the United States to maintain military readiness, advance badly-needed technological modernization, and provide the support that our men and women in uniform deserve.

Investing in Economic Growth While Maintaining Fiscal Responsibility

The Budget shows that investments in growth and opportunity are compatible with putting the Nation's finances on a strong and sustainable path. The Budget ends sequestration and makes critical investments while still addressing long-term fiscal challenges. It keeps deficits below three percent of GDP while stabilizing debt and putting it on a declining path through 2025—key measures of fiscal progress.

The Budget accomplishes these goals by more than paying for all new investments, achieving $2.9 trillion of deficit reduction over 10 years, primarily from health, tax, and immigration reforms. The Budget includes roughly $375 billion of health savings that grow over time, described further in Chapter 3, Meeting Our Greatest Challenges: Opportunity for All, and builds on the ACA with further incentives to improve quality and control health care cost growth.

The Budget also includes smart tax reforms that promote growth and opportunity, while strengthening tax policies that help middle-class families afford child care, higher education, and a secure retirement, also described further in Chapter 3. It achieves $955 billion in deficit reduction from curbing inefficient tax breaks for the wealthy and closing loopholes for high-income households, helping to bring in sufficient revenues to make vital investments while also helping to meet promises made to seniors. Changes in health and tax policies would help extend the life of the Medicare Hospital Insurance Trust Fund by over 15 years.

The Budget reflects the President's support for commonsense, comprehensive immigration reform along the lines of the 2013 bipartisan Senate-passed bill. CBO has estimated that comprehensive immigration reform along the lines of the Senate-passed bill would reduce the deficit by about $170 billion over 10 years and by almost $1 trillion over two decades. Immigration reform is a pro-growth policy that helps to directly address key fiscal challenges by helping to balance out an aging population, increase labor force participation, and raise productivity. The Social Security Actuary estimated that immigration reform would reduce Social Security's 75-year shortfall by eight percent.

The Budget also shows that responsible deficit reduction can be achieved without cuts in critical aid to poor Americans and without undermining commitments to seniors and workers. The Budget puts us on sound fiscal footing even as it modernizes benefits for workers, invests in evidence-based efforts to reduce poverty and promote opportunity, and protects Social Security and Medicare.

Under the President's leadership, there has been remarkable economic and fiscal progress, showing what is possible when strategic investment to grow the economy is paired with smart reforms that address the true drivers of long-term fiscal challenges. The Budget continues that approach, investing in America's future and laying out a path to address the Nation's greatest challenges.

MEETING OUR GREATEST CHALLENGES: INNOVATION TO FORGE A BETTER FUTURE

Scientific discovery, technological break-throughs, and innovation are vital for responding to the biggest challenges and opportunities we face as a Nation, including addressing climate change, improving the health of all Americans, enhancing access to clean water and healthy food, and ensuring the Nation's security. They are also key drivers of long-term economic growth and job creation.

Over the past seven years, the President has nurtured the American spirit of innovation. The Administration has prioritized research and development (R&D) funding and created a network of manufacturing institutes to bolster American innovation and increase exports. In addition, the largest investments in clean energy in American history have been made, creating hundreds of thousands of new jobs that will thrive in a low-carbon future. Pollution has been cut from power plants, vehicles, and agriculture, and the President has led the world in forging an unprecedented agreement to combat climate change.

However, there is still more work to do to harness technology and use it to drive economic growth and progress, not just for the year ahead, but for decades to come. Accelerating the pace of American innovation is essential to ensuring we keep up with the evolving economy and the rapidly changing world around us. As the President said in his 2016 State of the Union Address, we face the key question of "how to make technology work for us, and not against us, especially when it comes to solving urgent challenges like climate change."

The Budget makes significant investments to make technology work for us as we strive to meet the Nation's biggest challenges. It increases investment in our transition to climate solutions like clean energy, which will help to grow the economy and create new jobs. It invests in a new, sustainable transportation system that speeds goods to market while reducing America's reliance on oil, cuts carbon pollution, and strengthens our resilience to the effects of the changing climate. It invests in medical research to help develop treatments and cures that have the potential to save millions of lives and avoid heartbreak for countless families. It also provides critical funding to ensure that R&D keeps us on the cutting edge from manufacturing to space exploration to agriculture.

CREATING A CLIMATE-SMART ECONOMY

When the President visited Alaska in August 2015, he described the urgent and growing threat of a changing climate as "a challenge that will define the contours of this century more dramatically than any other." In 2015 the record set by 2014 as the warmest year on record was broken. Climate change is already disrupting the Nation's agriculture and ecosystems, water and food supplies, energy, infrastructure, and health and safety. If we address this growing challenge, we can minimize the damage to the economy and reduce threats to national security.

Climate change is not only a danger to avoid. It is an economic opportunity to seize. Not only can we act to protect the Nation from this threat, we can harness it to build a climate-smart economy of the future. Moving toward a climate-smart economy will improve the air we breathe, the soil we farm, and the water we drink. In doing so, we can create jobs and opportunity for millions of Americans by building the climate solutions the world needs.

The President has been focused on this challenge since his first inaugural address, when he committed this Nation to combating climate change and protecting the planet for future generations, and tremendous progress has been made. The United States has led by example, with historic investments in growing industries like wind, solar, and biofuels, creating a new and steady stream of middle-class jobs. We have set the first-ever nationwide standards to limit the amount of carbon pollution power plants can dump into the air. America is on track to double the distance cars can go on a gallon of gas. We are also making investments in communities smarter—to avoid future risks of flooding and sea level rise by establishing the Federal Flood Risk Management Standard. From Alaska to the Gulf Coast to the Great Plains, the Administration has partnered with local leaders who are working to help their communities protect themselves from some of the most immediate impacts of a changing climate.

The recent global climate agreement of 195 countries reached in Paris is a tribute to this U.S. leadership. The Paris Agreement is ambitious, with every nation committing to putting forward successive, ambitious, nationally determined climate targets in five-year intervals. It establishes strong and binding transparency requirements, including periodic reviews and independent assessments, to help hold every country accountable for meeting its commitments.

As we have made significant progress addressing climate change, the economy has continued to grow, evidence against the tired claims that we must choose between these critically important priorities. Economic output has reached all-time highs while carbon pollution has dropped to its lowest level in nearly two decades.

Yet we must do more domestically and internationally. Building on the historic Paris Agreement, the Budget makes critical investments in creating a climate-smart economy, one that lays the foundation to transform the Nation's transportation system, grows American leadership in clean energy, accelerates clean water innovation, helps communities prepare for the effects of climate change and become more resilient, protects the Nation's most treasured natural resources, and demonstrates America's global leadership in helping other countries reduce their carbon emissions and accelerate their transition to low-carbon economic growth.

21st Century Clean Transportation Plan

The Nation's transportation system was built around President Eisenhower's vision of interstate highways connecting 20th Century America. That vision enabled economic expansion and prosperity, fostered a new era for automobiles, and supported the growth of the Nation's metropolitan areas. Unfortunately, today the remains of that system—the crumbling highways, bridges, and passenger rail system—are not ready to meet the challenges of a growing 21st Century economy. Due to underinvestment, American infrastructure that was once the envy of the world is now ranked 19th behind countries such as Poland, Hungary, and Spain.

As we look to the future, we must invest in a new, sustainable transportation system that speeds goods to market, expands Americans' transportation options, builds resilient and connected communities, and integrates new technologies like autonomous vehicles into our infrastructure system. Furthermore, to address the challenges of the 21st Century, the Nation needs a transportation system that reduces reliance on oil, cuts carbon pollution, and strengthens our resilience to the impacts of climate change.

There have been important infrastructure investments to advance these priorities. Through the Recovery Act, the Administration invested over $48 billion for transportation, spurring more than 14,600 needed highway, transit, bridge, and airport projects across America, improving nearly 42,000 miles of roads, repairing or replacing more than 2,700 bridges, and helping transit agencies purchase more than 12,220 transit vehicles. Since 2009 the TIGER multi-modal competitive grant program has provided nearly $4.6 billion to 381 projects in all 50 States, the District of Columbia, and Puerto Rico, including 134 projects to support rural and tribal communities. The Build America Transportation Investment Center, established in July 2014, has provided technical assistance to increase infrastructure investment and economic growth by engaging with State and local governments and private-sector investors to encourage collaboration, expand the market for public-private partnerships, and put Federal credit programs to greater use. The Administration has worked with the Congress to pass the FAST Act, providing multi-year dedicated funding for surface transportation investments for the first time in a decade.

Yet much more remains to be done. To build a clean transportation system for the 21st Century, the Budget invests an average of $32 billion per year over 10 years into a multi-agency initiative to refocus Federal investments, reward local and State governments for innovation, accelerate integration of new vehicle technologies, and ensure the safety of the transportation system. The Plan will:

(1) Refocus Federal investment to enhance transportation options for American families.

The proposal invests nearly $20 billion per year above current spending to reduce traffic and provide new ways for families to get to work and to school by:

- Providing more than $10 billion on average per year for the Federal Transit Administration New Starts, Small Starts, and Transit Formula Grants programs to invest in the safety, performance, and efficiency of existing, new, and expanded transit systems. It also creates a new Rapid Growth Area Transit program for fast growing communities to implement multi-modal

solutions to challenges caused by rapid growth.

- Reaffirming the Administration's commitment to high-speed rail by investing on average almost $7 billion per year on a competitive basis, with an emphasis on incorporating advanced rail technologies.

- Providing an average of $1 billion per year for a multi-modal freight program that strengthens America's exports and trade by providing grants for innovative rail, highway, and port projects that seek to reduce both emissions and particulate matter that harm local community health.

- Nearly doubling the amount of grant funding available through the TIGER program to support innovative, multi-modal investments in the Nation's infrastructure to make communities more livable and sustainable.

(2) Reward State and local governments for innovations that lead to smarter, cleaner, regional transportation systems.

The proposal provides approximately $10 billion per year on average to transform regional transportation systems by shifting how local and State governments plan, design, and implement new projects, including:

- Proposing over $6 billion per year on average for a 21st Century Regions grant program to empower metropolitan and regional planners to implement regional-scale transportation and land-use strategies that achieve significant reductions in per capita greenhouse gas (GHG) emissions and vehicle miles traveled, while improving climate resilience.

- Providing nearly $1.5 billion per year on average in Clean Communities competitive grants to support transit-oriented development, reconnect downtowns, clean up brownfields, implement complete streets policies, and pursue other policies that make American cities and towns greener and better places to live.

- Providing nearly $1.7 billion per year on average for Climate-Smart Performance

Formula Funds that are designed to re-orient transportation formula funding by rewarding States that make investments to mitigate transportation impacts like air pollution.

- Providing $750 million on average per year for Resilient Transportation competitive grants to spur investments that bolster resilience to climate impacts. Cutting-edge projects would incorporate resilience strategies, such as adaptive materials, risk-sensitive design, and next generation transportation and logistics technology.

(3) Accelerate the integration of autonomous vehicles, low-carbon technologies, and intelligent transportation systems into our infrastructure.

The proposal includes just over $2 billion per year on average to launch a new generation of smart, clean vehicles and aircraft by expanding clean transportation R&D, launching pilot deployments of safe and climate smart autonomous vehicles, accelerating the transition to cleaner vehicle fleets and supporting the creation of regional fueling infrastructure for low-carbon vehicles by:

- Providing almost $400 million on average per year in funding over the next 10 years for the deployment of self-driving vehicles. Investments would help develop connected infrastructure and smart sensors that can communicate with autonomous vehicles, support R&D to ensure these vehicles are safe and road ready, and expand at-scale deployment projects to provide "proving grounds" for autonomous self-driving and connected vehicles in urban and highway settings.

- Expanding access to alternative fuels by 2020 and increasing the deployment of electric vehicles powered with clean sources of energy in communities across the United States by 2025 by providing an average of approximately $600 million per year for the Department of Energy (DOE) to develop regional low-carbon fueling infrastructure including electric vehicles, biofuels, and other low-carbon options.

- Dedicating an average of around $1 billion per year for DOE, the Environmental Protection Agency, and the National Aeronautics and Space Administration (NASA), to increase R&D in clean fuels and transportation technologies, including a new generation of low-carbon aircraft, and accelerate the Nation's transition to the deployment of a cleaner public vehicle fleet.

(4) Ensure transportation safety keeps pace with changing technology.

- The Plan focuses on catalyzing rapid changes in transportation technologies. Accordingly, it would invest an average of $400 million per year to ensure that these technologies are integrated safely into America's transportation system.

Overall, the 21st Century Clean Transportation Plan will increase American investments in clean transportation infrastructure by roughly 50 percent above current levels while reforming the transportation investments already being made to move America to more sustainable, low-carbon investments. Between the Plan and resource levels under current law, the Budget proposes to invest nearly $900 billion in the surface transportation system over 10 years through the Department of Transportation. The initiative will:

- **Strengthen the economy.** The investments would support hundreds of thousands of well-paying, middle-class jobs each year. It also would increase the competitiveness of U.S. businesses and the productivity of the U.S. economy by making it faster, easier, and lower-cost to move American-made products.

- **Reduce carbon pollution.** The plan would make public investments and create incentives for private-sector innovation to reduce America's reliance on oil and cut carbon pollution from our transportation sector, which today accounts for 30 percent of U.S. greenhouse gas emissions. The investments in vehicle research and deployment would put commercial autonomous vehicles on the road both more quickly and more safely while ensuring electric cars and other alternatives to oil-based vehicles have the technology and the charging infrastructure they need.

- **Make transportation easier for American families.** The plan would expand clean, reliable, and safe transportation options like transit and rail, making it easier for millions of Americans to get to work and take their children to school while reducing the seven billion hours that Americans currently spend in traffic each year.

The Plan would be funded by a new $10.25 per barrel fee on oil paid by oil companies, which would be phased in over five years. The fee raises the funding to make the new investments we need while also providing for the long-term solvency of the Highway Trust Fund to ensure we maintain the infrastructure we have. By placing a fee on oil, the President's plan creates a clear incentive for private-sector innovation to reduce America's reliance on oil and invest in clean energy technologies that will power our future. It continues the President's call to utilize one-time revenues from business tax reform to provide a temporary near-term surge in investment to set us on the right path for the years ahead. In addition to transportation investments, 15 percent of revenues would be allocated to provide assistance to families with burdensome energy costs, including a focus on supporting households in the Northeast as they transition from fuel oil for heating to cleaner forms of energy.

Doubling the Investment in Clean Energy R&D

Since the President took office, the Administration has made the largest investments in clean energy in American history and the impact is clear. In 2014, renewables accounted for half of new electricity generating capacity placed in service. As of October, renewables were on pace to account for over 60 percent of new generation capacity placed in service in 2015. Last year, the price of solar energy fell by 10 percent and installations climbed by 30 percent.

America's growing clean energy sector is also creating jobs and advancing American economic leadership; the solar industry adding jobs 12 times faster than the rest of the economy.

While we have made significant progress in deploying clean energy technologies, accelerating clean energy innovation is essential to addressing climate change.

That is why the President joined other world leaders on the first day of the recent Paris climate negotiations to launch Mission Innovation, a landmark commitment to dramatically accelerate public and private global clean energy innovation by investing in new technologies that will define a clean, affordable, and reliable global power mix.

Through this initiative, so far 20 countries have committed to doubling their governmental clean energy research and development investment over five years. These countries represent more than 80 percent of the world's clean energy R&D investment. Mission Innovation is complemented by the Breakthrough Energy Coalition, a separate, private sector-led effort whose purpose is to mobilize substantial levels of private capital to support the most cutting-edge clean energy technologies emerging from the R&D pipeline. At the same time, the Administration's Clean Energy Investment Initiative has catalyzed more than $4 billion in independent commitments by major foundations, institutional investors, and other long-term investors, along with executive actions to scale up clean energy innovation.

The U.S. Government is seeking to double its current base level Federal investment of $6.4 billion in 2016 to $12.8 billion in 2021. Initially, new funding would strategically target early stage R&D, which offers the greatest opportunities for breakthroughs and transformative change. However, the investment portfolio spans the full range of R&D activities—from basic research to demonstration. These programs address a broad suite of promising low-carbon technologies, including those that enable businesses and households to use energy more efficiently, bioenergy, renewable energy, nuclear energy, electric grid technologies, carbon capture and storage, and advanced transportation systems and fuels.

Doubling this investment would require the equivalent of about a 15 percent year-over-year increase in clean energy R&D funding in each of the five years of the pledge. The Budget goes beyond this increase for 2017 by providing $7.7 billion in discretionary funding for clean energy R&D across 12 agencies. About 76 percent of the funding is directed to DOE for critical clean energy development activities, including over $2 billion for energy efficiency and renewable energy technologies. For example, the Budget provides over $280 million for the EV Everywhere initiative and $169 million for emerging technologies in the building sector.

Investments in clean energy R&D at other agencies that drive progress toward our pledge include $512 million at the National Science Foundation (NSF) for research in a wide array of technology areas such as the conversion, storage, and distribution of diverse power sources, and the science and engineering of energy materials; $348 million at NASA for research in areas such as revolutionary aircraft technologies and configurations to enable fuel-efficient, low-carbon air transportation, and $106 million at the Department of Agriculture (USDA) for competitive and intramural research funding and education to support development of biobased energy sources that range from sustainable and economical forest systems and farm products to increased production of biofuels. These investments build on an ongoing commitment to advance renewable energy deployment and increase access to clean energy for all Americans.

The Budget also includes new mandatory funding across the clean energy research, development, demonstration, and deployment spectrum. The Budget provides $150 million in mandatory funding for DOE's ARPA-E in 2017, which is part of the ARPA-E Trust proposal that seeks to increase over five years the program's transformational clean energy technology R&D.

The Budget provides substantial support for clean energy R&D as part of the Administration's 21st Century Clean Transportation Plan.

Protecting and Increasing the Nation's Water Supply through Investment in Water Technology

The Nation's water supply is one of our most precious resources. Yet the increasing frequency and duration of droughts place extensive pressures on the vitality of communities and ecosystems across America. In 2012 alone, droughts affected about two-thirds of the continental United States, impacting water supplies, tourism, transportation, energy and fisheries, and costing the agricultural sector alone $30 billion. Future short-term droughts are expected to intensify in most regions of the United States, and longer-term droughts are expected to intensify in large areas of the Southwest, the southern Great Plains, and the Southeast. Climate change, along with population growth, land use, energy use, and socioeconomic changes, increases water demand and exacerbates competition among uses and users of water.

To increase the resilience of the Nation's water supplies to these stresses, the Administration has developed an aggressive two-part water innovation strategy with the goals of: first, boosting water sustainability through the greater utilization of water-efficient and water-reuse technologies; and, second, promoting and investing in breakthrough R&D that reduces the price and energy costs of new water supply technology.

By continuing to support efforts by U.S. businesses, industries, and communities to make efficient use of water—especially in water-stressed regions—and through better management practices and technology, we have the potential to considerably reduce water usage. High costs currently limit the ability of most communities to turn non-traditional water sources like seawater or brackish water into fresh water. Investing in innovative technologies designed to achieve "pipe parity" (the delivery of new supplies of clean and fresh water at a total cost, energy input, and carbon emission level equal to traditional supplies) can provide communities in water-stressed regions with new and more effective options to meet their increasing water supply needs. The Budget addresses these challenges by investing in water conservation and R&D of new water supply technology. The Budget provides:

- $98.6 million for the Department of the Interior's (DOI's) WaterSMART program through the U.S. Geological Survey (USGS) and the Bureau of Reclamation, which promotes water conservation initiatives and technological breakthroughs. This request is $10.3 million above the 2016 Budget.

- $4 million of new funding at USGS for near real-time assessment of water use during drought, which provides a regional and national picture of how water use is changing during drought.

- $28.6 million to support R&D at the Bureau of Reclamation. These funds include $8.5 million for the water technology solutions challenge program, an ambitious technology challenge prize focused on next-generation advanced water-treatment technologies; $5.8 million for desalination and water purification, and $2 million to continue the Open Water Data initiative to improve accessibility of data. This request is $8.6 million above the 2016 Budget.

- $25 million in new funding for DOE to launch a new Energy-Water Desalination Hub focused on developing technologies to reduce the cost, energy input, and carbon emission levels of desalination. DOE would also invest nearly $20 million in complementary R&D on desalination technologies relevant to fossil, concentrated solar power, and geothermal applications.

- $15 million in additional funding for USDA intramural research on safe and abundant water supplies to support U.S. agricultural production and agricultural practices that conserve water, such as building healthy soils that retain water. The agriculture sector is the largest consumer of fresh water in the United States.

- $88 million for NSF to support basic water research. The investment would enhance the scientific and engineering knowledge base and enable new technological solutions that will increase the Nation's water supply and the quality of potable water and clean water for use in agriculture and industry processes or cooling.

Partnering with Communities to Tackle Climate Risk

Across the Nation, the effects of climate change, including more frequent and severe storms, floods, droughts, and wildfires, thawing permafrost, and sea level rise, are felt by communities, households, governments at all levels, and individuals who are on the front lines of the devastation these events often bring. For example, over the last decade, the Federal Government has incurred over $350 billion in direct costs due to extreme weather and fire alone. Given its far-reaching impacts, it is our collective responsibility to better understand, prepare for, and adapt to our changing climate.

The Budget demonstrates the Administration's continued commitment to increasing the resilience of communities—and the ecosystems upon which they depend—in the face of growing climate-related risks. It invests in programs that advance our scientific understanding of projected impacts, assist communities in planning and preparing for future risks, and deliver risk reduction and adaptation projects on the ground. Through proactive investments in these areas, we can save lives and reduce long-term costs to families, communities and the Nation.

In all of these investments, the Administration recognizes that community demands and needs vary. For the past six years, the Administration has led efforts to transform the Federal Government into an effective partner that customizes support for local communities instead of relying on a one-size-fits-all approach. Place-based climate-preparedness efforts must be developed in partnership with those communities—by the people who live in them, work in them, and stand to benefit from them. As the Federal Government works with community partners to prepare for climate-related risks, the Administration is starting where it makes the most sense: meeting communities where they are.

Coastal Resilience. Climate change impacts are often most clear in coastal areas, where communities are witnessing their coastlines receding under the pressures of sea-level rise, storms, and coastal erosion. The Budget includes a package of proposals aimed at reducing these risks and building the resilience of communities and natural resources to these impacts in a fiscally responsible way.

First, the Budget proposes a $2 billion Coastal Climate Resilience program, which would provide resources over 10 years for at-risk coastal States, local governments, and their communities to prepare for and adapt to climate change. This program would be paid for by redirecting roughly half of the savings that result from repealing unnecessary and costly offshore oil and gas revenue sharing payments that are set to be paid to a handful of States under current law.

A portion of these program funds would be set aside to cover the unique circumstances that climate change forces some Alaskan communities to confront, such as relocation expenses for Alaska native villages threatened by rising seas, coastal erosion, and storm surges. The Budget also provides the Denali Commission—an independent Federal agency created to facilitate technical assistance and economic development in Alaska—with $19 million, including $5 million to coordinate Federal, State, and tribal assistance to communities to develop and implement solutions to address the impacts of climate change. It also includes complementary investments totaling approximately $100 million across a number of agencies and $150 million for a Coast Guard icebreaker in the Arctic to help address these challenges.

Second, the Budget invests $20 million, a fourfold increase above the 2016 enacted level, to help

coastal regions plan for and implement activities related to mitigating extreme weather, changing ocean conditions and uses, and climate hazards through the National Oceanic and Atmospheric Administration's (NOAA's) Regional Coastal Resilience grants program. These competitive grants to State, local, tribal, private, and non-governmental organization partners would support activities such as vulnerability assessments, regional ocean partnerships, and development and implementation of adaptation strategies.

Flood Resilience. Climate change is expected to increase heavy downpours and cause more rapid snowmelt, which is likely to intensify flooding in many areas of the United States. That increased flood intensity—coupled with development patterns that put people in harm's way—contributes to significant risks from future flood events. However, flood maps typically provide only a "snapshot" of flood risk at a certain time and become outdated as topographic, hydrologic, or climate conditions change, as development densities change or modify watersheds, or as engineering methods and models improve. To help communities and businesses understand the flood risks they face, the Budget includes $311 million for National Flood Insurance Program Risk Mapping efforts to update the Nation's flood maps.

Drought Resilience. The Budget continues the Administration's strong support for USDA in its efforts to integrate climate considerations into existing programs and to use programs to drive resilience. The Budget continues the collaborative effort initiated in 2016 to provide information on the latest technologies and risk management strategies to help farmers, ranchers, and landowners mitigate the impact of climate change through USDA's regional Climate Hubs. It also includes $10 million for NOAA's Regional Integrated Science and Assessments program, which would support expanded NOAA work with resource managers to utilize climate information to address drought and other challenges. The Budget's $98.6 million investment in DOI's WaterSMART program—which provides critical water data, promotes water conservation initiatives, and invests in technological break-throughs—complements this effort. (See the previous section on Protecting and Increasing the Nation's Water Supply through Investment in Water Technology.) In addition, the USDA's Natural Resources Conservation Service (NRCS) is leading efforts to promote soil health and integrate soil health management practices into conservation programs and technical assistance. The Budget also continues efforts by the NRCS, initiated in 2016, to develop a soil carbon monitoring network to support ongoing GHG monitoring. This network is a key component of USDA's Climate Strategy as it would allow USDA to verify, for the first time, the United Nations Framework Convention on Climate Change reporting and would also provide the foundation for a farm-scale database to house soil carbon data.

Wildland Fire Resilience. Warmer temperatures and drier conditions anticipated under climate change are projected to increase the frequency and intensity of future wildfires, increasing the risks they pose to nearby communities. It is a priority of the Administration to ensure adequate funds are available to fight wildland fires, protect communities and human lives, and implement appropriate land management activities to improve the resiliency of the Nation's forests and rangelands. To accomplish this, the Budget again proposes to establish a new budget framework for wildland fire suppression, similar to how other natural disasters are funded. This new framework includes a base funding level of 70 percent of the 10-year average for suppression costs within the discretionary budget cap, and a cap adjustment that would then be used for only the most severe fire activity, which comprises two percent of wildfires, but 30 percent of suppression costs. Paying for the most severe and costly wildfire suppression activity with a cap adjustment reduces the need to transfer funds from other important programs designed to more comprehensively manage wilderness landscapes, including the mitigation of losses to property and timber from wildfire.

Crop Insurance and Resiliency. The Budget includes proposals for USDA's crop in-surance program that would incentivize farmers to choose production practices that minimize climate-change impacts, discourage farming on environmentally sensitive lands and highly-erodable soils, and enhance resiliency in the future through soil protection. These include reducing the farmers' subsidy by 10 percentage points for harvest price revenue coverage and reforming coverage for prevented planting.

Multi-Hazard Resilience. The Budget invests in programs that provide the science and tools, technical assistance, and projects on-the-ground that enable communities to address the full range of climate-related hazards. It provides approximately $20 million to continue expanding and improving data and tools—available through the online Climate Resilience Toolkit—to help Tribes, communities, citizens, businesses, planners, and others manage climate-related risks and improve their resilience to extreme events.

The Budget provides $4 million to support a Resilience AmeriCorps pilot program at the Corporation for National and Community Service (CNCS) which would support roughly 175 AmeriCorps VISTA members to assist communities in planning for and addressing climate impacts. In addition to CNCS' investment, the Budget provides $2 million for NOAA to train the Resilience AmeriCorps members. The Budget also continues to support the Corps of Engineers programs that are already at work—such as the Flood Plain Management Services Program and the Silver Jackets—by providing $26 million for technical and planning assistance to local communities to help them develop and implement nonstructural approaches to reduce flood risk.

The Budget also invests $54 million in mitigation projects—including mitigation planning, facilities hardening, and buyouts and elevation of structures—through FEMA's Pre-disaster Mitigation Grant Program. Studies on mitigation activities conclude that Americans save approximately $4 for every dollar invested in pre-disaster mitigation.

Preserving and Protecting Public Lands and Oceans

America is home to some of the most beautiful landscapes on the planet. Our Nation is blessed with natural treasures from the Yosemite Valley to the Everglades, with verdant forests, majestic mountains, vast deserts, and lakes and rivers teeming with wildlife. These natural resources are not only beautiful, but are a vital economic engine, supporting hundreds of thousands of jobs in industries from recreation and tourism to timber and fishing and generating billions of dollars in economic activity.

America's natural landscapes face growing pressures, however, not only from agricultural, commercial, industrial, and residential development, but also from a changing climate that brings increased drought, wildfires and other dangers. As a result, the need for investments in natural and cultural resources on Federal and State lands is greater than ever. All of these forces necessitate coordinated efforts among Federal, State, tribal, local, and private land managers, who share a collective responsibility for preserving and restoring natural systems that are vital to mitigating climate impacts, such as soil and other carbon reservoirs.

The Budget includes robust funding to support such efforts. It invests in proven programs that allow Federal agencies and their partners to better understand, prepare for, and adapt to natural hazards, including those worsened by climate change. Public land management agencies administer programs that build the resilience of natural resources and communities to hazards, such as drought, coastal flooding, and wildland fire. These programs provide actionable science, data, and technical assistance that enhance the ability of natural resources to adapt to changing conditions, which in turn benefits our communities.

Land and Water Conservation Fund. Created 50 years ago, the Land and Water Conservation Fund (LWCF) is used to preserve historic resources, protect endangered wildlife, restore forest ecosystems, and provide recreational opportunities for millions of Americans in iconic places that range from Grand Canyon National Park to local parks in nearly every county across the Nation. The highly successful program reinvests royalties from offshore oil and gas activities into public lands, with the goal of using the benefits of one non-renewable resource for the protection of another—our irreplaceable landscapes. Through the LWCF, the Budget invests $900 million annually into conservation and recreation projects to conserve lands in or near national parks, refuges, forests, and other public lands. Through strategic and landscape-level land acquisition, public access to lands for sportsmen and hunters, and grants to States for recreation and conservation projects, the LWCF is a cornerstone of this Administration's conservation agenda.

National Park Service (NPS) Centennial. For over 100 years, NPS sites have preserved and shared our cultural and historical identity. The iconic places protected by NPS present America's unique history and draw tourists from across the United States and around the world. As we continue to celebrate the centennial anniversary of the Nation's great parks, the Budget proposes to increase park services for visitors and make targeted investments that would improve NPS facilities. This opportunity is an historic effort to upgrade and restore national parks and engage and inspire younger generations to visit and care for the Nation's parks into the future. With more and more American families living in urban spaces that often lack easy access to our great outdoors, it is vital to introduce a new generation to our public lands. That is why the Every Kid in a Park initiative provides all fourth-grade children free passes to U.S. public lands and waters. To support this effort, the Budget proposes $25 million for youth engagement and bringing youth from underserved communities to national parks and forests.

As NPS enters its second century, it is working to assess and build resilience to the effects of climate change in its 86 ocean and coastal parks and over its 12,000 miles of shoreline. The effects of climate change deteriorate park shorelines, threatening our resources, infrastructure, and public recreation opportunities. Working with scientists and other partners, NPS is developing adaptation strategies to protect these coastal resources and to boost their long-term resilience. Meanwhile, public lands continue to experience record visitation levels. Such visits do more than provide scenic views and inspiration— they drive an estimated $51 billion in economic impact, and support hundreds of thousands of jobs in local communities across the United States.

The Budget proposes $860 million in discretionary and mandatory funding to allow NPS, over 10 years, to make targeted, measurable, and quantifiable upgrades to all of its highest priority non-transportation assets and restore and maintain them in good condition. Doing so avoids increased deterioration and costs for future generations. The Budget also proposes matching funds to leverage contributions from the private sector for critical signature projects.

Sage-Grouse Protection. In September 2015 the DOI's Fish and Wildlife Service (FWS) issued a landmark determination that the greater sage-grouse does not warrant protection under the Endangered Species Act at this time. This decision was possible because of the collaborative strength of Federal, State, tribal, and private conservation efforts over many years and the continued commitment of all partners—including the Federal Government—to conserving the sagebrush habitat in what is arguably the largest landscape-level conservation effort in U.S. history. Moreover, the FWS determination and the conservation mechanisms in place provide the regulatory certainty needed for sustainable economic development across millions of acres of Federal and private lands throughout the western United States. The Administration is committed to meeting its responsibilities to conserve vital sagebrush ecosystems.

The Budget builds upon unprecedented investments provided in 2016 to protect the western United States' sagebrush ecosystems. On lands managed by the Bureau of Land Management and the U.S. Forest Service, the Administration

is committed to successful implementation of the sagebrush resource management plans, as well as the Administration's comprehensive rangeland fire strategy. The Budget proposes $23 million over the 2016 level within DOI—and more than twice the amount of funding enacted in 2015—for activities directly affecting sage-grouse protection. Across private lands, NRCS is investing $211 million by the end of 2018 to help hundreds of ranchers conserve or restore 3.7 million acres of additional habitat.

Ocean Science and Conservation. About a third of the carbon dioxide in the atmosphere dissolves into the ocean, and the increased global carbon dioxide levels are the main driver of ocean acidification, which in turn affects marine ecosystems. To address this complex issue and increase understanding of the consequences of ocean acidification on marine resources, the Budget includes $22 million, a $12 million increase over 2016 levels. To help fishing communities, which face significant climate challenges, become more resilient to the impacts of fisheries disasters, the Budget provides $9 million. These competitive funds would assist communities in becoming more environmentally and economically resilient through activities such as ecosystem restoration, research, and adaptation.

Leading International Efforts to Cut Carbon Pollution and Enhance Climate Change Resilience

Because climate change is a global challenge, it is imperative for the United States to couple action on climate change at home with leadership internationally, as called for in the President's Climate Action Plan. To support this objective, the Budget provides $1.3 billion in discretionary funding to advance the goals of the Global Climate Change Initiative (GCCI) through important multilateral and bilateral engagement with major and emerging economies. This amount includes $750 million in U.S. funding for the Green Climate Fund, which would help developing countries leverage public and private financing to invest in reducing carbon pollution and strengthening resilience to climate change.

Assisting these countries in meeting emissions reduction commitments and developing their economies along low-emissions pathways would play a vital role in mitigating some of the most serious risks from climate change both at home and abroad. Assisting developing countries in their climate adaptation efforts is critical to helping the poorest and most vulnerable nations prepare for, and build resilience to, the impacts of climate change. These efforts would not only help preserve stability and security in fragile regions that are of strategic importance to the United States, but also help open these regions to U.S. businesses and investment.

More broadly, GCCI funding enables the United States to provide international leadership through the Department of State, the U.S. Agency for International Development, and the Department of the Treasury to support our developing-country partners in their efforts to meet their emissions reduction commitments, including by expanding clean and efficient energy use, reducing deforestation and forest degradation, conserving the world's remaining tropical rainforests, and phasing down the production and consumption of substances with high global warming potential, such as such as hydrofluorocarbons. GCCI funding would help support U.S. commitments made in the context of the Paris Agreement and put the United States on a pathway to doubling U.S. grant-based support for international climate adaptation activities by 2020. Federal agencies will also systematically integrate climate-resilience considerations into international development investments so that U.S. investments overseas remain sustainable and durable and support the poorest and most vulnerable communities in their efforts to cope with the adverse impacts of extreme weather events and climate change.

INVESTING IN RESEARCH AND DEVELOPMENT

Because of the critical role that R&D plays in expanding the frontiers of human knowledge, tackling the Nation's biggest challenges, and driving the economy forward, the Administration has consistently prioritized robust R&D investments since the start of the Administration.

The Budget sustains the Administration's consistent prioritization of R&D with an investment of $152 billion for R&D overall through both discretionary and mandatory funding proposals. This reflects a four percent increase from 2016 and targets resources to the creation of transformative knowledge and technologies that can benefit society and create the businesses and jobs of the future. Specifically, the Budget prioritizes basic research, the type of R&D that is the most likely to have spillover impacts to multiple endeavors and in which the private sector typically under-invests. It also includes $7.7 billion in discretionary funding for clean energy R&D in 2017, the first step toward the Mission Innovation doubling goal.

Of the overall $152 billion investment in R&D, $4 billion is mandatory funding because the discretionary levels set by the Bipartisan Budget Act are not sufficient for the Nation to take full advantage of the opportunities for R&D investments to create jobs and grow the economy.

Revitalizing American Manufacturing

After a decade of decline, American manufacturing has added 878,000 new jobs since February 2010, new factories are once again opening their doors, and global investment in the U.S. manufacturing sector is increasing. The Budget proposes $2.0 billion in coordinated, cutting-edge manufacturing R&D, while also expanding industry-driven workforce training and providing additional resources through the

Manufacturing Extension Partnership to help America's small manufacturers access the technology and expertise they need to expand. This would help turn America's increased manufacturing competitiveness into a lasting advantage through smart, strategic investments that build on our strengths. Most importantly, the Budget makes new investments to grow a national network of innovative R&D hubs to help keep U.S. manufacturing in the lead on technology.

This network, the National Network for Manufacturing Innovation, plays an important part in this revitalization of American manufacturing. In his 2012 State of the Union Address, the President called for the creation of a network of manufacturing institutes to boost advanced manufacturing, foster American innovation, and attract well-paying jobs that would strengthen the middle class. Later that year, an interagency team led by the Department of Defense launched the first pilot institute. Proving that revitalizing American manufacturing is a topic we can all agree on, the Congress supported this initiative in a bipartisan fashion by passing the Revitalize American Manufacturing and Innovation Act in December 2014, which authorizes manufacturing innovation institutes to come together into a shared network and codifies authority for the Department of Commerce to coordinate this multi-agency initiative.

To date, the Administration has already awarded seven institutes. Those institutes represent more than $500 million in Federal resources matched by more than $1 billion of non-Federal resources, all focused on securing U.S. leadership in the emerging technologies that make America's industry more competitive today and ensure continued groundbreaking innovation tomorrow. The Budget builds on the seven institutes awarded, two more institutes with competitions already underway, and four more institutes funded in 2016 by proposing five additional manufacturing institutes in 2017 in the Departments of Commerce, Defense, and Energy. In total, the Budget proposes more than $250 million in discretionary resources to create and sustain manufacturing innovation institutes.

Each of these new institutes would bring together companies, universities, community colleges, and Government to co-invest in the development of world-leading manufacturing technologies and capabilities that U.S.-based manufacturers can apply in production. For example, the Digital Manufacturing and Design Innovation Institute in Chicago has attracted more than 140 partners and, in its first six months alone, hosted over 2,000 visitors to its smart factory demonstration facility, modeling state-of-the-art techniques for integrating digital technologies into a factory production line. Collectively, the institutes are attracting a swelling membership from across Fortune 500 companies, leading research universities, regional non-profits, and small businesses with over 800 members to-date. They have launched 147 R&D projects to accelerate transformative manufacturing technologies into production, demonstrating the significant momentum underway.

The Budget also includes a mandatory spending proposal of $1.9 billion to build out the remaining 27 institutes to create a national network of 45 manufacturing institutes over the next 10 years that would position the United States as a global leader in advanced manufacturing technology.

Advancing Biomedical Research at the National Institutes of Health (NIH)

The Budget provides $33.1 billion—including $1.8 billion in new mandatory funding—to support biomedical research at NIH. This funding would allow for almost 10,000 new and competing NIH grants that will help scientists better understand the fundamental biological mechanisms that underpin health and disease to improve health and save lives. The Budget provides increased resources for the President's Precision Medicine Initiative and continues support for the Brain Research through Advancing Innovative Neuroethologies (BRAIN) initiative, launched by the President in 2013, which is helping to revolutionize our understanding of the human brain.

Enhancing Investments in Cancer Research. As a part of the cancer "moonshot" the President announced in the State of the Union Address, the Budget provides an increase of $755 million to accelerate progress in preventing, diagnosing, and treating cancer. The increase is in addition to NIH's significant investment for the cancer moonshot in 2016. The Budget's multi-year cancer initiative, which begins in 2016, provides $680 million to NIH and $75 million to the Food and Drug Administration in 2017, to improve health and outcomes for patients through investments in research and infrastructure, and brings together researchers across sectors and scientific disciplines. Notably, these funds would significantly increase support for research to help realize the promise of cancer immunotherapy.

Precision Medicine Initiative. The Budget includes $300 million for NIH to continue the progress of the President's Precision Medicine Initiative, which was launched in 2016 to enable a new era of medicine for all by accelerating research into the development of treatments tailored to specific characteristics of individuals. The Budget supports efforts underway to establish a voluntary national research cohort of one million or more Americans, expand research to define cancer subtypes and identify new therapeutic targets, modernize the regulatory framework for DNA-sequence-based diagnostic tests, and improve health data sharing and interoperability so patients can access their health records for research, providers can recommend optimal treatments and researchers can use individual and population data to develop new insights and therapies. It also supports activities to engage patients, including those from historically underserved communities, and raise awareness about the promise of precision medicine for all.

BRAIN Initiative. The Budget includes $195 million for NIH for the BRAIN Initiative, a bold research effort to revolutionize our understanding of the brain and to uncover new ways to treat, prevent, and cure brain disorders like Alzheimer's, schizophrenia, autism, epilepsy, and traumatic brain injury. The initiative has grown since its launch in 2013 to include five agencies, and dozens of major foundations, private research institutions, universities, companies, and advocacy organizations have aligned their research efforts to advance the BRAIN Initiative.

Investing in Civil Space Activities

The Budget invests in space exploration and technological advancements, providing $19 billion, including $763 million in mandatory funding in 2017, to NASA to further U.S. leadership in space and at home. The Budget supports exploration of the Solar System, including robotic missions to Mars and to the Sun, and funds the development and operation of a fleet of spacecraft to study our own planet, increasing our understanding of the Earth and its climate. The Budget supports innovative public-private partnerships to enable new industries and capabilities in space and to ensure that our space programs are sustainable and affordable. The Budget also makes investments in new ground-breaking technologies, such as solar-electric propulsion that would allow us to push out into the Solar System not just to visit, but to stay.

Addressing Challenges in Agriculture through R&D

Recognizing the importance of science and technology to meet challenges in agriculture, the Budget increases investment in three major areas of agricultural R&D:

- Grants through USDA's flagship competitive peer-reviewed research program, the Agriculture and Food Research Initiative (AFRI), are funded at $700 million, including $325 million in mandatory funding. This is the full authorized level and double the 2016 funding level. It would enable USDA to accept many qualified research proposals that it previously would have rejected due to funding constraints. AFRI-supported research would enable USDA to respond to critical problems and challenges facing the Nation such as ensuring an abundant supply of safe water for agricultural uses, responding to climate change, understanding and restoring soil health, and improving food safety and quality.

- USDA's in-house research programs through the Agricultural Research Service are funded at almost $1.2 billion, which includes increases for current and new programs for climate change resilience and vulnerability, pollinator health, agricultural microbiomes, responding to antimicrobial resistance, as well as research on foreign animal diseases, soil health, avian influenza, and for safe and abundant water supplies to support agricultural production.

- The Budget provides $94.5 million for construction and renovation of key infrastructure investments based on USDA's facility modernization plan.

MEETING OUR GREATEST CHALLENGES: OPPORTUNITY FOR ALL

Since the onset of the Great Recession, we have restored economic growth and created millions of jobs. We have also laid the groundwork for long-term growth through investments in education, job training, infrastructure, and research and development that help businesses thrive and create high-paying jobs. But while the benefits of a growing economy are beginning to be more widely shared, too many hard-working Americans still are not experiencing those benefits. Too many are struggling to make ends meet.

This economic insecurity is due in part to changes in the U.S. economy that began long before the recession and will continue in the years to come. With increased globalization and automation in the workplace, workers have less leverage and job security. Because the face of the Nation's workforce has changed dramatically since many key benefit structures were established decades ago, those structures need updating.

As the President stated in the 2016 State of the Union Address, one of the Nation's key challenges is how to give everyone a fair shot at opportunity and security in this new economy. This is not only a moral imperative, but an economic one. The Nation does best when everyone shares in—and contributes to—our success. Failing to tap the potential of every American weakens the economy and harms us all. That is why the Budget makes a series of investments to ensure that if you work hard, you have a chance to get ahead and ensure a better future for your children.

The Budget invests in education from our youngest learners to those striving to complete college. It invests in job training to help workers get the skills they need to secure better paying jobs, updates worker benefits to reflect today's workforce and economy, and calls for a higher minimum wage and expanded working family tax credits. The Budget also takes new steps to reduce poverty and reinvigorate distressed communities.

It builds on the success of the Affordable Care Act to improve the health of all Americans, including through investments in mental health treatment and treatment for opioid use disorders. It supports meaningful criminal justice reform to break the cycle of poverty, criminality, and incarceration that traps too many Americans and weakens too many communities. The Budget also reforms the Nation's immigration system to make American society safer and more just, and to boost U.S. economic growth.

EDUCATING FOR THE FUTURE: FROM EARLY LEARNING TO COLLEGE

Americans must be prepared with the skills and knowledge necessary to compete in today's global economy and achieve economic security. Expanding educational opportunities is critical to equipping all children with these skills and positioning them to succeed as adults, and increasing educational attainment is central to the Nation's future economic strength.

We have made significant progress in expanding educational opportunities. By focusing on improving student outcomes and tying investments to evidence-based reform, the Administration has worked to support States and communities as they establish high academic standards that will prepare students for success in college and future careers, improve teacher effectiveness, and use data to ensure students graduate from high school prepared for college and a successful career. These investments have given teachers, school districts, and States the tools to turn around some of the Nation's lowest-performing schools. The Nation's high school graduation rate is at an all-time high and we have made college easier to access and afford.

However, there is more we must do to improve all levels of education, from early childhood through college, and ensure the Nation's workforce has the skills American businesses need. To meet this challenge, the Budget builds on our progress and reflects key developments over the past year, most significantly the reauthorization of the Elementary and Secondary Education Act, a bipartisan effort that was eight years overdue. The new law, the Every Student Succeeds Act (ESSA), embraces many reforms the Administration has long supported, including requiring States to define and set high standards for college and career readiness, ensuring that States are held accountable for the success of all students, spurring innovation in education, encouraging States to reduce unnecessary testing, and expanding access to high-quality preschool.

The Budget supports ESSA implementation and builds on its priorities. It reflects a strong commitment to ensuring that all students receive a high-quality education by improving access to early education, preparing elementary and secondary education students for success, increasing access to quality, affordable higher education, and continuing to build the evidence base for what works to improve student outcomes. The Budget provides $69.4 billion in discretionary funding for Department of Education programs, an increase of $1.3 billion from the 2016 enacted level adjusted for comparability.

Improving Access to High-Quality, Affordable Early Education

High-quality early education provides children with a foundation for success in school and puts them on a path toward realizing their full potential. Supporting children during this critical stage of development yields long-lasting benefits, providing a strong return on investment. This is particularly true for low-income children, who too often start kindergarten far less prepared than their peers.

Preschool for All. The Budget maintains support for the President's landmark Preschool for All initiative to ensure four-year-olds across the Nation have access to high-quality preschool programs. The Department of Education initiative establishes a partnership with States to provide all four-year-olds from low- and moderate-income families with high-quality preschool, while providing States with incentives to expand these programs to reach additional children from middle-class families and put in place full-day kindergarten policies. The initiative is paid for through an increase in tobacco taxes that will help reduce youth smoking and save lives.

With the support of Federal funding made available through the Administration's Preschool Development Grants (PDG) program, 18 States are currently developing and expanding high-quality preschool programs in targeted high-need communities. This work will continue under the newly authorized PDG program in ESSA, the first program in a major elementary and secondary education statute devoted solely to the expansion of high-quality preschool and early education, a clear recognition of the importance of preschool in ensuring students are successful in school.

The Budget provides $350 million for Preschool Development Grants at the Department of Health and Human Services (HHS)—which are jointly administered by HHS and the Department of Education under ESSA—an increase of $100 million from the 2016 enacted level. The Budget also provides $907 million for the Department of Education's early intervention and preschool services for children with disabilities, an increase of $80 million from the 2016 enacted level. This proposal includes up to $15 million for competitive grants for early identification of and intervention for developmental delays and disabilities, with a potential focus on autism, intended to help identify, develop, and scale-up evidence-based practices.

Head Start. The Budget provides $9.6 billion for HHS's Head Start program, which delivers comprehensive early childhood services to support the learning and development of America's neediest children. This funding level, a $434 million increase, includes a total of $645 million for the Administration's Early Head Start-Child Care Partnerships, through which local Early Head Start grantees partner with child care providers and leverage Early Head Start standards to expand access to high-quality early care and education for infants and toddlers. The Budget also builds on the nearly $300 million investment made in 2016 to increase the number of children attending Head Start in a full school day and year program, which research shows is more effective than programs of shorter duration and also helps meet the needs of working parents. The Budget continues funding for those programs that expand their full day and full year offerings with 2016 resources, and provides an additional $292 million to enable more programs to expand their full day and full year programs. Taken together, the 2016 and 2017 investments will mean that more than half of all Head Start children will now be provided a full school day and year program.

Home Visiting. The Budget invests $15 billion in new funding over the next 10 years to extend and expand evidence-based, voluntary home visiting programs, which enable nurses, social workers, and other professionals to work with new and expecting parents to help families track their children's healthy development and learning, connect them to services to address any issues, and utilize good parenting practices that foster healthy development and later school success. The program builds on research showing that home visiting programs can significantly improve maternal and child health, child development, learning, and success. As with Preschool for All, the proposal is paid for through an increase in tobacco taxes. To complement this investment, the Budget includes $20 million for a new initiative in rural home visiting that the Department of Agriculture (USDA) will administer in coordination with HHS. This initiative will focus exclusively on providing home visiting services in the most remote rural and tribal areas.

As discussed below under Making the 21st Century Economy Work for Workers, the Budget also makes historic investments in expanding access to quality, affordable child care. This investment is designed to meet two important purposes—help parents afford child care so they can work, and help children access quality care that supports their healthy development.

Putting Students on a Path to College and Careers

ESSA, the new elementary and secondary education law, cements many of the Administration's key education reforms and reflects the progress States and districts have made in implementing these important changes. Building on earlier Administration initiatives, it requires States to set high college and career standards for all students, invests in place-based and evidence-based strategies, supports the recruitment and retention of effective teachers and school leaders, and replicates high-quality charter schools. The Budget provides $24.4 billion to the Department of Education to support ESSA and related programs, an increase of $629 million above the 2016 enacted level.

Funding High-Poverty Schools and the Important Work of Improving Low-Performing Schools. The Budget proposes a $450 million increase for Title I, which ESSA maintained as the Department's largest K-12 grant program, and the cornerstone of the commitment to support schools in low-income communities with the funding necessary to provide high-need students access to an excellent education. Title I supports local solutions in States and school districts, while ensuring that students make progress toward high academic standards. As part of Title I, ESSA requires annual statewide assessments that measure student achievement, and ensure that the information about student achievement is available to teachers, school leaders, families, and communities. While retaining this critical accountability measure, the law also encourages States to reduce excessive standardized testing, aligned with the efforts of the Department of Education's testing action plan that supports maximizing the time students spend learning. ESSA also holds States and school districts accountable for improving their lowest-performing schools, requiring evidence-based interventions to turn them around. The Budget calls for dedicating additional funds within Title I to address the urgent need to improve the Nation's lowest-performing schools. This dedicated funding, which will be distributed based on the Title I formulas, will ensure States and school districts have the support necessary to successfully turn around these schools.

Supporting Computer Science for All and Rigorous STEM Coursework. There are currently more than 600,000 high-paying tech jobs open across the United States, and by 2020, 51 percent of all STEM jobs are projected to be in computer science-related fields. More than 9 of 10 parents want computer science taught at their child's school. However, by some estimates, just one quarter of all U.S. K-12 schools offer computer science with programming and coding even as other advanced economies, such as England, are making it available for all students between the ages of 5 and 16. Wide disparities exist even for those who do have access to these courses. For example, of the very few schools that offer advanced placement computer science courses, only 15 percent of enrollees are girls, and fewer than eight percent are African-American or Latino students. Disparities in computer science are emblematic of the large gaps in student access and engagement in STEM courses overall; only half of high schools offer calculus, and only 63 percent offer physics.

To address these disparities, the Budget provides resources to empower States and districts to create high-quality computer science learning opportunities in grades K-8 and access to computer science courses in high school. Under the Computer Science for All proposal, the Budget includes $4 billion in mandatory funding over three years for States to increase access to K-12 computer science and other rigorous STEM coursework by training more than 250,000 teachers, providing infrastructure upgrades, offering online courses, and building effective partnerships. Complementing the mandatory proposal, the Budget also dedicates $100 million in discretionary funding for Computer Science for All Development Grants to help school districts, alone or in consortia, execute ambitious computer science expansion efforts, particularly for traditionally under-represented students. Both the mandatory and discretionary proposals would also encourage States and districts to expand overall access to rigorous STEM coursework.

Redesigning and Strengthening America's High Schools. The Budget provides $80 million for a new, competitive program to promote the redesign of America's high schools by integrating deeper learning and personalized instruction, with a particular focus on STEM-themed high schools that expand opportunities for all students, including girls and other under-represented groups in STEM fields. This is complemented by the $375 million in private and public sector commitments that were announced in November 2015 as part of the White House Summit on Next Generation High Schools.

Promoting Student Support and Academic Enrichment. To compete in the 21ˢᵗ Century economy, students need a well-rounded education and rigorous coursework. To help ensure all students have such access, the Budget provides $500 million for Student Support and Academic Enrichment Grants, newly authorized in ESSA, which would provide funds for States and school districts to support student achievement and promote academic enrichment opportunities. This flexible funding can support expanding STEM opportunities and the arts, improving supports for student learning, and enhancing the use of technology for instruction.

Promoting Socioeconomic Diversity and School Choice. Poverty and negative educational outcomes are closely linked, with students who attend high-poverty schools often struggling to meet high standards and finish high school college- and career-ready. Research suggests that socioeconomically diverse schools can lead to improved outcomes for disadvantaged students. Based on this research and the work already underway in communities across the United States, the Budget supports a new initiative that would support new and ongoing State and local efforts to develop and implement strategies that increase socioeconomic diversity in the Nation's preK-12 schools.

The Stronger Together initiative would make $120 million in voluntary competitive grants available to school districts or consortia of school districts that are interested in exploring ways to foster socioeconomic diversity through a robust process of parental, educator and community engagement, and data analysis; and to school districts and consortia of school districts that already have set goals and developed strategies and are ready to begin implementation. The funding would be available for five-year projects.

In addition to this proposal, the Budget strengthens its support for investments in school choice programs designed to increase the supply of high-quality schools available to all students, including both magnet schools and charter schools. The Budget proposes $115 million for magnet schools, an $18 million increase compared to 2016, which would complement the Stronger Together program through a new provision under ESSA that allows districts to take into account socioeconomic diversity in the design and implementation of magnet school programs. The Budget also proposes $350 million for charter schools, a $17 million increase over 2016, for the start-up, replication, and expansion of effective charter schools that would improve students' access to high-quality educational opportunities regardless of their zip code.

Maintaining a Commitment to Evidence, Data, and Innovation. The Budget maintains a strong commitment to evidence, data, and innovation in education. The Budget provides $180 million for Education Innovation and Research, a new program authorized by ESSA. The program is modeled on the Investing in Innovation program, which has been the Administration's signature effort to develop and test effective practices that improve student outcomes, such as implementing college- and career-ready standards, using data to inform instruction and personalize learning, and improving low-performing schools. This funding level represents an increase of $60 million compared to Investing in Innovation's 2016 funding. The Budget amplifies this commitment by providing $209 million for the Institute of Education Sciences' Research, Development, and Dissemination program to produce strong evidence on effective strategies for improving student learning in early childhood, K-12, postsecondary, and adult education. An investment of $81 million in the State Longitudinal Data Systems program would support State and school district efforts to provide educators, parents, policymakers, researchers, and the public with information on the performance of schools and what works in education.

Supporting America's Teachers. The Budget invests $2.8 billion in discretionary funding for programs to provide broad support for educators at every phase of their careers, from ensuring they have strong preparation before entering the classroom, to pioneering new approaches to help teachers succeed in the classroom, and equipping them with tools and training they need to implement college- and career-ready standards. The Budget provides $250 million for the Teacher and School Leader Incentive program to drive improvements in school districts' human capital management systems through innovative strategies for recruiting, developing, evaluating, and retaining excellent educators. A new $125 million Teacher and Principals Pathways program, to be proposed in the next Higher Education Act reauthorization, would support teacher and principal preparation programs and nonprofits partnering with school districts to create or expand high-quality pathways into teaching and school leadership, particularly in high-need subjects such as STEM. A new program, Teach to Lead, would fund teacher-led projects to improve the quality of education, drawing on the knowledge and passion of teachers to identify, implement, and expand effective practices. Furthermore, the Budget includes RESPECT: Best Job in the World, a $1 billion mandatory initiative that would support a nationwide effort to attract and retain effective teachers in high-need schools by increasing compensation and paths for advancement, implementing teacher-led development opportunities to improve instruction, and creating working conditions and school climates conducive to student success. This proposal is a key strategy in the Department's efforts to ensure all students' equitable access to effective teachers.

Promoting College Affordability and Completion

Today's economy increasingly demands highly-educated workers. Higher education is one of the clearest pathways into the middle class, and decades of research has shown large returns to higher education in terms of labor market earnings, health, and well-being. In fact, research shows that the typical college graduate earns twice as much over his or her lifetime as the typical high school graduate. Further, over the next decade, jobs requiring education beyond high school will grow more rapidly than jobs that do not, with more than half of the 30 fastest-growing occupations requiring postsecondary education.

From the start of the Administration, the President has focused on making college more accessible and affordable for all Americans, with the goal of making the United States the leader once again in college completion, as it was a generation ago. The Administration ended the inefficient guaranteed student loan program and reinvested the savings into making college more

affordable, including strengthening and expanding the Pell Grant program, the cornerstone of opportunity for low- and moderate-income students. The Pell Grant program is now supporting scholarships for significantly more students to attend college than when the President took office.

In December, the American Opportunity Tax Credit (AOTC)—first enacted in the Recovery Act—was made permanent. The AOTC expands the level of support for college by providing a maximum credit of $2,500 per year for the first four years of college—up to $10,000 per student to cover tuition and educational expenses. The AOTC is partially refundable, so it provides critical college tuition help to low- and moderate-income families. The AOTC will cut taxes by over $1,000, on average, for nearly 10 million families in 2016.

Overall, since 2009, these investments in Pell Grants and tax credits have doubled, increasing the access and affordability of college for students.

The Administration has also made historic investments in the creation and expansion of community college programs aligned to in-demand jobs in high-growth industries from health care to information technology (IT). From 2011 through 2014, some $2 billion in funding reached more than half of all community colleges across the United States, enrolling over 176,000 students to date. Employers have donated thousands of dollars in equipment, scholarships, tuition, and more to support these programs.

The Administration also has made it easier and faster for students to apply for Pell Grants and other financial aid. Since taking office, the Department of Education has significantly simplified the Free Application for Federal Student Aid, known as the FAFSA. The Administration has reduced the time required to complete the FAFSA by two-thirds, to about 20 minutes, by revamping the online form for all families so they can skip questions that are not relevant to them and automatically retrieve needed tax information when filling out the FAFSA. More than six million students and parents took advantage of the ability to electronically retrieve their income information from the Internal Revenue Service (IRS) when completing their 2014-2015 FAFSA, an innovation that improves both speed and accuracy.

Building on this progress, starting in calendar year 2016, students and families will be able to fill out the FAFSA three months earlier—in October—so they can understand the financial resources available for them as they are applying to college. Families filling out the FAFSA in October 2016 will be able to fill it out immediately by electronically retrieving information from their 2015 tax returns. Families and students will no longer have to wait until the next year's tax season to finalize their FAFSAs and to learn about their financial aid. The Administration is working with college financial aid officers and State aid programs to ensure that they align their financial aid awards with the new Federal schedule so students have as much information as possible early in their college search process. These changes—coupled with further FAFSA simplification proposals in the Budget—could encourage hundreds of thousands of additional students to apply for and claim the aid they are eligible for.

Making Two Years of Community College Free for Responsible Students. The Budget ensures all Americans have the opportunity to pursue and succeed in higher education, with a goal of making at least two years of college as universal as high school. America's College Promise (ACP) would provide funding to support community colleges, as well as four-year Historically Black Colleges and Universities and other Minority-Serving Institutions, that undertake a set of reforms to improve the quality of their programs of study. The funding provided under ACP will offset tuition—fully in community colleges—before the application of Pell grants or student loans. This would allow students who qualify for Pell grants to use financial aid to cover additional costs, such as academic supplies and living expenses.

Since the President announced his plan, Tennessee's free community college program, Tennessee Promise, has helped increase enrollment in State colleges by over 4,000 students. Ten additional States and communities have created programs to provide free community college, including legislation enacted in Oregon and Minnesota, and new initiatives in Rhode Island, Richmond and Scotland Counties in North Carolina, and at Sinclair Community College (OH), Harper College (IL), Community College of Philadelphia (PA), Milwaukee Area Technical College (WI), Madison Area Technical College (WI), and Ivy Tech Community College (IN). Furthermore, legislation creating free community college has been introduced at the State level in at least 12 States.

There is Federal momentum as well. Senator Baldwin (WI) and Representative Scott (VA) have proposed the America's College Promise Act of 2015.

Building Effective Education and Training in High-Demand Fields. In addition to America's College Promise, the Budget includes $75 million for a complementary tuition-free investment in the American Technical Training Fund (ATTF). The ATTF would provide competitive grants to support the development, operation, and expansion of innovative, evidence-based, tuition-free job training programs in high-demand fields such as manufacturing, health care, and IT.

Promoting Completion through Pell Grants. The Budget continues the President's commitment to college affordability by ensuring that Pell Grants keep pace with inflation and by investing in new efforts that promote college completion. Data show that degree completion is critical to ensuring that the time and money invested in college pays off for students.

To promote completion, the Budget puts forward three important Pell Grant policies.

- *Pell for Accelerated Completion.* The Budget proposes to allow students to earn a third semester of Pell grants in an academic year so they can take courses year-round and make steady progress toward their degrees. The "year-round" Pell option was previously available to students, but cost more than anticipated and was eliminated in 2011 to preserve funding for the basic Pell award and close a funding shortfall. The Budget proposes to reinstate year-round Pell, but with changes to ensure that the additional aid is facilitating timely completion of a degree. In particular, the Budget proposes to allow students to access a third semester of Pell during a year if they have already completed a full-time course load of 24 credits to ensure that the third semester of eligibility is assisting students to accelerate progress toward completion.

- *Incentivizing Students to Take 15 or More Credits.* Since the beginning of the Administration, the President has increased the maximum Pell Grant by more than $1,000. To further incentivize students to enroll in enough credits to complete degree programs on time, the Budget proposes to increase the Pell Grant by an additional $300 for students taking at least 15 credit hours per semester in an academic year, the number of credits typically required for on-time completion.

- *Incentivizing Colleges to Do More to Promote Completion.* The Budget recognizes that schools themselves can and should do more to help disadvantaged students succeed in college and graduate. The Budget provides a College Opportunity and Graduation Bonus to schools that ensure that a large share of students receiving Pell Grants finish their degrees and to schools that improve their performance on this important metric of success.

Seeding Innovation. The Budget provides $100 million for the First in the World program (FITW) to develop, test, and scale-up new and promising strategies to help more students complete high-quality, affordable degrees. This proposal builds off of $60 million invested in 2015, and expands FITW to allow for greater piloting at-scale to facilitate wider adoption of evidenced-based practices that successfully support student persistence and lead to college completion. This investment is critical to ensure that students facing significant barriers to degree completion, such as adult learners and low-income students, can benefit from the cutting-edge research on student success at colleges and universities across the Nation.

Further Simplifying the FAFSA. While significant progress has been made in simplifying the FAFSA, many of the most time-consuming questions that remain cannot be completed with IRS data because they require information that is not reported on tax returns. To answer those burdensome questions, affected students have to collect information about assets and untaxed forms of income from multiple sources—even though these questions have little or no impact on aid eligibility in the vast majority of cases. The Budget proposes to eliminate up to 30 burdensome and unnecessarily complex questions, shortening the FAFSA application substantially, and making it easier for students and families to access critical resources to pay for college.

Ensuring High-Quality Service for Students and Borrowers. The Budget provides $1.6 billion for the Office of Federal Student Aid, which is responsible for administering the more than $140 billion in new financial aid made available each year to students at over 6,000 colleges and universities. This funding would be used to implement the Administration's ongoing efforts to ensure that student loan contractors provide high-quality loan servicing to students. These funds would also allow the Department of Education to provide enhanced oversight and strengthen enforcement activities, such as pursuing schools that engage in deceptive or misleading practices toward students, including veterans. Funds would also be used to provide students and families with clear information about how students who attend different colleges fare.

Creating Business Partnerships to Strengthen Community Colleges. The Budget also proposes a new tax credit to encourage businesses to invest in strengthening community college programs. While many regions face a shortage of skilled workers, community colleges providing training for in-demand fields often lack the needed regular investments in up-to-date equipment and highly-skilled instructors to meet the needs of employers and students. Under this proposal, businesses that help community colleges fill in these investment gaps would be eligible for up to $5,000 for each graduate they hire. Investing in workers' skills—

just as they invest in research, development, and physical equipment—is one way that businesses can promote long-term, shared growth.

Streamlining and Expanding Higher Education Tax Incentives. The Budget would streamline and expand education tax benefits by: 1) consolidating the Lifetime Learning Credit into an expanded AOTC; 2) exempting Pell Grants from taxation and the AOTC calculation; and 3) eliminating tax on student loan debt forgiveness, while repealing the complicated student loan interest deduction for new borrowers.

TRAINING AMERICANS FOR THE JOBS OF THE FUTURE

The record-setting 70 months of job growth in the United States reflects the strength of one of our Nation's greatest assets: a skilled, educated, and adaptable workforce. In the new economy, technology is allowing businesses to locate anywhere. In deciding where to locate jobs, employers seek the most educated, adaptable, and nimble workforce. A nation's ability to ensure a steady and consistent pipeline of highly skilled workers is one key ingredient to helping its economy grow and thrive. One of the surest paths to ensuring that the economy works for everyone is to expand access to job training and education for in-demand skills.

The Budget builds on the plan that the Administration released in July 2014 for a job-training system that, as the President has laid out, "trains our workers first based on what employers are telling us they're hiring for and helps business design training programs so that we're creating a pipeline into jobs that are actually out there." Since July 2014, agencies have awarded more than $1 billion in job training grants that incorporate seven essential elements that matter most for getting Americans into better jobs—stronger employer engagement, work-based learning approaches, better use of labor market information, accountability for employment outcomes, more seamless progression between education and

jobs, expansion of key support services, and regional partnerships. The Budget continues to support job-driven training.

Supporting Implementation of the Workforce Innovation and Opportunity Act (WIOA). Over the last several years, the Congress and the Administration have worked together to improve the Nation's job training system, including through the enactment and implementation of the bipartisan WIOA, which encompasses programs that serve about 20 million people annually. The reforms supported by WIOA—such as accountability for business engagement and new requirements to measure and report program outcomes—are allowing us to do more to make sure that training programs match in-demand jobs. The Budget helps to realize the goals of WIOA by funding the core Department of Labor (DOL) WIOA formula grants at their full authorized level—a $138 million, or five percent, increase over the 2016 enacted level. The Budget also gives DOL and States the funding they need to oversee and implement the extensive changes envisioned in the law. The Budget includes a $40 million investment to build State and local capacity to track the employment and educational outcomes of WIOA program participants, and give those seeking training meaningful information—including past participants' success in finding jobs—so they can make good choices about which program would best prepare them for the labor market.

Building a System of Apprenticeships. Apprenticeship is a proven strategy for preparing workers for careers. On average, apprentices who finish their program earn $50,000 a year and increase their lifetime earning potential by $300,000. The Administration has successfully expanded this proven model. There are now 75,000 more apprentices in training than when the President first launched the American Apprenticeship Initiative in 2014. The Budget further invests in this proven strategy, sustaining the new $90 million in grants provided in 2016—a landmark investment—and adding a $2 billion mandatory Apprenticeship Training Fund. These investments would help meet the President's goal to double the number of apprentices across the United States, giving more workers the opportunity to develop job-relevant skills while they are earning a paycheck.

Creating an American Talent Compact. A key to successful job training is ensuring that employers and training providers—including the Nation's community and technical colleges—work together so that students learn the skills needed for jobs and careers that are available in their communities. The Budget puts forward a substantial investment in this high-quality training by providing $3 billion in mandatory competitive funding for regional partnerships between workforce boards, economic development organizations, employers, K-12 career and technical education programs, and community colleges with the goal of training a half million people and placing them into jobs in high demand sectors.

Reconnecting Workers to Jobs. The Administration makes significant investments to reach those who have been left on the sidelines of the economic recovery. The Budget provides $1.5 billion in mandatory funding to States to fund Career Navigators in American Job Centers to proactively reach out to all people who have been unemployed for six months or more, those who

have dropped out of the labor force altogether, and people who are only able to find part-time work. These Career Navigators would help workers look for a job, identify training options, and access additional supportive services. The Budget also includes almost $190 million in discretionary funding to provide in-person reemployment services to the one-third of Unemployment Insurance (UI) beneficiaries most at risk of exhausting their benefits, as well as all returning veterans who are receiving UI. Evidence suggests these services are a cost-effective strategy that gets workers back into jobs faster with higher wages.

Empowering Workers, Training Providers, and Employers through Better Data. Each year, millions of Americans choose education and training programs with very little high-quality information and advice to go on. In a recent survey, only 40 percent of people knew post-graduation job placement rates before entering post-secondary education, and at most community colleges and secondary schools there is only one academic adviser per 800 to 1,200 students. One of the main tools we have to ensure that workers are making the best investments of time and money is empowering them with good data and information to make smart choices. In pursuit of that goal, the Budget proposes a $500 million mandatory Workforce Data Science and Innovation Fund that would invest in data systems in States to enable them to create easy-to-understand scorecards that provide key data on training participants' outcomes. In conjunction with the Departments of Commerce and Education, DOL would also develop new data standards, analytical data sets, and open source data products on jobs and skills to spur continued market innovation and provide key labor market actors with a more comprehensive view of local labor market demand. Finally, the Fund would establish a Center of Excellence with a best-in-class team of private sector researchers, statisticians, data scientists, and innovators to help States and localities find new ways to use technology and data analytics to improve training programs and consumer choice.

Opening Doors for Youth. Today, approximately six million Americans between the ages of 16 and 24 are out of school and work—a tremendous untapped resource for the Nation. Despite talent and motivation, these young Americans lack access to the education and training that can provide them with a pathway to better jobs and careers with advancement opportunities. The enactment of WIOA took a step toward addressing this problem by requiring that a minimum of 75 percent of WIOA Youth program funds be directed to out-of-school youth. The Budget fulfills this promise by fully funding the youth program at its authorized level, which would result in approximately $560 million in funding for out-of-school youth.

In addition, the Budget invests $5.5 billion in mandatory funding to engage young people in education and the workforce and set them on a path to a better future. Of this, $3.5 billion is devoted to giving more American youth the valuable experience of a paid learning opportunity; this includes $1.5 billion to support summer job opportunities, and $2 billion to create year-round first jobs for nearly 150,000 opportunity youth—those who are currently out-of-school and out-of-work but ready to take on a work opportunity. A critical component to the success of these programs is a strong focus on financial empowerment. To that end, all grantees receiving funds to support summer job opportunities or provide first jobs for opportunity youth must help participants establish bank accounts and directly deposit wages into those accounts. These accounts must be established with reputable banks and be affordable to youth. The accounts would be a tool to allow youth to learn sound money management practices, and would be used by youth employment programs to implement high-quality financial literacy education for participating youth.

The Budget also provides $2 billion to transform communities struggling with high rates of youth disengagement, high school dropouts, and unemployment into places of opportunity for young adults to help them succeed in school and the labor force. The program would provide funds to local governments to locate and reengage youth, and connect them with the counseling, support services, employment opportunities, and education they need to succeed.

Improving Interstate Mobility and Expanding Access to Jobs for Qualified Workers. The Budget builds on the investment provided in the 2016 Consolidated Appropriations Act (2016 Omnibus) and provides a total of $10 million for grants to States and partnerships of States to identify and address areas where occupational licensing requirements create an unnecessary barrier to labor market entry or mobility and where interstate portability of licenses can improve economic opportunity, particularly for dislocated workers, transitioning service members, veterans, and military spouses.

Protecting Workers

While most employers play by the rules, in too many cases workers need protection from employers who cheat workers out of their hard-earned wages or do not ensure a safe workplace. The Budget includes $1.9 billion in discretionary resources to ensure that DOL's worker protection agencies can meet their responsibilities to defend the health, safety, wages, working conditions, and retirement security of American workers. The Administration continues to pursue a combination of administrative and legislative actions to strengthen these laws and their enforcement, so workers can earn family-sustaining wages, be protected from discrimination, and return home safely at the end of a day's work. The Administration continues to support workers by:

Ensuring Workers Get Fair Pay for a Fair Day's Work. The Budget provides $277 million to enforce laws that establish the minimum standards for wages and working conditions in many of the workplaces in the United States, particularly in industries where workers are most at risk. The Budget also expands funding for efforts to ensure that workers receive back wages they are owed and cracks down on the illegal misclassification of some employees as independent contractors, a practice that deprives workers of basic protections like unemployment insurance, workers' compensation, and overtime pay.

Keeping Workers Safe. The Budget provides almost $1 billion for the Occupational and Mine Safety and Health Administrations (OSHA and MSHA) to ensure workers are protected from health and safety hazards on the job. In particular, the Budget provides resources to enhance safety and security at chemical facilities and improve response procedures when major incidents at these sites occur. The Budget also includes funds for OSHA to enforce the more than 20 whistleblower laws that protect workers from discrimination and retaliation when they report unsafe and unscrupulous practices. The Budget also pro-

---

Leveling the Playing Field through Wall Street Reform

In response to the destabilizing 2008 financial crisis, the Administration achieved landmark reform of the Nation's financial system in 2010 with enactment of the Dodd-Frank Wall Street Reform and Consumer Protection Act (Wall Street Reform). In the years since enactment, Federal agencies have helped make home, auto, and short-term consumer loan terms fairer and easier to understand for consumers, improved the transparency of financial markets, and made the system more resilient to downturns. These actions are already curbing excessive risk-taking, closing regulatory gaps, and making our financial system safer and more resilient. However, the financial services industry continues to rapidly evolve, expand and grow more complex. The agencies charged with establishing and enforcing the rules of the road are hampered by budget limitations. For example, resource constraints have forced the Commodity Futures Trading Commission (CFTC) to delay and even cut back on its examination of clearinghouses, critical points of systemic risk in our financial system. Similarly, without adequate staffing the Securities and Exchange Commission (SEC) is not able to examine investment advisors as frequently as it should, introducing significant risk to investors and the economy. To match these growing challenges and strengthen regulation of the financial system, the President is calling for doubling the funding of these agencies from their 2015 levels by 2021.

The Budget's 2017 down payment toward the five-year doubling target includes $1.8 billion for the SEC and $330 million for the CFTC. The Budget also reflects continued support for legislation to enable funding the CFTC through user fees like other Federal financial and banking regulators. Fee funding would shift the costs of regulatory services provided by the CFTC from the general taxpayer to the primary beneficiaries of the CFTC's oversight, and fee rates would be designed in a way that supports market access, liquidity, and the efficiency of the Nation's futures, options on futures, and swaps markets. Increasing the transaction fees that currently fund the SEC would particularly fall on high-frequency trading. In addition, the Budget takes other steps designed to reduce risk in the financial sector, such as leveling a fee on the largest financial firms on the basis of their liabilities. The Administration will also continue to oppose efforts to restrict the funding independence of the other financial regulators, including the Consumer Financial Protection Bureau, and will fight other attempts to roll back Wall Street Reform.

To finish addressing the weaknesses exposed by the financial crisis, the Government must reform the housing finance system and move forward to wind down the Government-sponsored enterprises (GSEs), Fannie Mae and Freddie Mac, which have been in conservatorship since September 2008. As part of the 2016 Omnibus, the Congress included a provision that limits the ability to return to the dysfunctional system in effect prior to conservatorship, and reinforces the need to enact comprehensive reform. A bipartisan bill developed in the Senate in the previous session includes many of the Administration's key housing finance reform principles, including ensuring that private capital is at the center of the housing finance system, and that the new system supports affordable housing through programs such as the Housing Trust and Capital Magnet Funds. The President stands ready to work with Members of Congress in both parties to enact commonsense housing finance legislation that embodies these core principles. (For additional discussion of the GSEs, see the Credit and Insurance chapter in the *Analytical Perspectives* volume of the Budget.)

vides MSHA the resources it needs to meet its statutory obligation to inspect every mine and address the risks posed to miners by the Nation's most dangerous mines.

MAKING THE 21ST CENTURY ECONOMY WORK FOR WORKERS

The economy and the Nation's workforce have changed significantly since the 1930s when many core worker protections and benefits, like unemployment insurance, were first established. Today, women are almost twice as likely to be in the workforce as they were eight decades ago and the issues of the intersection of work and family are more widely recognized. New industries and ways of organizing work continue to emerge. As the nature of work continues to evolve, it is important that we update key worker benefit structures to ensure that workers in the 21st Century economy can balance work and family obligations, save for retirement, and are protected during temporary periods of unemployment and upon return to work.

Helping Workers Balance Work and Family

Expanding Access to Quality Child Care for Working Families. The Budget reflects the President's commitment to quality, affordable child care, which research shows can increase parents' employment and earnings and promote healthy child development. The Budget invests $82 billion in additional mandatory funding over 10 years to ensure that all low- and moderate-income working families with children ages three or younger have access to quality, affordable child care. This landmark proposal makes significant investments in raising the quality of child care, including investments to improve the skills, competencies, and training of the child care workforce, and a higher subsidy rate for higher quality care. This increase in the subsidy rate, paired with investments in workforce development, would improve the quality of care that children receive in part by allowing for more adequate compensation of child care workers.

The Budget also provides $200 million in discretionary funding above the 2016 enacted level. This funding would help States implement the policies required by the new bipartisan Child Care and Development Block Grant Act of 2014, designed to improve the safety and quality of care while giving parents the information they need to make good choices about their child care providers. The new funding would help States improve quality while preserving access to care. The additional funding in the Budget would also go toward new pilot grants to States and local communities to help build a supply of high-quality child care in rural areas and during non-traditional hours. These grants focus on what low-income working families need most—high-quality, affordable care that is close to home and available during the hours they work and on short notice.

Cutting Taxes for Middle-Class Families with Child Care Expenses. The current tax benefits for child care are unnecessarily complex and provide too little help for families facing high child care costs. To ensure that all working families have access to high-quality, affordable child care, the Budget streamlines child care tax benefits, extends the child care tax credit to more middle-class families, and triples the maximum child care credit for families with young children, increasing it to $3,000 per child. This would benefit 5.3 million families, helping them cover child care costs for 6.9 million children, including 3.6 million children under five. This tax proposal complements the other substantial investments to improve child care quality, access, and affordability.

Encouraging State Paid Leave Initiatives and Creating Paid Leave for Federal Workers. Too many American workers face the difficult choice between caring for a new baby or sick family member and a paycheck they desperately need. The Family and Medical Leave Act allows many workers to take job-protected unpaid time off to care for a new baby or sick family member, or tend to their own health during a serious illness. However, millions of families cannot afford to use unpaid leave.

The United States is the only industrialized nation in the world that fails to offer workers paid maternity leave. Evidence shows that the availability of paid maternity leave increases the likelihood that mothers return to their jobs following the birth of a child, in addition to producing better outcomes for infants, yet employers are not required to offer paid leave in most States.

A handful of States and localities have enacted policies to offer paid family leave, and the Federal Government can encourage more States to follow their lead. The Budget includes more than $2 billion for the Paid Leave Partnership Initiative to assist up to five States to launch paid leave programs, following the example of California, New Jersey, and Rhode Island. States that choose to participate in the Paid Leave Partnership Initiative would be eligible to receive funds for the initial set up and three years of benefits. The Budget also includes funding for grants to help States and localities conduct analysis to inform the development of paid family and medical leave programs. These grants have helped recipients obtain the information they needed to understand how a paid family leave policy could work in their communities.

The Budget also proposes legislation that would offer Federal employees six weeks of paid administrative leave for the birth, adoption, or foster placement of a child. In addition, the proposal would make explicit the ability for mothers and fathers to use sick days to bond with a healthy new child. This proposal is part of a broader effort to expand the availability of paid family leave for the Federal workforce, and establish a Federal family leave policy that is on par with leading private sector companies and other industrialized nations so that the Government can recruit and retain the best possible workforce to provide outstanding service to American taxpayers. These proposals complement the President's

executive actions to expand paid leave for employees of Federal contractors.

Helping the Paychecks of Families Go Further. The Budget helps families' paychecks go further by cutting taxes for middle-class families when both spouses work. Two-earner couples can face higher marginal tax rates when both spouses work, even though the family incurs additional costs from commuting, professional expenses, child care, and, increasingly, elder care. The Budget proposes a new, simple second earner credit of up to $500 that recognizes the additional costs faced by families in which both spouses work. A total of 23.4 million couples would benefit from this proposal.

In addition, the Budget proposes a $100 million Financial Innovation for Working Families Fund within the Department of the Treasury to encourage the development of innovative private-sector financial products that would help low- to moderate-income workers build up "rainy day" reserves and provide a buffer against shocks to income and spending needs. Funds would be awarded to financial institutions and intermediaries that provide strong evaluation plans for promising programs.

Helping All Workers Save for Retirement

Our system of retirement benefits has not kept pace with a rapidly evolving economy. Approximately half of workers employed by firms with fewer than 50 workers and fewer than one-quarter of part-time workers have access to workplace retirement plans. Workers without access to a plan at work rarely save for retirement: fewer than 10 percent of workers without access to a workplace plan contribute to a retirement savings account on their own.

Helping Workers without Access to Workplace Retirement Plans. The Budget includes the following proposals that would make saving easier for millions of Americans currently without employer-based retirement plans:

- *Automatically Enroll Americans without Access to a Workplace Retirement Plan in an Individual Retirement Account (IRA).* Under the proposal, every employer with more than 10 employees that does not currently offer a retirement plan would be required to automatically enroll their workers in an IRA. Employers would not be required to contribute to the plan, and individuals would have the ability to opt out. There is strong evidence that making enrollment the default option results in greater participation. Under the proposal, approximately 30 million Americans would be automatically enrolled in an IRA. Other individuals not automatically enrolled could participate so long as they fall below the income cutoff, and could continue to make their own contributions even if they change jobs.

- *Provide Tax Cuts for Auto-IRA Adoption, and for Businesses that Choose to Offer More Generous Employer Plans or Switch to Auto-Enrollment.* To minimize the burden on small businesses, the Budget's auto-IRA proposal would provide any employer with 100 or fewer employees who offers an auto-IRA a tax credit of up to $4,500. The Budget also proposes to triple the existing "startup" credit and extend it to an additional year, so small employers who newly offer a retirement plan would receive a tax credit of up to $6,000, enough to offset administrative expenses. Furthermore, because auto-enrollment is the most effective way to ensure workers with access to a plan participate, small employers who already offer a plan and add auto-enrollment would get an additional tax credit of $1,500.

- *Expand Retirement Savings Options for Long-Term, Part-Time Workers.* Part-time workers are much less likely to have access to a retirement plan compared to their full-time colleagues, in part because employers can exclude them from participation. The Budget would provide approximately one million individuals with access to retirement plan coverage by requiring that employees who have worked for an employer at least 500 hours per year for at least three consec-utive years be eligible to participate in the employer's existing plan. Employers would not be required to offer matching contributions and participation by employees would be voluntary.

- *Encourage State Retirement Savings Initiatives.* Many States have been exploring options for creating retirement accounts for workers in the private sector who do not otherwise have access to a workplace retirement plan. Several States have created their own auto-IRAs or retirement marketplaces connecting small businesses and their employees to existing investment vehicles, with approximately 20 more considering similar measures or an alternative approach that would create a State-based 401(k). The Department of Labor has proposed regulations and guidance to provide a path forward for State retirement savings programs consistent with the Employee Retirement Income Security Act. To further State efforts, the Budget sets aside $6.5 million to allow a handful of States to pilot and evaluate State-based 401(k)-type programs or automatic enrollment IRAs.

- *Increase Coverage by Supporting New, More Flexible Benefit Models.* To expand access to retirement and other benefits, particularly for the self-employed and workers who frequently change employers, the Budget provides for the creation of open multiple employer plans (open MEPs) that allow multiple employers to offer benefits through the same administrative structure, but with lower costs and less fiduciary burden. The Budget proposes to remove the current requirement of a "common bond" between employers while adding significant new worker safeguards, thereby enabling more small businesses to offer cost-effective, pooled plans to their workers and potentially facilitating pooled plans of self-employed individuals. As an added benefit, if an employee moves between employers participating in the same open MEP, or is an independent contractor participating in a pooled plan using the open MEP structure, then he can continue contributing to the same plan even if he switches jobs. The Budget also funds pilots for States and non-profits to design, implement, and evaluate new approaches to expand retirement and other employer-provided benefit coverage, with a focus on developing models that are portable across employers and can accommodate contributions from multiple employers for an individual worker. Policies proposed in this Budget, as well as past Budgets, to expand access to IRAs should also increase portability since workers can continue contributing to their IRA even if they change jobs, though their employers cannot.

Finally, recognizing the challenges workers face in this new economy, the President proposes to allow long-term unemployed individuals to withdraw up to $50,000 per year for two years from any tax-preferred retirement account so they can draw upon their savings, not go further into debt, to make ends meet.

Protecting Workers' Retirement Security. The Pension Benefit Guaranty Corporation (PBGC) acts as a backstop to insure pension payments for workers whose companies or plans have failed. PBGC's single-employer program covers plans that are sponsored by an individual company; the multiemployer program covers plans maintained pursuant to one or more collective bargaining agreements involving more than one unrelated employer. Both programs are underfunded, with combined liabilities exceeding assets by $76 billion at the end of 2015. While the single-employer program's financial position is projected to improve over the next 10 years, in part because the Congress has raised premiums in that program several times in recent years, the multiemployer program is projected to run out of funds in 2024. Particularly in the multiemployer program, premium rates remain much lower than what a private financial institution would charge for insuring the same risk and well below what is needed to ensure PBGC's solvency.

To address these concerns, the Budget proposes to give the PBGC Board the authority to adjust premiums. The 2016 Budget proposed to raise premiums by $19 billion, with premiums to be split between the multiemployer and single-employer programs based on the size of their deficits. Given the $4 billion in recent premium increases enacted in the Bipartisan Budget Act of 2015, and the single-employer program's improving financial projections, the Budget directs the Board to raise $15 billion in additional premium revenue within the Budget window only from the multiemployer program. The Administration believes additional increases in single-employer premiums are unwise at this time and would unnecessarily create further disincentives to maintaining defined benefit pension plans. This level of additional multiemployer premium revenue would nearly eliminate the risk of the multiemployer program becoming insolvent over the next 20 years.

The Budget assumes that the Board would raise these revenues by using its premium-setting authority to create a variable-rate premium (VRP) and an exit premium in the multiemployer program. A multiemployer VRP would require plans to pay additional premiums based on their level of underfunding—as is done in the single-employer program. An exit premium assessed on employers that withdraw from a plan would compensate the PBGC for the additional risk imposed on it when healthy employers exit.

Helping Workers Who Lose Their Jobs and Reducing Job Loss

The Budget proposes a cost-neutral suite of reforms to strengthen and modernize the Unemployment Insurance (UI) program. UI provides critical income support to unemployed workers. But after cutbacks in coverage by States and broader changes in the evolving economy, fewer than one out of every three unemployed workers today receives UI benefits, the lowest level in half a century. The Budget's reforms would address this by providing coverage for more workers—including more part-time workers, low-wage and intermittent workers, and workers who must leave a job for compelling family reasons. The Budget would also help unemployed workers get back to work more quickly; reform UI to help prevent layoffs; make the UI program more responsive to economic downturns; and shore up the solvency of State UI programs so they are prepared if unemployment in their State rises. In addition, the Budget establishes wage insurance to help workers make ends meet if a new job pays less than an old one while encouraging workers to get off the sidelines quickly and stay in the workforce. The goal is a modernized, well-funded UI program that better serves the diverse set of workers in today's economy and better supports economic recoveries.

UI Solvency. Three out of five State UI programs are insolvent, and only 20 States have sufficient reserves to weather a single year of recession. Low State reserves remain a serious threat to UI for working Americans. The President's proposal would put State unemployment insurance programs on a path to permanent solvency while ensuring they have sufficient reserves to weather the next economic crisis. The proposal would modernize Federal unemployment insurance taxes and hold States accountable for maintaining sufficient reserves to provide benefits for at least six months of an average economic recession.

Expanded Access to UI Benefits and Services. The Budget makes changes to ensure that UI benefits and reemployment opportunities are available to more workers who need them. The Budget requires UI coverage for part-time workers and those who must leave a job due to compelling family reasons like domestic violence or family illness, and mandates the provision of at least 26 weeks of benefits, so workers have time to get back on their feet. Building on the success of the Recovery Act, the Budget also includes a $5 billion Modernization Fund to incentivize States to make other improvements in their UI programs' coverage, benefits, and connection to work. Through the Modernization Fund, States would be encouraged to allow workers to retool their skills to prepare for new job opportunities while receiving UI benefits and to create apprenticeship and on-the-job training programs to help the unemployed get back to work.

Wage Insurance. Wage insurance would provide a safety net for workers who lose their jobs and become reemployed at lower wages at least initially, often in new industries. The Budget proposes establishing wage insurance for all workers with at least three years of job tenure who are laid off and become reemployed in a lower-paying job at less than $50,000 per year. Wage insurance would pay half of the difference between the previous wage and the new wage, up to a maximum of $10,000 over a period of two years. The goal of the program is two-fold: help workers who return to work at lower wages on a temporary basis as they gain a foothold in their new jobs and provide workers an incentive to return to work, even if they must take a pay cut relative to their former employment.

Work Sharing. Work-sharing programs, also known as Short Time Compensation (STC), encourage employers to avoid layoffs by temporarily reducing hours when their need for labor falls and providing employees with a partial UI benefit to help compensate for their lower wages. Aided by incentives that were enacted in the Middle Class Tax Relief and Job Creation Act of 2012, about half the States are now operating STC programs. The Budget seeks to expand on this progress by renewing expired incentives for States to enact programs, providing for a 50-50 Federal cost share for STC benefits when State unemployment is high, and encouraging employers to use STC by allowing States to reduce employers' UI taxes for the portion of benefits that is paid by the Federal Government.

Extended Benefits During Recessions. The Budget seeks to create a more inclusive and responsive unemployment system by establishing a new Extended Benefits program to provide additional benefits during economic downturns. The new permanent Extended Benefits program would provide up to 52 weeks of additional federally-funded benefits for States seeing increased and high unemployment, with the number of weeks tied to the State's unemployment rate. This new program would ensure that the UI system responds quickly, providing critical support for unemployed workers in States where jobs are scarce, and helping to reduce the severity of recessions by providing timely economic stimulus.

Addressing Wage Stagnation and Helping Low-Wage Workers

While economic growth is strong, too many workers continue to see their wages stagnate, making it hard for them to get ahead. The Budget seeks to improve wage growth through a series of investments in the Nation's economy—from infrastructure to research and development—and also includes targeted policies to address wage stagnation directly.

Raising the Minimum Wage. In a Nation as wealthy as the United States, no one who works full time should have to raise his or her family in poverty. The value of the minimum wage, which has not increased in more than five years, has failed to keep pace with the higher costs of basic necessities for working families. The Administration supports raising the minimum wage so hard-working Americans can earn enough to support their families and make ends meet. Raising the minimum wage is good for workers, their families, and for the economy. Many companies, from small businesses to large corporations, recognize that raising wages is good for their bottom lines because it boosts productivity, reduces turnover and increases profits.

The President has already taken an important step by ensuring that those working on new and replacement Federal contracts receive a higher minimum wage. The Administration is encouraged that 17 States and the District of Columbia have passed increases in their minimum wage since the President called for a minimum wage increase during his State of the Union address in February 2013. Those increases will benefit an estimated seven million workers as of 2017. As the President continues to encourage States, cities, and businesses to act, he stands ready to work with the Congress to pass legislation to increase the minimum wage for the rest of the workforce as soon as possible.

Building on the Success of the Earned Income Tax Credit (EITC) and Child Tax Credit (CTC). The EITC and CTC are among the Nation's most effective tools for reducing poverty and encouraging people to enter the workforce. The 2016 Omnibus permanently extended Recovery Act expansions of the EITC and CTC for families with children that were scheduled to expire after 2017. These provisions provide a tax cut of about $900 on average for 16 million working families a year. If the expansions had been allowed to expire, more than 16 million people—including eight million children—would have fallen into, or deeper into, poverty in 2018. With the expansions in place, the EITC and CTC lift more children out of poverty than any other Federal program.

Because the EITC available to workers without children and to non-custodial parents is so small, they largely miss out on these antipoverty and employment effects of the EITC. The Budget would double the EITC for so-called "childless workers"—workers who are not raising dependent children, as well as noncustodial parents—and make the credit available to workers with earnings up to about 150 percent of the poverty line. It would also expand eligibility to single workers between the ages of 21 and 24 and ages 65 and 66, so that the EITC can encourage employment and on-the-job experience for young adults, as well as older workers, and harmonize the EITC rules with ongoing increases in the Social Security full retirement age. The proposal would reduce hardship and improve financial security for 13.2 million low-income workers struggling to make ends meet, while encouraging and supporting work.

The Budget also proposes providing funding for an EITC for Puerto Rico as part of a package to help the Commonwealth recover from an economic and fiscal crisis. (See text box below.)

Addressing Puerto Rico's Economic and Fiscal Crisis

The Commonwealth of Puerto Rico is in the midst of an economic and fiscal crisis which without action from the Congress could devolve into a humanitarian crisis. The 3.5 million Americans living in Puerto Rico have endured a decade of economic stagnation. Since 2006, Puerto Rico's economy has shrunk by more than 10 percent and shed more than 250,000 jobs. More than 45 percent of the Commonwealth's residents live in poverty—the highest poverty rate of any State or territory—and its 12.5 percent unemployment rate is more than twice the national level. These challenges have sparked the largest wave of outmigration since the 1950s, and the pace continues to accelerate. More than 300,000 people have left Puerto Rico in the past decade; a record 84,000 people left in 2014.

Consistent with the Roadmap for Congressional Action on Puerto Rico that the Administration established in October 2015, the Budget proposes a series of measures to provide Puerto Rico with the tools it needs to address its economic and fiscal crisis in a fair, orderly, and comprehensive manner while creating the foundation for recovery.

The President remains committed to the principle of self-determination for the people of Puerto Rico, and it is clear from the results of the 2012 referendum on the political status of Puerto Rico that the people of Puerto Rico want to resolve the issue. We believe that the Congress and this Administration have key roles to play to help Puerto Rico determine its future status through a fair, clearly defined, and transparent process—and we believe the outcome of that process should be respected and acted upon in the Congress.

There are four key elements of the Roadmap for Congressional Action on Puerto Rico in the Budget:

1. Provide tools for Puerto Rico to comprehensively address its financial liabilities. The Budget proposes to provide Puerto Rico with the necessary tools to restructure its financial liabilities in a fair and orderly manner under the supervision of a Federal court. Specifically, the Budget proposes a broad legal framework that allows for a comprehensive restructuring of Puerto Rico's financial liabilities. This framework should be reserved exclusively for U.S. territories. As under current law, States would remain ineligible to file for bankruptcy under this or any other bankruptcy regime.

2. Enact strong fiscal oversight and help strengthen Puerto Rico's fiscal governance. Puerto Rico must reform its fiscal governance in a credible and transparent way while implementing the changes needed to achieve financial stability. The Budget proposes to strengthen Puerto Rico's ability to implement a sound plan for achieving financial stability while also respecting Puerto Rico's unique status and local autonomy.

3. Strengthen Medicaid in Puerto Rico and other U.S. territories. To avoid a loss in coverage when one-time funds from the Affordable Care Act run out, and to better align territory Medicaid programs with the mainland, the Budget would remove the cap on Medicaid funding in the territories, gradually increase the Federal support territories receive through the Federal Medicaid match by transitioning them to the same level that is received on the mainland, and expand eligibility to 100 percent of the Federal poverty level in territories currently below this level. To be eligible for maximum Federal financial support, territories will have to meet financial management and program integrity requirements and achieve milestones related to providing full Medicaid benefits. (See details below in Building on the ACA to Improve Americans' Health.)

4. Reward work and support growth. The decade-long recession has taken a toll on Puerto Rico's finances, its economy, and its people. To reward work and break this vicious cycle, the Budget proposes an EITC for Puerto Rico. The EITC is already available to Americans living in the 50 States and the District of Columbia, and providing the EITC in Puerto Rico would create incentives for work and increase participation in the formal economy.

TAX REFORM THAT PROMOTES GROWTH AND OPPORTUNITY

A simpler, fairer, and more efficient tax system is critical to achieving many of the President's fiscal and economic goals. At a time when middle class and working parents remain anxious about how they will meet their families' needs, the tax system does not do enough to reward hard work, support working families, or create opportunity. After decades of rising income and wealth inequality, the tax system continues to favor unearned over earned income, and a porous capital gains tax system lets the wealthy shelter hundreds of billions of dollars from taxes each year. In a period where an aging population will put increasing pressure on the Federal budget, a wide range of inefficient tax breaks prevent the tax system from raising the level of revenue the Nation needs. While commerce around the world is increasingly interconnected, an out-of-date, loophole-ridden business tax system puts U.S. companies at a disadvantage relative to their competitors, while also failing to encourage investment in the United States.

The Budget addresses each of these challenges. As described above, it reforms and simplifies tax incentives that help families afford child care, pay for college, and save for retirement. The Budget expands tax benefits, like the EITC for workers without qualifying children, and creates new benefits, like a second earner tax credit, that support and reward work. It also makes important investments in the IRS that will improve taxpayer services, allow the IRS to fairly enforce the tax code, and takes steps to counter cybersecurity threats and protect taxpayers from identity theft.

Closing Tax Loopholes for the Wealthy, Imposing a Fee on Large Financial Firms, and Making Sure Everyone Pays Their Fair Share

The Budget pays for tax reforms that support work, help middle-class families get ahead, and reduce the deficit through numerous changes to make the tax code fairer, simpler, and more efficient, including by closing loopholes that let the wealthy pay less than their fair share and im-

posing a fee on large financial firms. Specifically, the Budget would:

- **Reform the Taxation of Capital Income.** The Budget would reform the taxation of capital income in two important ways: first, by increasing the top tax rate on capital gains and dividends to 28 percent (inclusive of the 3.8 percent Net Investment Income Tax (NIIT), the rate at which capital gains were taxed under President Reagan; and second, by ending "stepped-up basis," which allows hundreds of billions of dollars in capital gains to avoid income tax, while preventing undue burdens on middle-class families and small businesses through various exclusions.

- **Impose a Financial Fee.** The Budget would also impose a new fee on large, highly-leveraged financial institutions. Specifically, the Budget would raise $111 billion over 10 years by imposing a seven basis point fee on the liabilities of large U.S. financial firms—the roughly 100 firms with assets over $50 billion. By attaching a direct cost to leverage for large firms, this fee will reduce the incentive for large financial institutions to use excess leverage, complementing other Administration policies aimed at preventing future financial crises and making the economy more resilient.

- **Limit the Value of Itemized Deductions and Other Tax Preferences to 28 Percent.** Currently, a millionaire who deducts a dollar of mortgage interest enjoys a tax benefit that is more than twice as generous as that received by a middle-class family. The Budget would limit the value of most tax deductions and exclusions to 28 cents on the dollar, a limitation that would affect only couples with incomes over about $250,000 (singles with incomes over about $200,000).

- **Close Tax Loopholes.** The Budget would also close a number of inefficient, unintended, and unfair tax loopholes in the individual tax code. For example, it would end the "carried interest" loophole that allows certain investment fund managers to take advantage of preferential capital gains tax rates and prevent wealthy individuals from using loopholes to accumulate huge amounts in tax-favored retirement accounts.

- **Ensure that High-Income Individuals Pay into Medicare.** As in 2016, the Budget proposes to end the loophole that allows some high-paid professionals to avoid paying Medicare and Social Security payroll taxes. The Budget further closes gaps between the Self-Employment Contributions Act (SECA) tax and the NIIT to ensure that all high-income individuals fully contribute to Medicare, either through the NIIT or through payroll or SECA taxes. Revenue from the NIIT would be dedicated to the Medicare Hospital Insurance Trust Fund, extending Medicare's long-term solvency by more than 15 years.

- **Observe the "Buffett Rule."** As in past years, the Budget proposes to institute the Buffett Rule, requiring that wealthy millionaires pay no less than 30 percent of income—after charitable contributions—in taxes. This proposal acts as a backstop to prevent high-income households from using tax preferences to reduce their total tax bills to less than what many middle-class families pay.

Fixing America's Broken Business Tax System

In February 2012, the President proposed a framework for business tax reform that would help create jobs and spur investment, while eliminating loopholes that let companies avoid paying their fair share. The President's framework would cut the corporate rate to 28 percent—with a 25 percent effective rate for domestic manufacturing—putting the United States in line with other major countries and encouraging greater investment here at home. The rate reduction would be paid for by eliminating dozens of inefficient tax expenditures and through additional structural reforms. Together, these reforms would help achieve more neutral tax treatment of different industries, types of investment, and means of financing, improving capital allocation and contributing to economic growth.

Consistent with that framework, the Budget proposes a number of reforms that would make the business tax code fairer and more efficient, including a detailed international tax reform plan. The Budget includes improved incentives for research and clean energy investment and simplifies and cuts taxes on small businesses—allowing more than 99 percent of all businesses to dispense with many of the tax system's most complex rules and instead pay tax based on simpler, "cash" accounting.

The Budget details the President's full plan for reforming and modernizing the international business tax system, including a 19 percent minimum tax on foreign earnings that would require U.S. companies to pay tax on all of their foreign earnings when earned—with no loopholes or opportunities for deferral—after which earnings could be reinvested in the United States without additional tax. It would prevent U.S. companies from avoiding tax through "inversions"—transactions in which U.S. companies buy smaller foreign companies and then reorganize the combined firm to reduce U.S. tax liability—and prevent foreign companies operating in the United States from using excessive interest deductions to "strip" earnings out of the United States. The Department of the Treasury has taken steps within its authority to reduce the economic benefits of inversions, but the President has been clear that the only way to fully address the issue of inversions is through action by the Congress.

PARTNERING WITH COMMUNITIES TO EXPAND OPPORTUNITY

Since the start of the Administration, the President has called on the Federal Government to disrupt an outdated, top-down approach to working with communities, and to think creatively about how to make the our efforts more user-friendly and responsive to the ideas and concerns of local citizens. Too often in the past, innovative efforts to expand opportunity at the State and local level have been stymied by less flexible Federal approaches and a failure to recognize community assets alongside their challenges. In communities facing limited local revenues and capacity, the imperative for the Federal Government to serve as a strong partner only increases.

The need for this community-level focus and collaboration is clear. Groundbreaking new research shows that the place in which a child grows up has a significant impact on his or her prospects for upward economic mobility.[1] A child's zip code should never determine her destiny, but today, the neighborhood she grows up in impacts her odds of graduating high school, her health outcomes, and her lifetime economic opportunities. This inequality of opportunity in childhood is not just a moral failure, it is also an economic failure for the Nation and its cities and communities. Every year, the United States incurs an estimated half-trillion dollar cost as a result of allowing millions of America's children to grow up in poverty.[2]

Over the course of the past six years, the Administration has been steadily testing new ways of working in partnership with the communities that our programs serve—from southeastern Kentucky to Fresno, California to Detroit, and also in Indian Country. These collaborative efforts take a comprehensive approach to community revitalization instead of addressing problems in isolation; work with local leaders to support their vision for their communities; and embrace creative new solutions to old problems to learn and apply what works and stop doing what does not.

The first step in this approach is ensuring that the Federal Government is working in a coordinated way across agencies, and then improving how it interacts with individual communities as a partner. It also requires investments in the basic building blocks for program success, such as data infrastructure to measure outcomes and assess need across communities. By modernizing Federal programs to meet urban, suburban, and rural communities where they are, and updating Federal policies to respond to the ways that people live, we can better meet the demands of communities that are striving for a better quality of life.

Early initiatives such as Strong Cities, Strong Communities, which strengthens towns, cities, and regions by improving the capacity of local governments to develop and execute their local vision and strategies, and the Neighborhood Revitalization Initiative, which has helped nearly 200 communities pursue local solutions to revitalize and transform neighborhoods, have informed many other initiatives and programs as place-based approaches have spread.

The Budget increases the Administration's support for such holistic community solutions through investments that include the Administration's Promise Zone initiative, which establishes partnerships between the Federal Government, local communities, and businesses to create jobs, increase economic security, expand educational opportunities, increase access to quality, affordable housing, and improve public safety. The competitively-chosen Promise Zones are high-poverty urban, rural, and tribal communities that partner with local government, and business and community leaders to make investments that reward hard work and expand opportunity. In exchange, the Federal Government partners with these communities to help them secure the resources and flexibility

---

1   Chetty, Raj and Hendren, Nathaniel, "The Impacts of Neighborhoods on Intergenerational Mobility." Harvard University, April 2015, available at: http://www.equality-of-opportunity.org/images/nbhds_exec_summary.pdf

2   Holzer, Harry; Schanzenbach, Diane Whitmore; Duncan, Greg; & Ludwig, Jens, "The Economic Costs of Poverty: Subsequent Effects of Children Growing Up Poor." Center for American Progress, January 2007, available at: https://cdn.americanprogress.org/wp-content/uploads/issues/2007/01/pdf/poverty_report.pdf

they need to help them achieve their goals. To date, the President has designated 13 Promise Zones, and seven more will be announced in 2016. The Budget supports all 20 Promise Zones through intensive, tailored Federal assistance at the local level. The Budget continues to propose Promise Zone tax incentives to stimulate growth and investments in targeted communities, such as tax credits for hiring workers and incentives for capital investment within the Zones.

The Budget further supports efforts to transform distressed communities by expanding the Department of Education's Promise Neighborhoods program and the Department of Housing and Urban Development's (HUD) Choice Neighborhoods program. These programs have already provided critical funding for comprehensive and community-driven approaches to improving the educational and life outcomes of residents in over 100 distressed communities. The Budget provides $128 million for Promise

Neighborhoods and $200 million for Choice Neighborhoods, an overall increase of $130 million over 2016 enacted levels for the two programs. This additional funding would support implementation grants for approximately 15 new Promise Neighborhoods and six new Choice Neighborhoods, and numerous other planning grants for communities to engage with stakeholders to create plans for future revitalization.

To support private-sector partnerships and investments that play a key role in strengthening communities, the President also proposed to expand and make permanent the New Markets Tax Credit, which promotes investments in low-income communities. Under legislation signed into law by President Obama in December, $3.5 billion in New Markets Tax Credits will be available annually through 2019. The Budget would make the program permanent with an annual allocation of $5 billion.

HOUSING AND HOMELESSNESS

Improving Mobility with Housing Choice Vouchers. In addition to the studies mentioned above related to the impact of poverty on families and children new research demonstrates moving to higher-opportunity areas with a rental subsidy can generate large benefits for children's long-term earnings and educational attainment, especially for young children. These findings have significant policy implications. Though we must continue to prioritize revitalizing distressed communities, this research demonstrates the need to also invest in and make improvements to HUD's Housing Choice Voucher (HCV) program, which provides rental assistance to over 2.2 million extremely low- to very low-income households to enable them to rent modest units in the private market. The goal of the HCV program is not only to make decent, safe and sanitary housing affordable for low-income families, but also to improve the ability of families to rent in safer neighborhoods with more jobs and better schools.

The President proposes $20.9 billion for the HCV program in 2017, an increase of $1.2 billion over the 2016 enacted level, to expand opportunities for very low-income families. This includes additional funding for Public Housing Authorities' (PHAs) to ensure they have sufficient resources to promote mobility and greater access to opportunity, as well as cover fundamental functions, such as housing quality inspections and tenant income certifications.

In addition, the Budget requests $15 million for a new mobility counseling pilot designed to help HUD-assisted families move to and stay in higher-opportunity neighborhoods. These funds will be distributed to about 10 regional housing program sites with participating PHAs and/or private non-profits over a three-year period to provide outreach to landlords and counseling to voucher recipients on the benefits of opportunity-rich, low-poverty neighborhoods, as well as facilitate regional collaboration. A portion of the funding would also support an evaluation to measure the impact of the counseling pilot to further inform the policy process and design.

Ending Homelessness. In 2010, the President set the ambitious goal of ending homelessness in America. Since then significant progress has been made, especially in the area of veteran homelessness where the Administration, the Congress, local leaders, and nonprofit partners have committed to achieving the goal. Since 2010, the overall number of veterans experiencing homelessness on a single night has declined by 36 percent. Moreover, the number of homeless veterans on the streets has been nearly cut in half. Over 850 mayors, governors, and county executives have committed to ending veteran homelessness in their communities through the Mayors Challenge to End Veteran Homelessness. In the past year, communities across the Nation, including Las Vegas, Houston, Philadelphia, and the Commonwealth of Virginia, have successfully ended veteran homelessness—putting in place systems that ensure veterans and their families can get back into housing quickly and permanently if they experience homelessness.

The Nation's work to end veteran homelessness has proven that ending homelessness is possible. The Budget sustains funding to support programs dedicated to ending veteran homelessness, while also providing $11 billion in housing vouchers and rapid rehousing—a strategy that helps stabilize families' housing and then assists them to become more self-sufficient—over the next 10 years to reach and maintain the goal of ending homelessness among all of America's families by 2020. This significant investment is based on recent rigorous research that found that families who utilized vouchers—compared to alternative forms of homeless assistance—had fewer incidents of homelessness, child separations, intimate partner violence and school moves, less food insecurity, and generally less economic stress. Complementing this mandatory proposal, the Budget provides targeted discretionary increases to address homelessness, including 25,500 new units of permanent, supportive housing to end chronic homelessness, 10,000 new HCVs targeted to homeless families with children, $25 million to test innovative projects that support homeless youth, and 8,000 new units of rapid re-housing that provides tailored assistance to help homeless families stabilize in housing and then assists them to become more self-sufficient. This investment further builds the evidence base on this emerging intervention.

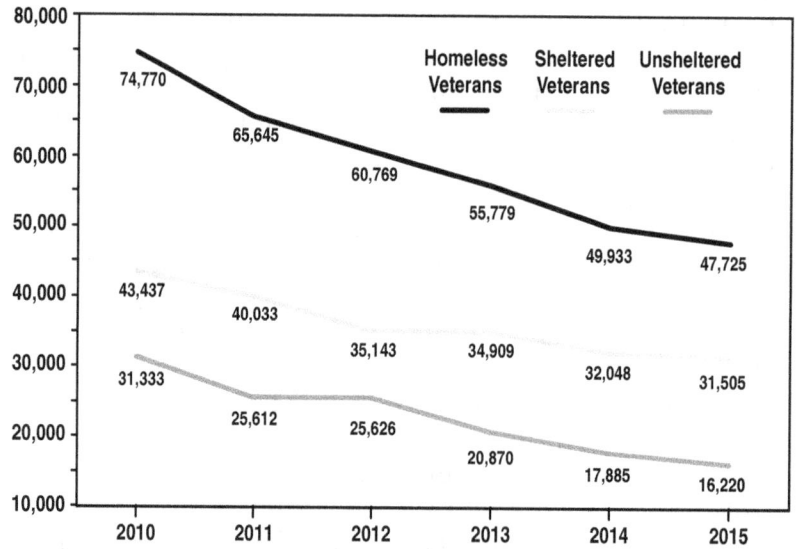

Veterans Homelessness Continues to Decline

Source: Department of Housing and Urban Development. The 2015 Annual Homeless Assessment Report to Congress, Part 1

STRENGTHENING EFFORTS TO HELP POOR FAMILIES SUCCEED

Between 2012 and 2014 child poverty fell farther than it had since 2000, indicating that the economic recovery is starting to improve prospects for poor families. Still, in 2014, 15.5 million children, or 21.1 percent of all children, were poor and nearly 6.8 million children lived in families with cash incomes that fell below half of the poverty line, or just $785 per month for a family of three. There is recent evidence showing that the number of very poor families with children living on less than $2 in cash income per person per day rose sharply after 1996: in 2011, roughly 1.5 million households had cash income of less than $2 per person per day.[3] While non-cash benefits such as the Supplemental Nutrition Assistance Program (SNAP), formerly known as food stamps, helps cushion the hardships these families face, their cash incomes are so low that they are at substantial risk of homelessness and hunger.

Improving the opportunity and economic security of poor children is both a moral and an economic imperative. Research shows that poverty has significant negative impacts on children's future prospects. For example, a large body of recent research finds that when children's families are more financially secure, children are healthier and do better in school. Importantly, this research shows that when poor families receive additional income, children's outcomes improve. In the 21st Century economy, the United States cannot afford for a large share of its children to have their learning and health hindered because of poverty.

Twenty years ago, The Personal Responsibility and Work Opportunity Reconciliation Act of 1996 created the Temporary Assistance for Needy Families Program (TANF), which replaced the Aid to Families with Dependent Children program. TANF gave States more flexibility in how they operate their cash welfare program, put in place work-related requirements that many States have found overly prescriptive, and capped and froze Federal funding. A strong

economy, work-supporting policies such as an expanded EITC and child care assistance, and changes to cash welfare programs contributed to an increase in employment rates among single mothers in the 1990s. However, that progress stalled and then reversed in the early part of the 2000s, ceding a significant portion of the earlier gains. In addition, too few families have worked their way into the middle class, while three million children are living on less than $2 a day in cash income. The rise in children living in such deep poverty is at least in part due to the declining role of TANF as a safety net. There is now substantial evidence that further reforms are needed to meet our 21st Century poverty challenges.

Given the need to do more to combat poverty and provide opportunity for all children, the Budget includes several proposals designed to reduce poverty, assist families in deep poverty or experiencing a financial crisis, and improve efforts to help parents find and keep jobs. These include:

Establishing Emergency Aid and Service Connection Pilots. For some financially stressed families, a needed car repair or a week of missed work due to the flu can bring the family to the brink of financial collapse—including the loss of a job or even homelessness. Some families have already hit bottom, living in extreme poverty without help. The Budget provides $2 billion for a robust round of pilots to test new approaches to providing emergency aid for these families, including both short-term financial assistance and connection to longer term supports for those who need them. Building on the lessons learned from the rapid rehousing approach, these pilots will seek to both prevent families from financial collapse when emergency help, such as fixing a car or paying a security deposit is needed, and connect families that need them to services and supports—such as TANF, employment assistance, SNAP, child care, or Medicaid—that can help them find jobs, stabilize their families, and become more financially secure. The pilots would be rigorously evaluated to inform future

[3]   Edin, K.J., & Shaefer, H.L. (2015). *$2.00 a Day*. New York, NY: Houghton Mifflin Harcourt.

policy and program decisions at the local, State, and Federal levels.

Strengthening TANF. TANF was designed to provide States with more flexibility while requiring them to engage recipients in work activities, but after 20 years there is strong evidence that the program can do more to help families get back on their feet and work toward self-sufficiency. Currently, some States use only a small share of their TANF funds to provide assistance to very poor families or to help parents find jobs. One major issue that has arisen is that a large share of poor families with children do not get any help at all from TANF, even when the parents are out of work and the family has no regular source of income. A particularly troubling indicator is the decline in the TANF-to-poverty ratio since TANF's inception: in 1996, for every 100 families in poverty, 68 received TANF assistance; by 2014, that number had dropped to just 23. Currently, just 32 percent of families that meet State eligibility requirements for TANF (such as income and asset rules) actually receive income assistance. Furthermore, when families do not receive income assistance, they also typically lose access to the employment services that TANF programs provide.

One contributing factor to this drop in help for poor families is the fact that TANF funding has remained frozen since it was created in 1996—after adjusting for inflation, TANF funding to States has fallen by about one-third over the last 20 years. Even with the resources available, too few TANF dollars are spent on the core purposes of supporting destitute families and helping them find jobs. In nearly half the States, the share of Federal and State TANF funds spent on basic income assistance to poor families, work programs, and child care is less than 50 percent. In addition, some Federal rules limit State flexibility in a way that hinders the effectiveness of TANF employment programs. Finally, TANF is not adequately responsive to recessions, which is why during the Great Recession, the Congress and the Administration had to create the temporary TANF Emergency Fund (now expired) to ensure that States had the resources required to meet the increased need.

In order to address these concerns, the Budget: 1) increases resources for TANF and ensures that States meet their State funding requirements without using funding gimmicks; 2) requires States to spend a majority of their funds (both Federal TANF funds and the funds States contribute to TANF) on core purposes of TANF, defined as welfare-to-work efforts, child care, and basic assistance, and ensures all TANF funds are spent on low-income families; 3) calls for providing States with more flexibility to design effective work programs in exchange for holding States accountable for the outcome that really matters—helping parents find jobs; 4) proposes that HHS be required to publish an annual measure or measures related to child poverty in States; and 5) creates a workable countercyclical measure modeled after the effective TANF Emergency Fund created during the Great Recession and utilized by governors of both parties. The Budget also builds on a prior proposal to redirect funds currently in the poorly designed contingency fund. The proposal would shift these funds to finance two important innovative approaches to reducing poverty and promoting self-sufficiency—subsidized jobs programs, and two-generation initiatives that seek to improve employment outcomes of parents and developmental and educational outcomes of children.

Ensuring Adequate Food for Children throughout the Year. With a consistent focus on raising a healthier next generation of kids, the Administration has made historic improvements in child nutrition programs, including through the Healthy, Hunger Free Kids Act of 2010, which updated nutrition standards for schools for the first time in 15 years. The Budget seeks to ensure all children have consistent and adequate access to nutritious food year round to learn and grow. During the academic year, school meals help meet this need for the nearly 22 million low-income children who rely on free and reduced price school meals. However, only a fraction of those children receive free and reduced price meals in the summer months. As a result, low-income children are at higher risk of food insecurity and poorer nutrition during the months when school is out of session. Rigorous evaluations of USDA pilots have found that providing additional food benefits on debit cards to low-income families with school-aged children during summer months can significantly reduce food insecurity. The Budget invests $12 billion over 10 years to create a permanent Summer Electronic Benefits Transfer for Children program that would provide all families with children eligible for free and reduced price school meals access to supplemental food benefits during the summer months.

Expanding Opportunity for Native American Youth. In December 2014, President Obama announced Generation Indigenous, a Native youth initiative focused on taking a comprehensive, culturally appropriate approach to help improve the lives of and opportunities for Native youth. The Budget builds on key investments the Congress made across several agencies in 2016 to support Generation Indigenous, providing $40 million at HHS to support youth-focused behavioral and mental health services, $23 million at the Department of Education (ED) for the Native Youth Community Projects, and $1 billion for Bureau of Indian Education (BIE) schools.

The additional resources provided in the Budget for Native youth would ensure that multiple agencies, including the Departments of the Interior (DOI), ED, HUD, HHS, USDA, and Justice (DOJ), are working collaboratively with Tribes and can successfully implement education reforms and address issues facing Native youth.

The Budget makes a number of investments in these priorities, including:

- $1 billion to support DOI's comprehensive redesign and reform of the BIE, including $138 million to improve facilities conditions and $25 million to extend broadband internet and computer access at BIE-funded schools and dormitories;

- $20 million for HUD-funded community facilities to support Native youth and teacher housing and $8 million for DOI's efforts to address teacher housing needs;

- $55 million in HHS's Substance Abuse and Mental Health Services Administration and Indian Health Service to support the Administration's priority of expanding access to mental health services to Native youth. The funding would provide youth-focused behavioral and mental health, and substance abuse services, and reduce the number of suicides among Native youth, which is currently the second leading cause of death among Native youth ages 8-24 and occurs at 2.5 times the national rate;

- $26.6 million for HHS's Administration for Children and Families to support Native youth resiliency and leadership development, implement special programs to increase and improve Native American language instruction across the educational continuum, and increase the ability of Tribes to effectively serve Native youth involved in the child welfare system, as well as $242 million in mandatory funding over 10 years to strengthen the capacity of tribal child welfare systems, including tribal courts; and

- A $30 million increase to the Native Youth Community Projects at ED to support community-driven, comprehensive strategies to improve college- and career-readiness of Native youth.

These investments build on current efforts to better serve Native youth by coordinating and demonstrating results across the Federal Government.

Reducing Rural Child Poverty. According to a 2015 report by USDA's Economic Research Service, roughly one in four rural children live in poverty. Not only is rural child poverty pervasive, it is persistent: approximately 80 percent of persistent child poverty counties—that is, counties with 20 percent or more of their child populations living in poverty over the last 30 years—are rural. To address these challenges, the Budget invests in innovative strategies to increase rural families' access to promising and evidence-based programs and services. The Budget makes unprecedented investments in two-generation approaches—aligning high-quality early childhood education for children with high-quality workforce development for parents to put the entire family on a path to educational success and permanent economic security. The Budget provides $20 million for two-generation demonstration projects within USDA to fight rural child poverty and $16 million to support an integrated model for early childhood development and parental involvement for American Indian families in BIE-funded schools. As discussed above, the Budget also introduces a new rural home visiting program that complements HHS's evidence-based Maternal, Infant, and Early Childhood Home Visiting program to serve more high-risk, high-need children and families in remote rural areas.

Promoting Permanency, Safety, and Well-Being for Children and Youth in Foster Care. On any given day, there are more than 400,000 young people in the Nation's foster care system, with over 100,000 waiting to be adopted. The Budget includes a package of investments designed to do more to prevent the need for foster care and assist children and families so that children can either be reunited with their biological parents or placed in a permanent home where they can thrive. The Budget includes funding to provide critical preventative services to vulnerable families and children to address hardships early, keeping more children out of foster care and with their families, as well as funding to promote family-based care for children with behavioral and mental health needs to reduce the use of congregate care—which can have negative effects on children. The Budget also provides funding to help improve the training and skills of the child welfare workforce, individuals working with some of the most vulnerable children and youth in the Nation, including funding to help caseworkers obtain a Bachelor or Master's degree in social work and incentivize State child welfare agencies to hire and retain caseworkers

with this specialized education. The Budget continues to include funding for Tribes to build their child welfare infrastructure, and for tribal children and youth removed from their homes to remain in their communities.

Improving Health Outcomes for Children and Youth in Foster Care. The Budget continues to propose a Medicaid demonstration project in partnership with HHS's Administration for Children and Families to encourage States to provide evidence-based psychosocial interventions to address the behavioral and mental health needs of children in foster care and reduce reliance on psychotropic medications to improve overall health outcomes.

Helping Families Achieve Self-Sufficiency through the Upward Mobility Project. The Budget continues to support the Upward Mobility Project, which would allow up to 10 communities, States, or a consortium of States and communities more flexibility to use funding from up to four Federal programs for efforts designed to implement and rigorously evaluate promising approaches to helping families achieve self-sufficiency, improving children's education and health outcomes, and revitalizing communities. Projects will have to rely on evidence-based approaches or be designed to test new ideas, and will have a significant evaluation component that will determine whether they meet a set of robust outcomes. The funding streams that States and communities can use in these projects are currently block grants—the Social Services Block Grant, the Community Development Block Grant, the Community Services Block Grant, and the HOME Investment Partnerships Program—that share a common goal of promoting opportunity and reducing poverty, but do not facilitate cross-sector planning and implementation as effectively as they could. The Budget also provides $1.5 billion in additional funding over five years that States and communities can apply for to help support their Upward Mobility Projects.

BUILDING ON THE ACA TO IMPROVE AMERICANS' HEALTH

For decades, too many Americans went without the security of health insurance. Since the ACA's coverage provisions have taken effect, 17.6 million Americans have gained health insurance coverage through the Health Insurance Marketplace, Medicaid, and other sources. Now, fewer than 1 in 10 Americans lack health insurance for the first time in history. The dramatic decline in the uninsured rate shows the ACA is working, making health care more affordable and accessible for millions of people.

The ACA also provides Americans the economic security they deserve. Because of the ACA, American families no longer need to worry about losing coverage due to economic setbacks, such as lay-offs or job changes, or due to pre-existing conditions, such as asthma, cancer, or diabetes. In addition, health insurance plans cannot bill patients into debt because of an illness or injury, or limit annual or lifetime dollar benefits. Americans have benefited from these changes. For example, the number of people in households that faced problems paying medical bills fell by 12 million from 2011 to 2015.

Further, the ACA has taken historic and significant steps toward putting the Nation back on a sustainable fiscal course, while laying the foundation for a higher quality health care system. It is improving the quality of care that Americans receive and reducing cost growth by deploying innovative new payment and delivery models that incentivize more efficient, higher-quality care.

With the ACA as a solid foundation, the Budget makes additional health care investments and reforms to further improve the Nation's health care system and the health of all Americans. With approximately $375 billion in health savings that will grow over time, the Budget would extend the exceptionally slow cost growth of recent years. It builds on the dependable health insurance provided to Medicare, Medicaid, and Children's Health Insurance Program (CHIP) beneficiaries, supports an aggressive agenda to transform the Nation's health care delivery system into one that better incentivizes quality and efficiency, reins in growing drug costs while improving quality and transparency, and includes proposals that extend the life of the Medicare Hospital Insurance Trust Fund by over 15 years.

Implementing the ACA and Improving Health Care in America

The Budget fully funds the ongoing implementation of the ACA and makes a number of improvements to the health care system.

Supporting Medicaid Expansion. The ACA expanded affordable health insurance coverage to millions of low-income Americans by offering significant Federal financial support to States that expand Medicaid eligibility to non-elderly individuals with income below 133 percent of the poverty line, roughly $26,700 for a family of three. In the 30 States (and the District of Columbia) that expanded Medicaid by the end of 2015, the share of people without health insurance has fallen significantly, along with the cost of uncompensated care. The Budget provides further incentive for States to expand Medicaid by covering the full cost of expansion for the first three years regardless of when a State expands, ensuring equity between States that already expanded and those that will expand in the future. Previously, the ACA covered the full costs through calendar year 2016 before gradually reducing the level of support to 90 percent.

Protecting Consumers and Other Reforms. The Budget makes targeted improvements to the ACA's private insurance programs, including proposals to help eliminate unexpected health care charges and provide for uniform health care billing documents, among other reforms. It also proposes to standardize the definition for American Indians and Alaska Natives used in the ACA. The Budget bolsters program integrity efforts with additional investments and a proposal to allow the Centers for Medicare & Medicaid Services (CMS) access to new data sources to improve the accuracy of eligibility determinations for Marketplace financial assistance.

Improving the Excise Tax on High-Cost Employer Coverage. The ACA included an excise tax on the highest-cost employer-sponsored health insurance plans to give employers an incentive to make those plans more efficient. The Budget proposes to modify the threshold above which the tax applies to be equal to the greater of the current law threshold or the average premium for a Marketplace gold plan in each State. This reform would protect employers from paying the tax only because they are in high-cost areas and ensure that the tax remains targeted at the highest-cost plans in the long term. The Budget would also make it easier for employers offering flexible spending arrangements to calculate the tax. Finally, the proposal would require the Government Accountability Office to conduct a study of the potential effects of the tax on firms with unusually sick employees, in consultation with the Department of the Treasury and other experts.

Strengthening Medicare, Medicaid and CHIP

Together, Medicare, Medicaid, and CHIP provide affordable health coverage to support longer, healthier lives and economic security for the Nation's seniors, people with disabilities, and low-income working Americans and families. Today, Medicare provides about 55 million Americans with dependable health insurance. State Medicaid and CHIP programs provide health and long-term care coverage to more than 70 million low-income Americans. The Budget strengthens the Medicare and Medicaid programs through reforms that expand and extend health coverage in Medicaid and CHIP, encourage high-quality and efficient care, and continue the progress of reducing cost growth.

Expanding Health Coverage by Improving Access to Medicaid and CHIP Coverage and Services. The Budget gives States the option to streamline eligibility determinations for children in Medicaid and CHIP

and to maintain Medicaid coverage for adults by providing one-year of continuous eligibility. The Budget also extends full Medicaid coverage to pregnant and post-partum Medicaid beneficiaries, expands access to preventive benefits and tobacco cessation for adults in Medicaid, streamlines appeals processes, and ensures children in inpatient psychiatric treatment facilities have access to comprehensive benefits. The Budget also fully covers the costs of the Urban Indian Health Program (UIHP) clinics for Medicaid services provided to eligible American Indians and Alaska Natives, supporting the expansion of UIHP service offerings and improving beneficiary care.

Preserving Coverage through CHIP. CHIP currently serves more than eight million children of working parents who are not eligible for Medicaid. While the Medicare Access and CHIP Reauthorization Act extended CHIP funding through 2017, the Budget proposes to extend funding for CHIP through 2019, ensuring continued, comprehensive, affordable coverage for these children.

Strengthening Medicaid in Puerto Rico and other U.S. Territories. The Medicaid programs in Puerto Rico and the other U.S. territories of American Samoa, Guam, Northern Mariana Islands, and the U.S. Virgin Islands are fundamentally different from the Medicaid program in the States, leading to a lower standard of care than may be otherwise experienced on the mainland. Medicaid funding in Puerto Rico and the other territories is capped; beneficiaries are offered fewer benefits; and the Federal Government contributes less on a per-capita basis than it does to the rest of the Nation. The ACA increased the Federal match rate and provided $7.3 billion above the territory funding caps between July 1, 2011 and the end of 2019. To avoid a loss in coverage when the supplemental funds provided in the ACA run out and to better align Puerto Rico and other territory Medicaid programs with the mainland, the Budget would remove the cap on Medicaid funding in Puerto Rico and the other territories. It also would gradually increase the Federal support territories receive through the Federal Medicaid match by transitioning them to the same level of Federal support as is received on the mainland, and expand eligibility to 100 percent of the Federal poverty level in territories currently below this level. To be eligible for maximum Federal financial support, territories would have to meet financial management and program integrity requirements and achieve milestones related to providing full Medicaid benefits.

Promoting Access to Long-Term Care Services and Supports (LTSS). The Administration has made it a priority to help more older Americans and people with disabilities with Medicaid coverage have the choice to receive home and community-based services (HCBS) rather than institutional care. The Administration has focused on implementing key initiatives in this area, including supporting State efforts to transition disabled and elderly individuals from institutions to community-based care. The Budget builds on these efforts by expanding and simplifying eligibility to encourage more States to provide HCBS in their Medicaid programs. The Budget also includes a comprehensive long-term care pilot for up to five States to test, with enhanced Federal funding, a more streamlined approach to delivering LTSS to support greater access and improve quality of care. In addition, the Budget includes an increase of $10 million for HCBS provided through HHS's Administration for Community Living, which provides supportive services such as in-home personal care, respite care, and transportation assistance.

Improving Care Delivery for Low-Income Medicare-Medicaid Beneficiaries. The Budget proposes to streamline enrollment for the Medicare Savings Programs, which assist low-income beneficiaries with their Medicare premiums and cost-sharing, by setting a national standard for income and asset definitions. The Budget also proposes to implement simpler, faster processes for Federal-State review of marketing materials and beneficiary appeals for managed care plans that serve Medicare-Medicaid enrollees. In addition, the Budget proposes to permanently

authorize a demonstration that provides retroactive drug coverage for certain low-income Medicare beneficiaries through a single plan, establishing a single point of contact for beneficiaries seeking reimbursement for claims.

Strengthening the Medicare Advantage Program. The Budget proposes a package of reforms that encourage greater quality and efficiency in Medicare Advantage. First, the Budget proposes to reform payments to Medicare Advantage plans by using competition to set payment rates. Under the Budget's proposed competitive bidding system, Medicare Advantage payment rates would be based on plans' bids, ensuring that plan payments reflect plans' costs for covering Medicare beneficiaries. The proposal also preserves most beneficiaries' access to a Medicare Advantage plan that provides supplemental benefits, without paying an additional premium. In addition, the Budget includes higher payments to high-quality Medicare Advantage plans to encourage quality improvement and attainment. These reforms would save about $77 billion combined.

Encouraging High-Quality, Efficient Care among Medicare Providers. The Budget includes new proposals to expand competitive bidding to additional durable medical equipment and to encourage efficiency among hospice providers through changes to payments. The Budget continues a robust set of proposals that build on ACA initiatives to help extend Medicare's solvency while encouraging provider efficiencies and improved patient care among hospitals and post-acute care providers. Together, these proposals would save almost $180 billion over 10 years.

Reducing Cost Growth by Encouraging Beneficiaries to Seek High-Value Services. The Budget includes structural changes to encourage Medicare beneficiaries to seek high-value health care services and improve the financial stability of the Medicare program. It also includes new proposals to improve coverage of colonoscopies and incentivize primary care delivery. The Budget continues to propose several modifications for new beneficiaries starting in

2020, such as a modified Part B deductible and a modest copayment for certain home health episodes. Together, these proposals would save approximately $54 billion over 10 years.

Making Targeted Reforms to Increase Quality and Maximize Cost-Effectiveness in Medicaid and CHIP. The Budget proposes to limit the portion of Medicaid and CHIP managed care dollars spent on administration and incentivize more investments in quality health care services by establishing a Medical Loss Ratio (MLR) ratio of 85 percent. This would modernize Medicaid and CHIP managed care by aligning program requirements with those in Medicare Advantage and private insurance. Furthermore, it will strengthen State and Federal financial management of managed care contracts with a requirement to return payments in excess of the minimum MLR. The Budget extends funding for the Medicaid adult quality program, and continues to propose better aligning Medicaid Disproportionate Share Hospital Payments, which compensate hospitals that treat high numbers of uninsured patients, with expected levels of uncompensated care.

Cutting Waste, Fraud, and Abuse in Medicare and Medicaid. The Administration has made targeting waste, fraud, and abuse in Medicare, Medicaid, and CHIP a priority and is aggressively implementing new tools for fraud prevention provided by the ACA. In 2014, the Government's health care fraud prevention and enforcement efforts recovered $3.3 billion in taxpayer dollars from individuals and companies attempting to defraud Federal health programs, including programs serving seniors, persons with disabilities, and low-income individuals. In addition, further development of the CMS Fraud Prevention System, a predictive analytic model similar to those used by private-sector experts, continues to support CMS' efforts to identify and prevent wasteful, abusive, and potentially fraudulent billing activities. Building on this progress, the Budget proposes a series of policies that would save nearly $3.4 billion over the next 10 years by:

- Requiring prior authorization for power mobility devices and advanced imaging, which could be expanded to other items and services at high risk of fraud and abuse;

- Supporting efforts to investigate and prosecute allegations of abuse or neglect of Medicaid beneficiaries in non-institutional health care settings;

- Strengthening the Federal Government's ability to identify and act on fraud, waste, and abuse through investments in the Medicaid Integrity Program;

- Providing the Secretary of HHS with greater authority to reject claims for certain items and services in areas of the United States where there is evidence of fraud and abuse;

- Ensuring Federal and State governments can confidentially share data algorithms developed to detect waste, fraud, and abuse;

- Improving the Recovery Audit Contractor (RAC) program by authorizing CMS to pay RACs after the second-level of appeals, and by requiring RACs to maintain a surety bond or other form of protection to cover overturned recovery auditor decisions; and

- Requiring States to suspend Medicaid payments when there is a significant risk of fraud.

In order to decrease waste, fraud, and abuse and strengthen program integrity in the Medicare prescription drug program, the Budget also provides the Secretary the authority to suspend coverage and payment for questionable Part D prescriptions and establishes a program to reduce prescription drug abuse in Medicare.

Transforming the Nation's Health Care Delivery System

The Administration continues to support an aggressive reform agenda to transform the Nation's health care delivery system into one that better incentivizes quality and efficiency. These reforms are designed to not only improve Americans' health, but also to help further slow growth in health care costs and increase quality in Medicare and Medicaid.

Supporting Alternative Payment and Delivery Models. In January 2015, the Administration announced the goals of tying 30 percent of Medicare payments to quality and value through alternative payment models by 2016 and 50 percent by 2018. The Administration is on track to exceed the 2016 milestone by the end of 2016. This was the first time in Medicare's history that the Administration set explicit goals for alternative payment models and value-based payments.

In addition, the Administration is supporting more than 20 demonstration projects through the Center for Medicare & Medicaid Innovation (Innovation Center) to test new innovative payment and service delivery models targeted at reducing program expenditures while preserving or enhancing the quality of care. One demonstration, the Pioneer Accountable Care Organizations, generated over $300 million in savings to Medicare over its first three years while delivering high-quality patient care. Beginning in April 2016, approximately 800 hospitals will be engaged in a mandatory demonstration to drive quality improvement and cost reduction in hip and knee replacements.

The Budget builds on the ACA as well as the Administration's current demonstration projects and other actions to further delivery system reform. It proposes bundled Medicare payments for post-acute providers, such as nursing homes and home health agencies. The Budget also includes proposals that enhance the ability of Accountable Care Organizations to increase quality and reduce costs, and includes a proposal to incentivize hospitals to engage with qualifying alternative payment models. The Budget also reduces incentives for physicians to inappropriately order services from which they would financially benefit, establishes quality bonuses for the highest rated Part D plans, and modifies incentives in the Medicare prescription drug program to encourage patient engagement in health care decisions.

In addition, the Administration also is working to implement the Medicare Access and CHIP Reauthorization Act to accelerate physician participation in high-quality and efficient health care delivery systems, align incentives, and improve care coordination.

To facilitate system-wide change, the Administration launched the Health Care Payment Learning and Action Network to bring together private payers, providers, employers, State partners, consumer groups, individual consumers, and many others to accelerate the transition to alternative payment models.

Improving Health IT and Transparency. Health information exchange is essential for a transformed delivery system. To support improvement in this area, the Administration is promoting health IT interoperability and increasing access to health care information, including cost and quality information, so that clinicians, patients and their family members, and businesses can make informed health care choices.

To improve transparency and distribution of information, the Administration continues to improve access to Federal data through the Open Data Initiative, release Medicare data on cost and quality, and invest in innovative ways to collect and share data, from the way we measure the quality of care to the way health care is documented and communicated to consumers. For example, in December 2015, the Administration released an interactive tool that can be used to examine spending and price trends for medications that are fiscally significant to Medicare.

The Budget increases support to advance interoperable health IT while protecting patient privacy. The Budget includes new incentive payments for certain behavioral health providers to adopt and meaningfully use certified electronic health records, which would further enhance the integration of physical and behavioral health care. In addition, the Budget supports the Office of the National Coordinator for Health Information Technology in developing and advancing policies that help consumers and providers access electronic health information when and where they need it to make health care decisions, including development of interoperable tools and implementation of efforts to deter and remedy information blocking.

Investing in Public Health and Safety and the Health Care Workforce

Combating Prescription Drug Abuse and Heroin Use. More Americans now die every year from drug overdoses than in vehicle crashes, and the majority of these overdoses involve opioids—a class of drugs that includes prescription painkillers and heroin. Prescription opioid-related overdoses alone cost tens of billions in medical and work-related costs each year. The Administration has promoted and expanded community-based efforts to prevent drug use, improve opioid prescribing practices, and increase access to opioid use disorder treatment services. However, too many Americans are abusing opioids and too few are getting treatment. Individuals who want to but do not undergo treatment often report cost and lack of access as reasons why they do not get treatment.

The Budget takes a two-pronged approach to address this epidemic. First, it includes approximately $500 million to continue and expand current efforts across HHS and DOJ to expand State-level prescription drug overdose prevention strategies, increase the availability of medication-assisted treatment programs, and improve access to the overdose-reversal drug naloxone. A portion of this funding is targeted specifically to rural areas, where rates of overdose and opioid use are particularly high.

Second, the Budget includes $1 billion in new mandatory funding over the next two years to boost efforts to help individuals seek treatment, successfully complete treatment, and sustain recovery. States would receive funds based on the severity of the epidemic and on the strength of their strategy to respond to it. States can use these funds to expand treatment capacity and make services more affordable to those

who cannot afford it. This funding would also help expand the addiction treatment workforce through the National Health Service Corps and support the evaluation of treatment services. This investment, combined with other efforts underway to reduce barriers to treatment for substance use disorders, would help ensure that every American who wants treatment can access it and get the help they need.

Expanding Access to Mental Health Care. Too often mental health is thought of differently than other forms of health, yet mental health is essential to overall health and wellness. Recovery from and management of mental health conditions is possible and those who receive treatment can go on to lead happy, healthy, productive lives. One in five American adults experience a mental health issue at some point in their life, yet millions do not receive the care they need. The Budget includes $500 million in new mandatory funding over two years to help engage individuals with serious mental illness in care, improve access to care by increasing service capacity and the behavioral health workforce, and ensure that behavioral health care systems work for everyone. In addition to these funds, the Budget expands the President's Now is the Time initiative to improve access to mental health services for young people; support communities in developing comprehensive systems to intervene when an individual is experiencing a mental health crisis; and funding new strategies to address the increasing number of suicides by older adults.

Investing in Native American Health Care. The Budget provides the Indian Health Service (IHS) with $5.2 billion, a total increase of more than $400 million over the 2016 enacted level, to expand health care services and to make progress toward the construction of health care clinics in Indian Country. The Budget proposes to fund contract support costs fully, through discretionary funds in 2017 and through mandatory funds beginning in 2018.

Strengthening HIV and Hepatitis C Services. The Budget expands access to HIV prevention and treatment activities for millions of Americans through the continued implementation of the updated National HIV/AIDS Strategy, with a focus on three key elements of the Strategy. First, the updated Strategy calls for providing more people with highly effective prevention services such as pre-exposure prophylaxis (PrEP) to reduce new HIV infections. PrEP has been shown to reduce the risk of HIV infection by up to 92 percent in people who are at high risk. The Budget also includes $20 million for a new innovative pilot program to increase access to PrEP and allow grantees to use a portion of funds to purchase treatment and other health care services as the payer of last resort. Second, the Strategy calls for improved screening for Hepatitis C, which disproportionally affects Americans living with HIV. The Budget includes funding for a new initiative to increase screening and expands access to Hepatitis C care and treatment among people living with HIV. Third, the Strategy calls for prioritizing HIV/AIDS resources within high-burden communities and among high-risk groups, including gay and bisexual men, Blacks/African Americans, and Latino Americans, which is reflected throughout the Budget.

Combating Antibiotic Resistant Bacteria (CARB). The Budget includes $1.1 billion across the Federal Government to prevent, detect, and control illness and death related to infections caused by antibiotic-resistant bacteria and to support research on innovative ways to reduce or manage resistance. These resources would also help support the advancement of rapid diagnostics and new types of therapies for the treatment of bacterial infections, including managing the patient's microbiome and targeting bacterial virulence factors, as outlined in the CARB National Strategy and National Action Plan. The Budget also continues to support implementation of surveillance, prevention, and stewardship activities as outlined in the Strategy and the Action Plan.

Improving Access to Primary Care Health Care Providers. The Budget includes increased investments to strengthen the primary care workforce. The Budget expands the number of National Health Service Corps clinicians who practice primary care in areas of the Nation that need it most, to 15,000 providers between 2018 and 2020. In addition, the Budget supports primary care residency training in medically underserved areas. To continue encouraging provider participation in Medicaid, the Budget reestablishes increased payments for primary care services delivered by certain physicians through calendar year 2017, with modifications to expand provider eligibility and better target primary care services.

Addressing the High Cost of Drugs

The Administration is deeply concerned about rapidly growing prescription drug prices, driven in part by the shift to specialty therapeutics, the slowdown in patent expirations, and challenges in measuring drug value. To address this issue, the Budget includes a package of proposals focused on Medicare, Medicaid, and drug price transparency.

Improving Quality and Lowering Drug Costs for the Medicare Program. The Budget includes proposals to lower drug costs while improving transparency and evidence development in the Medicare Part D program. The Budget proposes to increase data collection to demonstrate the effectiveness of medications in the Part D program in the Medicare population and to inform real world clinical treatment. The Budget continues to provide the Secretary of HHS the authority to negotiate drug prices for biologics and high-cost drugs in Medicare Part D and includes a new proposal to incentivize Part D plan sponsors to better manage care provided to beneficiaries with high prescription drug costs.

To help ensure access and affordability of treatments, the Budget proposes to accelerate discounts for brand name drugs for seniors who fall into Medicare's coverage gap by increasing manufacturer rebates from 50 percent to 75 percent in 2018. In addition, the Budget proposes to require drug manufacturers to provide rebates generally consistent with Medicaid rebate levels for drugs provided to low-income Part D beneficiaries. Together, these proposals would save

Medicare approximately $140 billion over 10 years.

Lowering Medicaid Drug Costs for States and the Federal Government. The Budget includes targeted policies to lower drug costs in Medicaid. It provides States with a new, voluntary tool to negotiate lower drug prices through the creation of a Federal-State Medicaid negotiating pool for high-cost drugs. In addition, the Budget continues to support and build on previously proposed reforms to the Medicaid drug rebate program. These reforms enhance manufacturer compliance with rebate requirements, and improve access to medications. In addition, the Budget corrects and improves the ACA Medicaid rebate formula for new drug formulations, such as by exempting abuse deterrent formulations. These proposals are projected to save the Federal Government approximately $11.4 billion over 10 years.

Increasing Transparency of Prescription Drug Pricing and Ensuring Access to Generic Medications. The Budget proposes to provide the Secretary of HHS with the authority to require drug manufacturers to publicly disclose certain information, including research and development costs, discounts, and other data as determined through regulation. It also includes three previously proposed reforms designed to increase access to generic drugs and biologics by stopping companies from entering into anti-competitive deals intended to block consumer access to safe and effective generics, by awarding brand biologic manufacturers seven years of exclusivity, rather than 12 years under current law, and by prohibiting additional periods of exclusivity for brand biologics due to minor changes in product formulations. These proposals would save the Federal Government $21 billion over 10 years.

ENSURING SAFETY, FAIRNESS, AND COMMUNITY TRUST IN THE CRIMINAL JUSTICE SYSTEM

The President is committed to ensuring the criminal justice system is fair and effective for all Americans. Since the President took office, the rate of violent crime has fallen to levels not seen in decades. In 2014—for the first time in over 30 years—the Federal prisoner population decreased, following updates to Federal sentencing guidelines and implementation of DOJ's Smart on Crime initiative. The Budget proposes to accelerate criminal justice reform in the States, improve post-incarceration outcomes, remove barriers to reentry, support the enhancement of community policing practices across the Nation, support DOJ's efforts to focus its resources on the most serious threats to public safety, and to strengthen trust between the brave men and women of law enforcement and the communities they serve.

Incentivizing Justice Reform. The Administration continues to support criminal justice reform that simultaneously enhances public safety, avoids excessive punishment and

unnecessary incarceration, and builds trust between the justice system and communities. The Budget provides $500 million per year over 10 years—a $5 billion investment—for a new 21st Century Justice Initiative. The program will focus on achieving three objectives: reducing violent crime; reversing practices that have led to unnecessarily long sentences and unnecessary incarceration; and building community trust. Specifically, States would focus on one or more opportunities for reform in both the adult and juvenile systems, including: examining and changing State laws and policies that contribute to unnecessarily long sentences and unnecessary incarceration, without sacrificing public safety; promoting critical advancements in community-oriented policing; and providing comprehensive front-end and reentry services.

Reducing Gun Violence. The Administration maintains its commitment to reduce gun violence by providing funding to hire 200 new special agents and investigators for the Bureau of Alcohol, Tobacco, Firearms, and Explosives, enhance the National Integrated Ballistics Information Network, and improve the National Instant Background Check System (NICS). The NICS reforms by the Federal Bureau of Investigation (FBI) and the U.S. Digital Service include processing criminal background checks 24 hours a day, seven days a week and improving notification of local authorities when certain prohibited persons unlawfully attempt to buy a gun. The FBI will hire more than 230 additional examiners and other staff to help process these background checks. In addition, within the resources provided, the Departments of Defense, Justice, and Homeland Security (DHS) will conduct or sponsor research into gun safety technology to reduce the frequency of harm from accidental discharge or unauthorized use.

Community Policing Initiative. The President's Community Policing Initiative aims to build and sustain trust between law enforcement and communities. The Budget provides $97 million to expand training and oversight for local law enforcement, increase the use of body-worn cameras, provide additional opportunities for police department reform, and facilitate community and law enforcement engagement in 10 pilot sites, with additional technical assistance and training for dozens of communities and police departments across the Nation.

Improving Post-Incarceration Outcomes. The Administration continues working to address the problem of unnecessary and harmful collateral consequences of criminal convictions, which too often undermine the ability of the formerly incarcerated to reenter society and earn their second chance. For example, the Administration has emphasized the importance of investing in reentry programs and "banning the box" in employment applications, including taking steps to delay inquiry into criminal history for hiring in the Federal Government.

Reviewing and Reforming the Use of Restrictive Housing. The Administration has also sought to promote policies that provide inmates with programs and services that reduce recidivism and improve outcomes, including an ongoing DOJ review to study and reform the use of restrictive housing, often called solitary confinement, in prisons. The Budget invests $24 million to begin implementing the Department's proposals, which includes expanding mental health programming in Federal facilities. DOJ will also assist States and localities with implementing the recommendations.

Funding the New FBI Headquarters Facility. The Administration seeks $1.4 billion to support the full consolidation of the FBI headquarters operations in a new, modern, and secure facility that brings together all of the existing disparate headquarters locations and functions. This funding would be a combination of $759 million in the General Services Administration's Federal Building Fund and $646 million in the FBI Construction account for a total of $1.4 billion dedicated toward construction of the project in 2017. This substantial funding commitment illustrates the Administration's recognition of the importance of the FBI as a critical member of the U.S. intelligence community, as well as its role in national security and in enforcing the Nation's laws and protecting civil liberties.

FIXING OUR BROKEN IMMIGRATION SYSTEM AND SECURING OUR BORDERS

Immigration Executive Actions

In November of 2014, the President announced a series of actions consistent with his authority to fix what he can of our broken immigration system. These actions are improving accountability in our immigration system, strengthening our national security and our economy, and building on our past efforts to enforce immigration laws with common sense and compassion.

According to the Council of Economic Advisors, the President's executive actions, if fully implemented, would boost the Nation's economic output by up to $250 billion and raise average annual wages for U.S.-born workers by 0.4 percent, or $220 in today's dollars, in 10 years. Though the new deferred action policies announced in 2014 have been put on hold in litigation, the Administration will continue fighting to implement them. The Supreme Court of the United States has accepted DOJ's petition to review these policies.

The President's other immigration executive actions continue to move forward. DHS implemented new enforcement priorities and strengthened engagement with local law enforcement in order to better focus our limited resources on those who are threats to our national security, public safety, and border security. Over 98 percent of individuals removed by U.S. Immigration and Customs Enforcement (ICE) currently fall into DHS's enforcement priorities. DHS also ended the Secure Communities Program and replaced it with the Priority Enforcement Program (PEP). PEP is a commonsense program that works with local law enforcement and communities to apprehend priority individuals in local custody. It is tailored to the needs of each jurisdiction in order to keep communities safe, while preserving community trust. Today, the vast majority of local law enforcement agencies are working with DHS to keep America's communities safe. These include 15 of the top 25 jurisdictions that had previously declined to fully participate in ICE's efforts to apprehend individuals held in their custody.

Through new regulations and policies, the Administration is also modernizing the legal immigration system for families, employers, students, entrepreneurs, and workers. For example, DHS finalized a regulation that allows the spouses of certain high-skilled workers on their path to becoming lawful permanent residents to apply for work authorization. As a result, over 30,000 of these spouses are now able to work and contribute to their families and the economy. In addition, the White House released a report that announced further steps to modernize and streamline the legal immigration system so that

we can transform the largely paper-based system into a 21st Century, electronic system.

Finally, as a part of the immigration executive actions, the President established the White House Task Force on New Americans, a Government-wide effort tasked with better integrating and welcoming immigrants and refugees into American communities. Last April, the Task Force released its strategic plan with 48 recommendations to advance these goals. In December, the Task Force released its one-year progress report, highlighting the actions taken over the last year. These included the launch of the Building Welcoming Communities Campaign, which includes 48 communities to date and strives to support municipalities seeking to build more inclusive welcoming communities, and the "Stand Stronger" Citizenship Campaign, which works to raise awareness about the rights and responsibilities of U.S. citizenship.

These actions, however, are only a first step toward fixing our system, and the Administration continues to count on the Congress for the commonsense comprehensive reform that only legislation can provide and that the American public strongly supports. The reform supported by the President and passed by the Senate in 2013 would have fixed the Nation's broken immigration system by continuing to strengthen U.S. border security, cracking down on employers who hire undocumented workers, modernizing the Nation's legal immigration system, and providing a pathway to earned citizenship for hardworking men and women who pay a penalty and taxes, learn English, pass background checks, and go to the back of the line.

The Administration supports the bipartisan Senate approach, and calls on the Congress to act on comprehensive immigration reform this year. Although the President's executive actions will provide temporary relief while demanding accountability for those whose cases are not an enforcement priority, the Administration urges the Congress to act to permanently fix the Nation's broken immigration system. In addition to contributing to a safer and more just society, comprehensive immigration reform would also boost economic growth, reduce deficits, and strengthen Social Security.

Improving Border Security

Our long-term investment in border security and immigration enforcement has produced significant and positive results. Under this Administration, the resources that the DHS dedicates to security at the Southwest border are at an all-time high. Compared to 2008, today there are 3,000 additional Border Patrol agents along the Southwest border. Border technology, such as unmanned aircraft surveillance systems and ground surveillance systems, as well as border fencing, has more than doubled since 2008. The Administration's approach toward border security focuses on a risk-based approach that pursues heightened deterrence, enhanced enforcement, stronger foreign cooperation, and greater capacity for Federal agencies to ensure that the U.S. border remains secure.

Even as overall unauthorized Southwest border crossings remain near the lowest levels in decades, there continue to be significant fluctuations in the level of unauthorized crossings by both families and unaccompanied children. The Administration is working to address the increase in such crossings in recent months and the Budget calls for flexible contingency funding for both DHS and HHS so that adequate funding is available if the number of such illegal crossings continues to rise. The Administration supports strengthening and improving due process for all those in immigration proceedings, including unaccompanied children and families. We need every element of the court process to work effectively to accomplish the goal of both honoring humanitarian claims and processing those who do not qualify for relief. That is why DOJ is working to hire the 55 additional immigration judges funded in 2016, and is maintaining

funding in the Budget for several programs that provide legal representation and help to ensure that individuals know their rights and responsibilities in removal proceedings.

The Budget continues to invest in border security by supporting U.S. Customs and Border Protection (CBP) front line operations, funding additional border security technology, recapitalizing aging radios and vehicles for field personnel, expanding and enhancing intelligence and targeting capabilities, and investing in initiatives that support transparency and accountability across CBP.

The Budget supports 21,070 Border Patrol Agents and 25,891 CBP Officers, including 2,070 new Officers supported by proposed increases to user fees. The Budget includes over $353 million for the acquisition and sustainment of technology and tactical infrastructure along U.S. borders. These technology investments provide CBP with increased situational awareness on the border, as well as the ability to effectively respond to border incursions. The Budget also provides $55 million for recapitalization of aging non-intrusive inspection equipment at ports of entry, which would help CBP more efficiently detect security threats and facilitate lawful trade and travel. The Budget includes an increase of $95 million to support the purchase and deployment of mission-critical equipment, including radios and vehicles. The Budget also funds a total of $529 million in CBP intelligence and targeting activities that provide cutting-edge analytic support to Agents and Officers in the field. The Budget also includes targeted investments in initiatives that support transparency and accountability, including funding a Spanish-language call center, hiring additional Internal Affairs criminal investigators, funding the purchase of less-lethal weapons, and supporting the testing, evaluation, and deployment of body worn cameras.

MEETING OUR GREATEST CHALLENGES: NATIONAL SECURITY AND GLOBAL LEADERSHIP

Since the start of the Administration, the Nation has grown stronger and better prepared to both address global threats and seize opportunities to demonstrate global leadership.

We have renewed our alliances from Europe to Asia. Our rebalance to Asia and the Pacific is yielding deeper ties with a more diverse set of allies and partners. When complete, the Trans-Pacific Partnership will generate trade and investment opportunities—and create high-quality jobs at home. These alliances lay the groundwork for increasing U.S. economic power and harnessing the power of collective action to address problems of global concern, such as preventing a nuclear-armed Iran, stopping the threat of Ebola, and leading international efforts to pursue a lasting peace in Syria.

Leadership means a wise application of military power and rallying the world behind causes that are right. The United States has moved beyond the large ground wars in Iraq and Afghanistan that defined much of U.S. foreign policy over the past decade, dramatically reducing the number of troops deployed in both countries and saving more than $100 billion per year. At the same time, a strong military remains the bedrock of national security. The Nation must continue to reform and invest in our military—the finest fighting force the world has ever known—to ensure its dominance in every domain, to remain ready to deter and defeat threats to the homeland, and to be postured globally to protect our citizens and interests.

Investments in national defense and the security of Federal networks and critical infrastructure must be sustained because we continue to face serious challenges to our national security, including from violent extremism and evolving terrorist networks that pose a direct and persistent threat to America and our allies, cyber-threats on our Nation's critical infrastructure, Russian aggression, the accelerating impacts of climate change, and the outbreak of infectious diseases. The Administration is clear-eyed about these and other challenges and recognizes that the United States has the unique capability to mobilize and lead the international community to overcome them.

ADVANCING NATIONAL SECURITY PRIORITIES

In accordance with the Bipartisan Budget Act of 2015, the President's Budget includes $583 billion for the Department of Defense (DOD), a $2 billion, or 0.4 percent, increase from the 2016 enacted level, to provide the military the resources needed for the President's national security strategy. These resources will enable our military to protect the homeland, including by providing support for ongoing military operations to defeat terrorist threats; build security globally; project power; and, should deterrence fail, win decisively against any adversary.

DOD's base budget is $524 billion, which is $2 billion, or 0.4 percent, above the 2016 enacted level. These resources will support our military's readiness and posture to address current security challenges and arm our military with the capabilities needed to deter and, if necessary, respond to future threats. These capabilities include investments in 4th and 5th generation fighters, unmanned systems, a new long-range bomber, lethality upgrades to the Stryker combat vehicle, and technologies such as advanced torpedoes, electromagnetic railguns, high-speed long-range weapons, and new systems for electronic, space, undersea, and cyber warfare.

In addition to investments in advanced capabilities, the Budget promotes innovation to prepare for the future, including by modernizing personnel systems and introducing human capital best practices, funding cutting-edge research and technology initiatives, and promoting more agile warfighting strategies and concepts.

In an increasingly complex and competitive security environment, and in anticipation of major modernization and recapitalization costs beginning in the 2020s, the Budget also proposes a number of critical defense reforms that are needed to reduce spending on unnecessary or outdated force structure, modernize military health care, and reduce wasteful infrastructure and overhead.

DOD's Overseas Contingency Operations (OCO) request is $59 billion, which is roughly equal to the 2016 enacted level, and is the level set by the Bipartisan Budget Act of 2015. It provides the funding needed to combat diverse terrorist groups, such as the Islamic State of Iraq and the Levant (ISIL), so that they do not threaten Americans at home. It also supports a responsible transition in Afghanistan, counters Russian aggression toward neighboring countries, and reassures allies and partners in Europe.

The Budget provides $52.7 billion for the Department of State and Other International Programs (State/OIP), including $37.8 billion in base funding and $14.9 billion in OCO, which is a $0.1 billion decrease from the 2016 enacted level, excluding emergency funding. The Budget supports strategic investments in instruments of national security, diplomatic power, and development priorities. These include funding the President's signature initiatives in global health, food security, and climate change; deepening our cooperation with Allies and regional partners; continuing America's leadership in the United Nations and other multilateral organizations; supporting democratic societies and advocating for human rights; and investing in and protecting U.S. diplomatic personnel and facilities abroad. At a time when the demand for U.S. leadership and engagement has never been greater, the Budget provides America's diplomats and development professionals with the tools they need to advance the Nation's interests and build a safer and more prosperous world.

The President's Budget also recognizes that protecting our security requires long-term planning and stable resourcing, as well as investments in the economic security on which our national security depends. Starting in 2018, the President's Budget once again proposes to end sequestration for both defense and non-defense spending, and replace the savings by closing tax loopholes for the wealthy and cutting inefficient spending. Accepting the return of sequestration in 2018 and beyond would add risk to our national security by threatening the size, readiness, posture, and capability of our military, as well as critical national security activities at non-defense agencies such as the Departments of State and Homeland Security. Instead, the Budget builds on the bipartisan agreements that provided sequestration relief from 2014 through 2017, and which have enabled us to recover military readiness, advance badly-needed technological modernization, and provide the support our men and women in uniform deserve. Moreover, it provides the stable long-term base budget funding that is critical to military planning. As Secretary Carter has said, "we need to base our defense budgeting on our long-term military strategy, and that's not a one-year project."

ADDRESSING TODAY'S CHALLENGES

Destroying ISIL

The President's highest priority is keeping the American people safe. That is why the United States is leading the global coalition that will destroy ISIL. Our comprehensive strategy draws on every aspect of American power and enables the United States and its partners to continue delivering blows to ISIL's leaders, attack plotters, infrastructure, and revenue sources. The Budget provides robust funding for DOD and the Department of State so that the United States can continue to hunt down terrorists, provide training and equipment to forces fighting ISIL on the ground, help stabilize communities liberated from ISIL in Syria and Iraq, disrupt ISIL's financing and recruitment, counter ISIL's expansion, and support a political solution to the Syrian civil war. In Iraq, we will meet immediate and evolving stabilization needs, promote inclusive and responsive governance to bridge the sectarian divide, and provide for additional credit support and an expanded package of technical assistance to support economic reforms for greater fiscal stability, which is crucial to sustained success against ISIL. Specifically, the Budget provides $7.5 billion to DOD to continue our military campaign, Operation Inherent Resolve, which is expelling ISIL from Syrian and Iraqi territory and disrupting ISIL efforts to plan external attacks through the use of precision airstrikes, Special Operations forces, intelligence collection and exploitation, and the development of capable local ground forces in Iraq and Syria. The Budget provides $4.0 billion for State/OIP to pursue this effort, strengthen U.S. regional partners, provide humanitarian assistance to those impacted by the conflict, address needs in refugee host communities, and counter the ISIL narrative.

Combatting Global Terrorism

The Budget provides robust funding to support a sustainable and effective approach for combating global terrorism, with a focus on protecting the homeland, U.S. persons and interests abroad, and empowering partner nations facing these terrorist threats. The Administration continues to implement its strategy to address recent domestic terror incidents and the emergence and ongoing efforts by groups—such as al Qaeda and ISIL—that are attempting to recruit, radicalize, and mobilize Americans to commit violence by empowering communities and their local partners to prevent violent extremism. It commits the Federal Government to improving engagement with and support to communities, including sharing more information about the threat of radicalization, building government and law enforcement expertise for prevention, and challenging terrorist propaganda through words and deeds while helping communities protect themselves, especially online.

The Department of Justice's Countering Violent Extremism (CVE) initiative is an Administration priority and directly aligns with and bolsters United Nations' efforts to address the threat of foreign terrorist fighters. The Budget provides additional resources to support community led-efforts, including $4 million to conduct research targeted toward developing a better understanding of violent extremism and advancing evidence-based strategies for effective prevention and intervention, $6 million to support flexible, locally-developed CVE models, $2 million to develop training and provide technical assistance, and $3 million for demonstration projects that enhance the ability of law enforcement agencies nationwide to partner with local residents, business owners, community groups, and other stakeholders to counter violent extremism.

The Department of Homeland Security's (DHS) newly created Office of Community Partnerships will formalize and continue efforts to build relationships and promote trust with communities, focusing on innovative, community-based approaches that seek to discourage violent extremism and undercut terrorist narratives and propaganda. The Budget also includes for DHS $50 million in Federal assistance specifically for efforts to respond to emergent threats from violent extremism and prevent, prepare for, and respond to complex, coordinated attacks. In addition, CVE programs and activities are considered generally eligible to receive Federal assistance funding through other DHS grant programs, such as the Urban Area Security Initiative and the State Homeland Security Grant Program.

As part of the Administration's global efforts, the Budget provides DOD and State/OIP funding to expand and deepen the global coalition to combat terrorism and counter the spread of extremist narratives. The Budget requests resources to enhance DOD's counterterrorism activities and support ongoing engagements for partner capacity building through such mechanisms as institutional reform and training and equipping programs. Within State/OIP, the Budget supports programs that engage governmental and non-governmental organizations to build community-based partnerships against violent extremism, disrupt the flow of foreign terrorist fighters to conflict zones, and weaken the legitimacy and resonance of extremist messaging.

21ˢᵗ Century Cybersecurity: Securing the Digital Economy for All Americans

The President has made clear that cybersecurity is one of the most important challenges we face as a Nation. Like so many of the world's evolving technologies, the internet was not initially designed to be used, and consumed, by everyone. In 1985, about 2,000 people used the internet, and almost all of them had a deep understanding of how the technology worked. Today, 3.2 billion people use the internet. What started out as a useful tool for a few is now a necessity for all of us—as essential for connecting people, goods, and services as the airplane or automobile. The U.S. economy, national security, educational systems, and social lives have all become deeply reliant on this connectivity.

Yet while these advancements have created great opportunities, the risks have also increased. As more and more sensitive data are stored online, as critical functions increasingly rely on networked technologies, as the economy becomes ever more digital in nature, the consequences of malicious cyber activity grow more dire each year. Our adversaries know this, as evidenced in the steady stream of reports about cyber incidents. Cyber threats to critical infrastructure are growing in scope, sophistication, and persistence. Cyber-enabled theft of innovators' intellectual property persists and identity theft is the fastest growing crime in America.

The Federal Government is also vulnerable. Many Federal departments and agencies are reliant on aging applications running on outdated hardware and infrastructure that is difficult and costly to defend against modern cyber threats. Fragmented governance, insufficient policy, and a shortage of skilled cybersecurity professionals add to the challenges the Federal Government must address. Innovators and entrepreneurs have reinforced U.S. global technology leadership and grown the economy, but with each revelation of a Government database infiltrated, a high-profile company hacked, or a neighbor defrauded, more Americans are left to wonder whether technology's benefits may someday be outpaced by its costs.

That is why, since 2009, the President has executed a comprehensive strategy to defend the Nation against cyber threats. The strategy brings all elements of government together with private industry, academia, international partners, and the public to raise the level of cybersecurity in both the public and private sectors; deter and disrupt adversary activities in cyberspace; improve capabilities for incident response and resilience; and enact legislation to remove legal barriers to and incentivize cybersecurity threat information-sharing among private entities and between the private sector and the Government.

The Budget builds on these achievements by enhancing ongoing work, investing resources, and focusing leadership attention on new broader reforms—including fundamental changes to the way the Federal Government manages cyber risks. The Budget invests over $19 billion, or a roughly 35 percent increase from 2016, in overall

Federal resources for cybersecurity to support a broad-based cybersecurity strategy for securing the Government, enhancing the security of critical infrastructure and important technologies, investing in next-generation tools and workforce, and empowering Americans to take better control of their digital security. In particular, this funding would support the Cybersecurity National Action Plan, which aims to dramatically increase the level of cybersecurity in both the Federal Government and the Nation's digital ecosystem as a whole. Key initiatives that are part of this investment package include the creation of a Federal Chief Information Security Officer, better securing high-value Federal assets, retiring or upgrading Federal legacy information technology (IT) systems that cannot be appropriately secured, rationalizing how Federal IT and cybersecurity are delivered, educating Americans so that they are more empowered to keep their information secure, upgrading the skills of the Nation's cybersecurity workforce by expanding cyber education at academic institutions, and securing commonly used software, protocols, and standards that the internet relies upon. These initiatives would also continue to develop partnerships with industry to share actionable information more effectively and rapidly, and increase the cyber defenses of our critical infrastructure.

With this Budget, a pivotal moment is reached in the approach to the cybersecurity challenges facing the Nation. The investments in the Budget would allow America to better defend against cyber threats, but just as cyber threats evolve at a relentless pace, so must the Nation's approach to the challenge. This problem will not be solved in one year or by one Administration. These challenges require that we take bold, aggressive steps, sustain those efforts over time, and fundamentally change the way we as a Nation think about issues of security, privacy, and digital identity in the online age. Yet, no single company or government agency has all the answers for what these steps should be or how to implement them. Therefore, to gather the best ideas from across industry, academia, and government, the President is also establishing a Commission to identify recommendations for the President, future Administrations, and the Nation to enhance cybersecurity within the Government and across the private sector, and to empower Americans to take better control of their digital security.

Strengthening Federal Cybersecurity

The Federal Government is responsible for issuing, handling, and storing much of America's most important data—including Social Security numbers, tax returns, medical benefits, student loans, and top secret documents. The Government also operates critical functions, from satellites to financial payment systems, which rely upon networked technologies to function. It is critical that the Government take responsible actions for securing data and systems from those who would do us harm.

In 2015, the Office of Management and Budget (OMB), in coordination with the National Security Council, DHS, the Department of Commerce, and other departments and agencies, led a comprehensive review of the Federal Government's cybersecurity policies, procedures, and practices. The review found that many Federal IT systems are antiquated, making them difficult to secure, update, and defend, enabling adversaries to gain and maintain access. The review also revealed that current Federal Government budgeting and management structures do not allow for the consistent application of effective cybersecurity. In addition, the review found that the Federal Government does not have enough cybersecurity or privacy professionals, as shown by the difficulty agencies have in recruiting and retaining these personnel. These challenges are relics of systems, policies, and practices that were put in place before the onset of modern cyber risks and which have been updated only incrementally since then.

To begin to address these challenges, OMB directed a series of actions to further secure Federal information systems through the Cybersecurity Strategy and Implementation Plan for Federal civilian agencies. These actions and others have improved cybersecurity across the Federal landscape. Examples of such action include: Federal civilian agencies urgently patching critical vulnerabilities; identifying high-value assets; tightly limiting the number of privileged users with access to authorized systems; and dramatically accelerating the use of Personal Identity Verification cards or an alternative form of strong authentication for accessing networks and systems. Since the Cybersecurity Sprint, an intensive effort conducted in July 2015 to assess and improve the health of all Federal assets and networks, Federal civilian agencies have nearly doubled their use of strong authentication for all users from 42 percent to 81 percent.

However, given the magnitude of the challenge, we will continue to build on these actions. That is why the Budget includes substantial funding for the Federal Government-focused portions of the Cybersecurity National Action Plan. Immediate steps are being taken to improve the Federal Government's cybersecurity while laying the foundation for more strategic structural transformation in the future. To address legacy technology problems, the Budget creates a $3.1 billion revolving fund to retire antiquated IT systems and transition to new, more secure, efficient, modern IT systems, while also ensuring that Federal agencies maintain the security posture of their critical systems through reliable lifecycle management and keeping abreast of new technologies and security capabilities. Ultimately, retiring or modernizing vulnerable legacy systems will not only make us more secure, it will also save money. Agencies will also invest resources in identifying and better securing their high-value information assets.

The Budget also funds initiatives to expand the availability of cybersecurity services and tools across the Government. For example, the Budget invests $275 million for the DHS to accelerate implementation of the Continuous Diagnostic and Mitigation program, with the long-term goal of increasing common cybersecurity platforms and services that protect the Federal civilian Government as a holistic enterprise. This program would assist agencies in managing cybersecurity risks on a near

real-time basis. The Budget also invests $471 million to continue deployment of the National Cybersecurity Protection System (better known as EINSTEIN) across the Federal civilian Government. EINSTEIN detects and blocks cybersecurity threats before they can impact Federal agencies.

Securing the Digital Ecosystem

The Federal Government also has a responsibility to protect the Nation from threats in cyberspace. Citizens and businesses should have the tools they need to protect themselves. Just as one does not have to be an expert mechanic and professional driver to safely operate one's car, one should not have to be a technology expert to safely go online. Accordingly, the Budget sustains and expands on the Administration's previous work in this area as part of the Digital Ecosystem portion of the Cybersecurity National Action Plan.

Individuals increasingly rely upon online identities for essential services and for their social lives, but most current approaches to establishing and authenticating those online identities are easy to compromise and challenging to use. The Budget supports efforts to develop effective identity proofing and multi-factor authentication methods for users trying to obtain certain online Federal Government services by funding the General Services Administration's development of enhanced identify proofing and authentication services. These services would be more secure than systems relying on user names and passwords and would allow individuals to use the same credential with multiple Federal agencies, thereby making it easier to use as well.

Software is too often produced without sufficient consideration and design for security. This is especially true for much of the core software, standards, and protocols upon which users of the internet rely. These core technologies are often developed and maintained through an open source model, and often do not have sufficient funding to ensure security and reliability. To help secure widely used software, standards, and protocols, the Budget proposes $24.2 million to support the DHS Science and Technology Directorate's software assurance efforts.

The Nation's critical infrastructure is also increasingly under threat from disruption by cyber means. Such disruption could have severe adverse impacts on U.S. national security, economic security, and public health and safety. The Budget funds DHS and Sector-Specific Agency efforts to secure critical infrastructure, such as programs designed to increase the security and resilience of the electric grid. It also supports efforts to promote greater usage of the National Institutes of Standards and Technology's Cybersecurity Framework and best practices by industry and on-going efforts to deepen our partnership with critical infrastructure owners and operators. In addition, the Budget proposes up to $4 million within the Department of Health and Human Services to increase the agency's ability to utilize auditing and investigation authorities with respect to cybersecurity, as well as to increase cyber threat information sharing within the health care sector, and improve awareness of cybersecurity by patients, practitioners, and medical companies.

The Budget also supports key initiatives for the larger national digital ecosystem by investing $62 million to address the cyber workforce shortages and skill gaps that we face by creating a cybersecurity reservist program and expanding cybersecurity educational programs at academic institutions across the Nation. Current software engineering practices do not always produce software that is sufficiently secure and reliable, and training for developers on how to design software securely is uneven. These educational programs would strengthen training for software developers to improve the security and reliability of software that individuals and businesses rely on.

In addition, investments in cybersecurity research and development (R&D) provide the science and technology foundation needed to provide more effective and efficient security, secure fast-emerging information technologies, and thwart ever evolving cyber threats and adversaries. The Budget includes $318 million in R&D investments at Federal civilian agencies to address these ongoing challenges and continue investment in innovative cybersecurity technologies.

Disrupting and Deterring Malicious Cyber Activity. Even as we pursue initiatives to enhance U.S. cyber defenses, we must also invest in the capabilities needed to disrupt our adversaries' malicious activities, deter them from taking action in the future, and hold them accountable for their actions. The Budget includes funding to support the use of all the tools of U.S. national power to achieve this goal—including diplomatic, economic, law enforcement, intelligence, and military activities.

For example, the Budget includes funding to further enhance or establish programs across the civilian and defense agencies that would augment existing capabilities to defend the Nation against cyber threats and provide the President options in crisis or contingency. In support of this effort, DOD has established a trained and ready cyber operations workforce—including the Cyber Mission Forces (CMF)—with all the technical capabilities necessary to complete missions and support full-spectrum operations. The Budget fully supports this multiyear effort to improve defensive and offensive cyberspace operations capabilities and capacity, building on prior investments in tools, training, skills, and technology. The Budget also focuses on developing cyber tools to deter state and non-state actors from conducting malicious cyber acts, producing new capabilities and tools, including systems to support CMF missions, integration and improvements to the CMF platforms, and launching improved and consistent training for cyber forces. These investments are guided by the 2016 Federal Cybersecurity Research and Development Strategic Plan that was recently delivered to the Congress and will provide the Nation with science and technology elements to deter adversaries, protect cyberspace, detect malicious activities, and adapt to threats, vulnerabilities, and attacks.

The Budget expands law enforcement capabilities with the Federal Bureau of Investigation and other relevant agencies. It sustains the Department of State and the Department of the Treasury's ability to use their respective diplomatic and economic tools to impose costs on our adversaries. While we will use these tools judiciously and with restraint, the President has made clear that we will take action to defend U.S. citizens and our interests.

Improving the Response to Cyber Incidents. Despite the best efforts to raise our defenses and more effectively disrupt malicious activity, cyber incidents—intrusions, thefts, and even destructive events—will still occur. The Federal Government must be ready to respond effectively and rapidly when such events occur. Therefore, the Budget continues to invest in improvements to the Federal Government's incident response capabilities. In particular, the Budget enables the Cyber Threat Intelligence Integration Center to assume its role as a cornerstone of the Government's cybersecurity capabilities by fusing intelligence and "connecting the dots" regarding malicious foreign cyber threats to the Nation. We will also invest the resources required to be ready to work with the private sector to respond to incidents and, if necessary, to take action to protect U.S. interests, both domestically and abroad.

The digital age has already changed our lives in countless remarkable ways, and perhaps most remarkable of all, its potential still remains largely untapped. Ultimately, our vision is for an internet, cyberspace, and digital life that is inherently secure. If we modernize our approach to security, and prioritize keeping Americans safe, we will unlock more of that potential, and continue to deliver on the promise of this incredible age.

Supporting the Transition in Afghanistan

The Budget continues to support long-term national security and economic interests in Afghanistan and helps sustain political, economic, and security gains in the country as the United States draws down its forces and assistance levels gradually decline. It also includes resources to reinforce Afghanistan's security and development by supporting military training and assistance as well as health, education, justice, economic growth, governance, and other civilian assistance programs necessary to promote stability and strengthen diplomatic ties with the international community. The Budget also supports the U.S. military mission to train, advise, and assist the Afghan National Security Forces and maintain a counterterrorism capability.

Countering Russian Aggression and Supporting European Allies

In response to increasing attempts by the Russian Federation to constrain the foreign and domestic policy choices of neighboring countries, the Budget includes over $4.3 billion for political, economic, public diplomacy, and military support to build resilience and reduce vulnerabilities to Russian aggression among NATO allies and partner states in Europe, Eurasia, and Central Asia. To increase resilience within the governments and economies most targeted by Russian aggression, foreign assistance will support efforts to improve democracy and good governance, increase defense capabilities, strengthen rule of law and anti-corruption measures, and promote European integration, trade diversification, and energy security. This includes bolstering capabilities across the region to counter Russian aggression, with a particular focus on Ukraine, Georgia, and Moldova. In addition, through continued investments in U.S. public diplomacy and international media activities, the United States will seek to engage vulnerable populations in periphery countries, expand U.S. support for freedom of the press and independent journalism in the region, and advance America's foreign policy interests.

To increase security and reassure our NATO allies and partner states in Europe, the Budget provides over $3.4 billion for DOD's European Reassurance Initiative (ERI). ERI funding would enable the United States to increase military exercises and training, sustain a larger continuous rotational presence in Europe, enhance U.S. preparedness to reinforce NATO allies through the prepositioning of equipment, and build the capacity of partner states in Europe to enhance interoperability with the United States and NATO to strengthen regional security.

Providing Further Support for the Central American Regional Strategy

The Budget supports the U.S. Strategy for Engagement in Central America by investing in a long-term, comprehensive approach designed to address the root causes of migration of unaccompanied children and families from the region. The Budget builds on the funding the Congress enacted in 2016 by providing $1 billion to further support the Strategy, including financing support, to continue progress toward advancing security, prosperity, and economic growth in the region. This effort is designed to promote economic opportunities for the Central American people; build democratic, accountable, transparent and effective public institutions, and provide a safer and more secure environment for its citizens. The Budget request anticipates increased public and private investments in the region, which would increase economic growth and provide the necessary stability to counter illicit activities undermining Central American security. The Budget assumes continued coordination with international financial institutions, the private sector, civil society, and other international partners to promote prosperity through well-coordinated plans to address economic growth challenges. Executing the Strategy is inextricably linked to the readiness of the Central America governments and their ability to demonstrate continued will to undertake substantial political and economic commitments to bring about positive change in the region. Accordingly, the Strategy would continue to complement the "Alliance for Prosperity" plan jointly developed by the El Salvador, Honduras, and Guatemala governments to accelerate longer-term reforms and improvements in the lives of ordinary citizens.

Advancing the Rebalance to Asia and the Pacific

The Budget supports the Administration's commitment to a comprehensive regional strategy in Asia and the Pacific that reinforces a rules-based order and advances security, prosperity, and human dignity across the region, as described in the highlights below. Recognizing that security in the Asia-Pacific region underpins regional and global prosperity, the Budget aligns resources and activities to strengthen U.S. alliances and partnerships with emerging powers, promote regional economic cooperation, and build a constructive relationship with China that simultaneously supports expanding practical cooperation on global issues while candidly addressing differences. It also provides the necessary resources to implement the Trans-Pacific Partnership (TPP), a historic, high-standard trade agreement with 11 countries of the region that levels the playing field for American workers and American businesses. Through TPP, the United States will lead the way in revitalizing the open, rules-based economic system that will boost American exports while creating jobs at home by promoting strong labor, environmental, and intellectual property protections.

To promote universal and democratic values, the Budget provides support for educational and cultural exchanges and strengthens regional cooperation with organizations, such as the Asia-Pacific Economic Cooperation forum and the Association of Southeast Asian Nations. The Budget also provides resources and advances regional cooperation in counterterrorism, countering violent extremism, and nonproliferation.

In pursuit of security cooperation, the Budget enhances and modernizes U.S. defense relationships, posture, and capabilities with a focus on maritime security. DOD funding remains consistent with the priorities identified in the 2012 Defense Strategic Guidance and the 2014 Quadrennial Defense Review. DOD's most significant efforts to support the rebalance include implementing the Southeast Asia Maritime Security Initiative; increasing the number of ships assigned to the Pacific Fleet outside of U.S.

territory by approximately 30 percent, which improves the Navy's ability to maintain a more regular and persistent maritime presence in the Pacific; rotating four Littoral Combat ships through the region through 2017; and deploying the first P-8 Poseidon maritime patrol aircraft off Singapore. DOD continues to develop its defense relationship with India through the Defense Technology and Trade Initiative, the Joint Working Group on Aircraft Carrier Technology Cooperation, and the Jet Engine Technology Joint Working Group.

Growing Partnerships in Africa

The Budget supports the Administration's commitment to a broad partnership with countries in Africa that spans security, economic, and democracy and development priorities.

The Budget provides funding to ensure the U.S. will uphold the commitments it made during the U.S.-Africa Leaders Summit in 2014, including with respect to Power Africa, Trade Africa, the Security Governance Initiative, the Young African Leaders Initiative, the African Peacekeeping Rapid Response Partnership, and the Early Warning and Response Partnership. It also provides resources for implementing the peace agreement in South Sudan and helping the transitional government build the institutions it needs for a sustainable peace; supporting regional efforts to end the threat posed by the Lord's Resistance Army; delivering expanded security assistance to Nigeria and its regional partners to counter Boko Haram; securing governance and security gains in Somalia; and supporting preparations for peaceful and credible democratic elections on the continent.

PREPARING FOR THE FUTURE

In addition to addressing today's changing security environment, the Budget makes significant investments to maintain our military's superiority and ensure the United States always has an operational advantage over any potential adversary. DOD does this by driving smart and essential innovation: pursuing new research and technology development; updating and refining operational concepts and warfighting strategies; identifying and supporting capacity building among local partners; building the Force of the Future; and pursuing additional enterprise reform.

Building the Force of the Future

The United States has the world's finest fighting force, and our people are our most enduring advantage. The Budget invests in the health of today's force, maintaining the current end strength ramps for our military services, continuing to recover readiness, and providing competitive compensation for our service men and women. It continues efforts to care for our military families, veterans transitioning to other employment, and our wounded warriors and

families of the fallen. The Budget also invests in the Force of the Future to ensure our people remain the best. These investments include attracting a new generation to service, integrating data into our human capital processes, creating dynamic links among the active force, the private sector, and reserve component, and investing in the health and well-being of our military personnel and their families.

Maintaining Technological Superiority

For generations the United States has relied on technological superiority to remain dominant across the domains of air, land, sea, and space as well as the cyber arena. In recent years, potential adversaries have accelerated their investments in military modernization and advanced technologies, narrowing the U.S. technological advantage. In the 2016 Budget, the Administration prioritized research, development, test, and evaluation (RDT&E) spending at a nine percent increase over the 2015 enacted level. The Budget continues that trend, raising the RDT&E budget levels to $71.8 billion while remaining focused on innovation across DOD.

Unprecedented collaboration among the military services and with other agencies, especially the intelligence community, are creating new concepts and applications of current, first-rate weapon systems operated by trusted, agile, expert operators that will expand technological superiority. The Budget also continues to prioritize the necessary long-term investments in early-stage science and technology at $12.5 billion to fund future technologies to reshape the battlespace, such as hypersonics, unmanned, and autonomous systems. New and innovative efforts in technology transfer are set to take advantage of early-stage basic research investments made throughout the Government. Cooperative efforts with both industry and academia are creating game-changing opportunities for national security in areas ranging from advanced manufacturing to new technologies for training. The combination of simultaneous investments in future defense system technologies and programs that deploy new technologies faster, leverage adapted commercial off-the shelf technologies, and develop strategic capabilities that bend the cost curve will change the calculus of warfare for our potential opponents both today and into the foreseeable future.

Strengthening Space Security

Space capabilities are vital to U.S. national security and the ability to understand emerging threats, project power globally, support diplomatic efforts, and enable global economic prosperity. It is the shared interest of all nations to act responsibly in space to help prevent mishaps, misperceptions, and mistrust. The Budget supports a variety of measures to help assure the use of space in the face of increasing threats to U.S. national security space systems. In addition, it supports the development of capabilities to defend and enhance the resilience of these space systems. These capabilities help deter and defeat interference with, and attacks on, U.S. space systems.

Making the Military More Effective and Efficient through Defense Reforms

Successfully executing the defense strategy requires prioritizing every dollar and spending it effectively. The Budget supports this goal by adjusting force structure, modernizing DOD's health care system, and further reducing wasteful overhead and infrastructure. The 2017 reform proposals build on the success of recent initiatives, such as the effort with the Congress to slow growth in compensation costs and enact a modern, military retirement system featuring both defined benefit and defined contribution plans. The Department of Defense's annual acquisition performance reports also strongly indicate that Better Buying Power initiatives are reducing cost growth and significantly lowering prices paid for major weapons systems.

Yet the need for reform remains urgent. Savings from reform can take years to fully achieve, and current reform proposals will be especially critical as they reach their full effect in the 2020s, when several major defense costs will converge. By then, the Department will be simultaneously recapitalizing the tactical air fleet and the nuclear triad, as well as other weapons systems. These recapitalization efforts form only one part of a broader investment strategy required to confront the threats posed by the accelerating military modernization programs of advanced competitors, and the rapid evolution of asymmetric technology, such as missile threats. If reforms do not begin now, the security and fiscal choices of the next administration will be much more challenging, with consequences for taxpayers, servicemembers, and national security.

The Department of Defense is responsible for implementing the Nation's defense strategy, but depends on congressional authority to execute force structure shifts that match capability with strategy. The Budget re-proposes retiring, restructuring, and modernizing a range of systems, to ensure that the military has the most capable, versatile, and survivable systems to perform its missions. Examples of critical force structure shifts that better match capability with current and emerging threats include the Army's Aviation Restructure Initiative and the Navy's phased approach to cruiser modernization—both of which require congressional support.

In modernizing its health care system, the Department will simplify TRICARE—the health care program of the Military Health System—while adding choices for beneficiaries and encouraging the use of existing military treatment options.

The Budget reduces overhead and waste, such as through continued reductions to DOD's major headquarters and the establishment of Service Requirements Review Boards across the Department to identify further efficiencies and cost-savings. The Budget also requests that the Congress authorize another round of Base Realignment and Closure (BRAC), which is critically important to re-align resources currently consumed by maintaining unneeded facilities. The need to reduce excess facilities is so critical that, in the absence of authorization of a new round of BRAC, the Administration will pursue new options to reduce wasteful spending on surplus infrastructure within existing authorities.

SUSTAINING THE PRESIDENT'S DEVELOPMENT AND DEMOCRACY AGENDA

The successful pursuit of sustainable global development and democracy is a central pillar of U.S. foreign policy and national security and is essential to building a more stable and prosperous world. The Budget continues to advance the Administration's development and democracy initiatives and activities as it seeks to reduce extreme poverty, encourage broad-based economic growth, and support democratic governance and human rights, and to drive progress toward meeting the global development vision and priorities adopted in the 2030 Agenda for Sustainable Development.

The Budget provides $1.0 billion for Feed the Future, the President's food security initiative, which uses development programs to reduce hunger sustainably, address the root causes of food insecurity, improve economic resilience, nutrition, and agricultural productivity, and develop regional markets and trade. The Budget also supports greater climate resilience and low-emission economic growth in partner countries, especially the poorest and most vulnerable, through $1.3 billion in funding for the Global Climate Change Initiative (GCCI). (See additional discussion of the GCCI in Chapter 2.) It also includes $300 million for Power Africa, which aims to expand electricity access in sub-Saharan Africa to more than 60 million new households and businesses by helping to catalyze private investment in new and cleaner power generation projects and increasing the capacity of African governments and utilities to develop and manage their domestic energy sectors.

More generally, the Budget provides $9.0 billion for the Development Assistance and Economic Support Fund accounts, $2.3 billion for the Department of the Treasury's international programs, and $1.0 billion for the Millennium Challenge Corporation, which continues to provide a powerful example of an evidence-based approach to development. Together, this funding supports activities across numerous sectors of development—including agriculture and nutrition, environmental sustainability and biodiversity, effective and accountable democratic governance and institutions, infrastructure, education, addressing corruption and financial mismanagement in countries working toward reform, promoting the rights of women and girls around the world, and enabling sustained and inclusive economic growth.

Mobilizing the Private Sector to Advance Sustainable Development

To ensure that investments in global development have long-term and transformative impacts, the United States has increasingly focused these investments to achieve sustainable development outcomes, mobilize increased private capital flows, diversify the range of private sector and nongovernmental partners with whom we work, and enable developing countries to better mobilize and use their own domestic resources. The Administration has championed a new model for development assistance that aims to catalyze private sector and third party investment, understanding that the sheer cost of investments needed to achieve the next generation of development goals is unattainable by Official Development Assistance alone. Development programs that mobilize the private sector advance U.S. interests, deliver tangible results within the realm of complex development finance, and in some cases also support U.S. economic growth.

The Budget includes roughly $200 million for the Overseas Private Investment Corporation, the Trade and Development Agency, and the U.S. Agency for International Development's (USAID's) Development Credit Authority, and supports efforts to catalyze private sector funding through other avenues such as the Millennium Challenge Corporation, in order to mobilize billions of dollars to support the Administration's priority development projects. These efforts build on the models of the Administration's flagship development initiatives like Power Africa and the New Alliance for Food Security and Nutrition, which have successfully showcased how U.S. taxpayer dollars can mobilize greater investments from the private sector, other donors, and foreign governments. The Budget also supports efforts to build developing countries' capacity to mobilize and effectively use domestic resources—including through improved revenue and fiscal management—and to attract domestic and foreign private investment to finance their own development and reduce their dependence on foreign aid. For example, the "Doing Business in Africa" initiative facilitates access and exports for American companies on a continent that has six of the top 10 fastest growing countries in the world.

Addressing Humanitarian Needs

The Budget maintains strong support for food aid and other humanitarian assistance, providing about $6.2 billion to help internally displaced persons, refugees, and others affected by natural or man-made humanitarian disasters. The United States has provided over $6 billion annually in humanitarian assistance for the past several years and continues to be the largest single humanitarian donor. Current trends show a greater number of people in need throughout the world due to more protracted crises and more extreme weather events. Meeting urgent humanitarian needs saves millions of lives and is integral to advancing the Administration's long-term goals of assisting people in crisis and reducing extreme poverty.

For the Syrian crisis alone, the United States provided over $4.5 billion in humanitarian assistance through 2015 to address the impacts of conflict and mitigate the need for affected populations in Syria and in countries of first asylum. Refugee resettlement is an important component in our multifaceted response to the global refugee crisis and the Budget supports the admission of at least 100,000 refugees to the United States. In maintaining our long-standing tradition of providing refuge to some of the world's most vulnerable people, we will continue to strengthen our robust screening protocols, as we have no higher priority than safeguarding the American public.

Advancing Global Health

The Budget maintains support for effective global health programs, including for the President's Malaria Initiative and the President's Emergency Plan for AIDS Relief (PEPFAR). To support the President's call to end the scourge of malaria, the Budget includes an increase of $71 million for the President's Malaria Initiative, for a total of $745 million. Also, the Budget proposes to use an additional $129 million out of the remaining Ebola emergency funding to combat malaria. The Budget includes $1.35 billion for the Global Fund to Fight AIDS, Tuberculosis and Malaria. When combined with $243 million in 2016 enacted funds above the President's matching pledge to the Global Fund's Fourth Replenishment, the United States will be able to contribute nearly $1.6 billion by 2017 toward a Fifth Replenishment contribution. Building on the President's September 2015 announcement of U.S. HIV/AIDS prevention, care, and treatment targets through 2017, the Budget includes $4.65 billion for U.S. bilateral PEPFAR efforts, including enduring support for PEPFAR's Impact Fund to focus on reducing HIV infections in high-burden populations and areas. The Budget also increases support for Gavi, the Vaccine Alliance as part of the $1 billion, four-year U.S. pledge, and continues strong support for other programs to end preventable child and maternal deaths.

The Administration continues to be vigilant on Ebola and to prepare to respond to future outbreaks. The Ebola epidemic in West Africa spotlighted the need to urgently strengthen global health security in vulnerable countries around the world that have poor infrastructure, limited capacity, high population density, and major transport hubs. The Budget increases support for programs to advance the Global Health Security Agenda (GHSA) at USAID and the Centers for Disease Control and Prevention, and continues support for DOD to improve disease surveillance, laboratory capacity, and biosecurity in support of the GHSA.

Supporting Let Girls Learn

In March 2015, the President and First Lady launched Let Girls Learn, which brings together the Department of State, USAID, the Peace Corps, and the Millennium Challenge Corporation, as well as other agencies and programs like PEPFAR, to address the range of challenges preventing adolescent girls from enrolling, completing, and succeeding in school. Over the past year, the initiative has launched a $25 million Challenge Fund, supported Peace Corps Volunteers in 13 countries, and forged adolescent girls' education partnerships with several countries. The Budget provides more than $100 million in new funds for Let Girls Learn, which will augment ongoing investments that support adolescent girls. Let Girls Learn will continue to leverage public-private partnerships, and challenge organizations, governments, and private sector partners to commit resources to improve the lives of adolescent girls worldwide.

Building Strong Democratic Institutions

The Budget continues to provide robust support for democracy, human rights and governance programs, recognizing that promoting democracy and good governance reflects American values and is essential to achieving our broader global development and national security objectives. U.S. democracy programs foster good governance, promote access to justice, strengthen civil society and reinforce effective and accountable institutions at all stages of countries' democratic transitions. The Budget includes funding for programs in the areas of rule of law and human rights, good governance, political competition and consensus-building, and civil society capacity-building. It also supports key Administration initiatives, including the Open Government Partnership and Stand With Civil Society initiative.

HONORING OUR COMMITMENT TO VETERANS

The Budget includes $75.1 billion in discretionary 2017 resources for the Department of Veterans Affairs (VA), a 4.9-percent increase over 2016. The Budget also includes an advance appropriation request of $66.4 billion for 2018 medical care, a 2.2-percent increase over the revised 2017 request. This funding would ensure continued investment in the five pillars the President has outlined for supporting the Nation's veterans: providing the resources and funding they deserve; ensuring high-quality and timely health care; getting veterans their earned benefits quickly and efficiently; ending veteran homelessness (which has dropped 36 percent since 2010, as measured by the yearly Point-in-Time count); and helping veterans and their families get good jobs, an education, and access to affordable housing.

Improving Veteran Access to Quality Health Care

The Budget provides $65.1 billion for health care and continues to support the Administration's goal of providing timely, high-quality health care for the Nation's veterans. Building on the increased access made possible by the Veterans Access, Choice, and Accountability Act of 2014, the Budget proposes resources and legislative changes to further improve veterans' ability to access care, as described in the "Plan to Consolidate Programs of the Department of Veterans Affairs to Improve Access to Care," which was submitted to the Congress on November 1, 2015. These administrative improvements will increase efficiency when veterans are best served by seeing non-VA medical providers. Further, following the anticipated release of recommendations from the Commission on Care in mid-2016, the Administration will determine how to best meet veterans' current and future needs using VA and community resources.

Speeding the Processing of Disability Compensation Claims and Appeals

The VA continues to make tremendous progress reducing the veteran disability claims backlog, which is down from a high of over 611,000 in March of 2013 to approximately 75,000. However, with approximately 11 percent of all initial claims decisions appealed by veterans, the increased completion of initial claims has created a corresponding increase in the number of appeals. The Budget includes legislative proposals to streamline the appeals process and provides additional funding to support technological improvements and the hiring of additional employees to continue to reduce both initial claim and appeal backlogs. Further, the Budget funds continued efforts to ensure consistent, personalized, and accurate information about services and benefits, especially in compensation and pension claims processing.

A GOVERNMENT OF THE FUTURE

"In this democracy, we the people recognize that this government belongs to us, and it's up to each of us and every one of us to make it work better... We all have a stake in government success—because the government is us."

—President Barack Obama

The President is committed to driving lasting change in how Government works—change that makes a significant, tangible, and positive difference in the economy and the lives of the American people. Over the past seven years, this Administration has launched successful efforts to modernize and improve citizen-facing services, eliminate wasteful spending, reduce the Federal real property footprint, and spur innovation in the private sector by opening to the public tens of thousands of Federal data sets and innovation assets at the national labs. Yet, despite this progress, there is more work to be done. The President's Management Agenda is addressing this by improving the way Government works and delivers for citizens.

The President's Management Agenda has four pillars: 1) Effectiveness—delivering a Government that works for citizens and businesses; 2) Efficiency—increasing quality and value in core operations; 3) Economic Growth—opening Government-funded data and research to the public to spur innovation, entrepreneurship, and job opportunities; and 4) People and Culture—unlocking the full potential of today's Federal workforce and building the workforce we need for tomorrow. The Administration is executing the President's Management Agenda through Cross-Agency Priority (CAP) Goals, which were introduced by this Administration to improve coordination across multiple agencies to help drive performance on key priorities and issues. Performance for each CAP goal is regularly tracked throughout the year and goal teams are held accountable for results, which are updated quarterly on *Performance.gov.* In addition to the Management Agenda, the Budget also supports the President's commitment to using evidence to drive policy decisions and his plan to reorganize the Federal Government so that it does more for less, and is best positioned to assist businesses and entrepreneurs in the global economy.

EFFECTIVENESS: A GOVERNMENT THAT WORKS FOR CITIZENS AND BUSINESSES

A more effective Government will not only better deliver services for citizens, but will also use taxpayer dollars more efficiently. Ultimately, the Federal Government must be able to deliver the user experience and engagement that the American people and businesses expect and deserve. The Budget provides resources to continue the progress toward implementing the

President's Management Agenda, focusing on four key areas: delivering smarter information technology (IT); strengthening Federal cybersecurity; delivering world-class customer service; and reshaping engagement with communities and citizens.

Delivering Smarter IT

The Administration has embarked on a comprehensive effort to fundamentally improve the way that the Government delivers technology services to the public, called the Smarter IT Delivery Agenda. The Agenda is focused on recruiting top technologists and entrepreneurs to work within agencies on the highest priority projects, leveraging the best processes to increase oversight and accountability for IT spending, and ramping up Government contracting with innovative companies. To date, these and other efforts have saved over $3.5 billion.

Recruiting the Best Talent. A key component of the Smarter IT delivery strategy is recruiting the best talent to work as part of, and with, the Federal Government. In 2014, the Administration piloted the U.S. Digital Service (USDS)—a group of select private-sector innovators, entrepreneurs, and engineers recruited to Government service to improve and simplify the digital experience between individuals, businesses, and the Government. Digital Service experts have worked in collaboration with Federal agencies to implement streamlined and effective digital technology practices on the Nation's highest priority programs. The team has also worked to disseminate best practices such as the U.S. Web Design Standards, an open source visual style guide to create consistent and superb user experiences across U.S. Federal Government websites.

USDS teams have also reimagined how Government services should be provided to the public. The USDS supported the United States Citizenship and Immigration Services (USCIS) transition to electronic filing and processing of Form I-90 to renew, or replace, a green card and the Immigrant Visa Fee payment. Closing down the old Electronic Immigration System will save the agency millions of dollars per year in ongoing operations, maintenance, and licensing costs, and the newly launched myUSCIS makes it easier for users to access information about the immigration process and immigration services. USDS supported *HealthCare.gov* during the 2015 open enrollment season, and worked between open enrollment seasons to dramatically improve site performance and save millions of dollars per year in operating expenses. In addition, USDS launched the new College Scorecard with the Department of Education to give students, parents, and their advisors the clearest, most accessible, and most reliable national data on college cost, graduation, debt, and post-college earnings. This new College Scorecard provides students and families with information on college performance that can help them identify colleges that are serving students of all backgrounds well and providing a quality and affordable education. It empowers Americans to search for colleges based on what matters most to them and allows them to compare the value offered by different colleges to help improve their decision. Within the first month, the College Scorecard had over one million users, more than 10 times the users its predecessor had in a year. Over a dozen other organizations have used the Scorecard data to launch new tools to support students in their college search and application processes.

To facilitate requests for short-term support, USDS created a new Rapid Response team in 2015. This team's work included restoring service for the Department of State's Consolidated Consular Database, after an outage led to a two-week suspension of visa issuances worldwide. In 2016, the USDS is partnering with the Internal Revenue Service (IRS) to bolster electronic authentication procedures, laying the groundwork for unified and secure taxpayer access to all IRS digital services.

To institutionalize the dramatic improvements that this approach has demonstrated, the Budget funds the development of digital services teams at 25 agencies. These small, high-impact teams will drive the quality and effectiveness of the agencies' most important digital services. The Budget also funds the USDS headquarters to maintain and expand the team that can coordinate these efforts across the Federal Government. As an example, USDS will work closely with agencies to provide the new agency teams with hiring, training, and procurement support.

To dramatically improve customer satisfaction with Federal technology services, there is a critical need for IT specialists to serve on digital services teams. To that end, the Budget supports the Administration's aggressive goal of hiring and placing 500 top technology and design experts to serve in the Government by January 2017. In addition, USDS worked with the Office of Personnel Management (OPM) to create a term-appointment hiring authority for Digital Services Experts to more quickly get talent into Government service. Working with OPM to expand these flexible hiring options and spread proven hiring practices across the Federal Government will remain a priority in 2016 and 2017.

Finally, the Administration has been expanding opportunities for the current Federal IT workforce to rise to the challenge and sharpen their skills by increasing training opportunities for these professionals. For example, this past year the Chief Information Officer (CIO) Council, Chief Acquisition Officer Council and the Office of Management and Budget (OMB) launched the IT Solutions Challenge. Throughout the course of several months, over 40 IT and acquisition professionals worked in teams to develop innovative solutions for some of the Federal Government's most challenging IT problems. These types of training programs work in tandem with an enhanced focus on expanding the Government's digital acquisition expertise. In the past year, 30 Federal acquisition professionals piloted an innovative approach to digital IT acquisition training.

Leveraging the Best Processes. The passage of the first major IT reform legislation in almost 20 years, the Federal Information Technology Acquisition Reform Act (FITARA) in December 2014, gave the Administration's ongoing work under Smarter IT Delivery an added boost. To aid in Government-wide implementation, OMB released guidance to agencies on FITARA implementation—Management and Oversight of Information Technology Resources. This guidance empowers Federal executives to help ensure that IT resources and tools are used effectively and strategically to help programs better meet their missions. It also places an emphasis on the IT workforce by focusing on the relationship between bureau and departmental CIOs, requiring agencies to have a robust IT workforce planning process, and positioning CIOs so that they can reasonably be held accountable for how effectively their agencies use modern digital approaches.

The Administration has also encouraged data-driven processes to provide effective oversight of Government IT. For example, the Administration's PortfolioStat process—a data-based review of agency IT assets—has not only strengthened Federal IT, but made it significantly more cost effective. PortfolioStat and other IT reform efforts have helped the Government achieve more than $3.5 billion in savings over the past four years while ensuring agencies are efficiently using taxpayer dollars to deliver effective and innovative solutions to the public. PortfolioStat promotes the adoption of new technologies, such as cloud computing and agile development practices. As a result of these continuing efforts, the Federal Government now spends approximately 8.2 percent of its IT budget on provisioned services, such as cloud computing. In addition, agile development—an incremental, fast-paced style of software development that reduces the risk of failure—is now used for half of new software projects compared to just 35 percent in 2012 and IT hardware spending has declined 25 percent from 2010 levels. In 2017, the use of PortfolioStat to increase efficiency in the Federal IT portfolio will continue.

Contracting with Innovative Companies. The Federal Government must work with private-sector innovators to ensure the best use of proven and emerging technologies and practices, which requires rethinking procurement rules, processes, and practices to reduce barriers to entry. The President has taken bold steps to create an environment that opens more Federal contracting opportunities to new companies—especially to help solve IT challenges—and these efforts are paying off with almost 200 new small businesses winning Federal contracts for IT software development investments in 2015. In 2017, these efforts to increase digital acquisition capability within agencies, train agency personnel in digital IT acquisitions, and test innovative contracting models will expand.

Strengthening Federal Cybersecurity

Strengthening the cybersecurity of Federal networks, systems, and data is one of the most important challenges the Nation faces. As cyber risks have grown in severity over recent years, the Administration has executed a comprehensive strategy to address cybersecurity across the Nation, as outlined in the National Security Chapter. Building upon the Administration's broader efforts for 21st Century Cybersecurity, in 2015 OMB, in coordination with the National Security Council (NSC), the Department of Homeland Security (DHS), the Department of Commerce, as well as other departments and agencies, executed a series of actions to bolster Federal cybersecurity and secure Federal information systems through the Cybersecurity Strategy and Implementation Plan (CSIP).

In 2015, these actions and others led to areas of significant progress across the Federal Government. Federal civilian agencies took action to patch critical vulnerabilities, identify high-value assets, tightly limit the number of privileged users with access to authorized systems, and dramatically accelerate the use of Personal Identity Verification cards or alternative forms of strong authentication for accessing networks and systems. Since the Cybersecurity Sprint, an intensive effort conducted in July 2015 to assess and improve the health of all Federal assets and networks, both civilian and military, Federal civilian agencies have nearly doubled

their use of strong authentication for all users from 42 percent to 81 percent.

Still, as outlined in the CSIP, challenges remain. The Federal Government has identified three primary challenges:

- *Outdated Technology.* The Federal Government relies significantly on hard-to-defend legacy hardware, software, applications, and infrastructure, which make it particularly vulnerable to malicious cyber activity, as well as costly to defend and protect.

- *Fragmented Governance.* Governance and management structures are unable to consistently provide effective, well-coordinated cybersecurity across the Federal Government.

- *Workforce Gaps.* Workforce shortages and skill gaps, including training, education, and recruitment and retention of cybersecurity and privacy professionals, are significant.

To address these challenges and continue moving the needle on cybersecurity for the Federal Government, the Budget invests over $19 billion, or a roughly 35 percent increase from 2016, in overall Federal resources for cybersecurity.

Enhancing Federal IT to Secure Federal Information and Assets. The technology, architectures, and processes underpinning Federal Government operations need to be modernized to improve cybersecurity. Of the $52 billion in Federal civilian IT spending planned for 2017, approximately 71 percent ($37 billion) is dedicated to maintaining legacy IT investments. Improving Federal cybersecurity will require an accelerated push to strengthen the Government's most high-value IT and information assets and to retire, replace, or upgrade hard-to-defend legacy IT. This will require not just modernizing hardware and software, but also improving how we manage the lifecycle of IT investments so that security gains can be sustained over time. This approach will improve the Government's risk management capability, improve the cyber-defense landscape, and enhance the ability to respond to changing threats. Therefore, the Administration is proposing a revolving fund at the General Services Administration (GSA), seeded with an initial capital injection of $3.1 billion, to transition to new, more secure, efficient, modern IT systems, while also establishing long-term mechanisms for Federal agencies to regularly refresh their networks and systems based on up-to-date technologies and best practices.

A project review board, comprised of experts in IT acquisition, cybersecurity, and agile development, will review agency business cases and select projects for funding to ensure prioritization of projects with the greatest risk profile, Government-wide impact, and probability of success. The board would identify opportunities to replace multiple legacy systems with a smaller number of common platforms—something that is difficult for agencies to do when acting on their own with limited insight into other agencies' operations. As a result, the central fund would achieve a far greater and more rapid impact than if the funds were allocated directly to agencies. In addition, a team of systems architects and developers would provide additional oversight and development capabilities to make these major changes. The revolving fund would be self-sustaining by requiring agencies to re-pay the initial investments through efficiencies gained from modernization, ensuring the fund can continue to support projects well beyond the initial infusion of capital. Seed funding of $3.1 billion would address an estimated $12 billion worth of modernization projects over 10 years.

Finally, the Budget includes $275 million in funding to accelerate implementation of the DHS continuous diagnostics and monitoring program.

Streamlining Governance and Ensuring Effective Oversight. Over the long term, the Federal Government will need to move away from a model of IT and cybersecurity governance where individual departments and agencies build, provision, and manage nearly all aspects of their IT and cybersecurity, from infrastructure to platforms to applications. Instead, IT systems and cybersecurity capabilities will need to be built, acquired, and managed in a more holistic way, one that treats the Federal Government as an enterprise and that relies more on shared platforms and common services. This Budget lays the foundation for shifting to this more effective approach to Federal cybersecurity by supporting investments in common IT solutions for small agencies, more secure, enterprise-wide e-mail systems, and common cybersecurity tools and services. Further, the Federal Government needs to improve not only its hardware and software, but how it acquires technology, so that it can keep up to date with industry best practices and emerging technologies in the future.

Today's sophisticated cyber incidents have also demonstrated the need for more coordinated and nimble Government efforts when they occur. In such instances, the Government may need to play an important coordinating role. Moving forward, the Budget supports the Federal Government's efforts to continue developing policy and plans that establish a foundation for a scalable, flexible, and cooperative approach to significant cyber incident coordination involving both public- and private-sector stakeholders, and anchors it within the broader National Preparedness System.

In 2016 and 2017, the Administration, including OMB and NSC staff, will also coordinate with DHS to continue working with agencies to identify and remediate weaknesses in cybersecurity programs while ensuring agency progress toward the Cybersecurity CAP Goal through CyberStat reviews. These reviews provide the opportunity for agencies to identify the cybersecurity areas where they may be facing implementation and organizational challenges.

Strengthening the Cybersecurity Workforce. There is a shortage of skilled cybersecurity experts and privacy professionals throughout the IT industry as a whole, and that shortage is more acute within the Federal Government. The Budget includes $62 million for three initiatives to address this recruitment challenge by:

- Expanding the National Science Foundation's (NSF) CyberCorps® Scholarship for Service program to establish a sustainable cadre of cyber reservists and enhance opportunities for career cybersecurity experts across departments and agencies that can serve the Federal Government to help rapidly respond to cybersecurity challenges across the Government;

- Developing a foundational cybersecurity curriculum for academic institutions to consult and adopt; and

- Providing grants to academic institutions to develop or expand cyber education programs as part of the National Centers of Academic Excellence in Cybersecurity Program.

In addition to funding these foundational workforce initiatives, this Budget also invests over $37 million to expand standing teams of cybersecurity experts within DHS to provide readily-available cybersecurity capabilities to departments and agencies.

As malicious cyber activity becomes increasingly sophisticated and persistent in the digital age, so must actions to tackle them. Cyber threats cannot be eliminated entirely, but they can be managed much more effectively. Through these investments, the Administration continues to lead a broad, strategic effort to combat cyber threats, update and modernize Federal cybersecurity policies and procedures, and strengthen the Federal Government's overall cybersecurity infrastructure through modernization efforts.

To complement these steps and focus on long-term challenges in cybersecurity, the Budget also supports the creation of the first Federal Chief Information Security Officer, and the establishment of a blue ribbon commission consisting of leaders in the fields of cybersecurity, technology, privacy, national security, and Government that will identify recommendations for the President, future Administrations, and the Nation to enhance cybersecurity awareness and protections inside and outside of Government and to empower Americans to take better control of their digital security.

Delivering World-Class Customer Service

The Administration is continuing its efforts to improve the quality, timeliness, and effectiveness of Federal services through three major customer service initiatives. First, the customer service Community of Practice (COP) established in 2014 is developing standards, practices, and self-assessment tools for agencies to use on how to better serve the American people. For example, the COP has developed a draft assessment framework for programs to use to identify strengths and weaknesses in their existing customer service that will be piloted in 2016.

Second, the Federal Customer Service Awards program recognizes individuals and teams who provide outstanding customer service directly to the American people and identifies effective practices that can be replicated within and across agencies. The inaugural awards, announced in December 2014 by the President and awarded in December 2015, exemplify how the Federal Government delivers excellent service to its customers—the public. For example, the BusinessUSA Veteran Entrepreneur Initiative streamlined a complicated process to provide veterans with easier access to resources on how to start a new business. Since its launch, the Veteran Entrepreneur Initiative has served over 250,000 veterans and increased the number of first-time veteran users to the BusinessUSA website from 558 to 53,993 users. A second awardee, the Department of State consular team serving in Dhahran, Saudi Arabia, used social media, technology, and innovative strategies to deliver a range of consular services to U.S. citizens without requiring a visit to the Consulate. This saved time and money for American citizens leading to high customer service ratings for the consular team.

Through a third customer service initiative, the Administration increased opportunities for the collection and use of customer feedback data, which are critical to helping the Government better respond to the needs of the public and improve overall service delivery. In August of 2015, GSA launched the pilot of FeedbackUSA, a simple tool that uses kiosks located in local Federal offices—such as passport offices and Social Security Administration (SSA) card centers—to allow customers to rate their experience. Customers can also provide more detailed feedback using the FeedbackUSA web portal. Federal agencies can use FeedbackUSA to solicit, aggregate, and analyze customer service transactional feedback in real time so that they can resolve issues and improve their services to the public. The pilot was launched in 27 Department of State passport processing centers and at 14 SSA card centers. The Transportation Security Administration is set to join in the spring of 2016.

FeedbackUSA has achieved high initial response rates and levels of satisfaction, and agencies are able to use the data collected to conduct meaningful analysis and take immediate action. Going forward, the Administration will continue to build and expand on this progress by improving the collection and use of customer feedback data across Government programs that provide services to the public in order to make tangible improvements in customer interactions.

The Budget supports continued investments in improving the quality of service the public receives when they interact with their Government. For example, the Budget includes an increase of more than $100 million, or eight percent, for IRS services to taxpayers, including for critical activities to improve and modernize its public-facing IT infrastructure. Although the 2016 Consolidated Appropriations Act reversed a five-year trend of irresponsible cuts to the IRS budget—which threatened the integrity of the tax system and resulted in unacceptable levels of taxpayer services—the IRS operating budget is still almost $1 billion below 2010 levels, even before accounting for inflation, and more resources are needed to achieve satisfactory levels of customer service. The 2017 investments in the Budget would enable the IRS to provide taxpayers with the same level of online service as they have come to expect from their financial institutions, and would return IRS telephone service levels to acceptable levels, reducing the average wait time for taxpayers who call the IRS

by half compared with 2015, and nearly doubling the share of callers that reach a live assister. The Budget also supports the SSA's field operations and provides the funding necessary to reduce the disability hearing backlog, as well as ensure timely assistance to the public who call the SSA help line. SSA is continuing to improve on-line customer service with the addition of new services to the "my Social Security" portal including click-to-chat, secure messaging, and online Social Security replacement cards. Each year, more than six million customers sign up for eServices and SSA conducts 87 million transactions online. At the same time, the Budget provides funding to ensure that SSA can provide high-quality face-to-face and phone services to individuals who need or prefer them. SSA serves over 40 million customers in person at 1,200 field offices nationwide each year. According to the Foresee e-Government 2015 Report Card, five of the top 10 ranked Federal websites were SSA online customer service products.

Reshaping the Way Government Engages with Citizens and Communities

Too often in the past, the Federal Government has taken a "one-size-fits-all" approach to working with local communities, ignoring the unique challenges and resources of each place. Such an approach fails to fully leverage local knowledge and leadership in maximizing the impact of Federal resources and Federal-local collaboration. Addressing entrenched poverty or improving resilience in the face of climate change requires cross-sector solutions that bring together different agencies and different assets from local, State, Federal, public and private stakeholders.

From day one, the President called on the Federal Government to disrupt this outdated, top-down approach, and to think creatively about how to make our efforts more user-friendly and responsive to the ideas and concerns of local citizens. This new approach is simple. First, we partner with communities by seeking out their plans or vision. Second, we take a one-government approach that crosses agency and program silos to support communities in implementing their plans for improvement. Lastly, we focus on what works, relying on evidence and using data to measure success and monitor progress, fostering communities of practice to share and build on local innovations.

As a result, the collaborative initiatives launched in the last six years have led to progress on numerous challenges facing America's communities. From sparking economic growth, to building ladders of opportunity, to combating climate change, initiatives such as Promise Zones, Investing in Manufacturing Communities Partnership, Partnership for Sustainable Communities, and Performance Partnership Pilots for Disconnected Youth (P3) have supported holistic responses to pressing issues. Today over 1,800 communities nationwide—including cities, towns, counties, and regions—are implementing place-based initiatives that support their integrated goals by busting through Federal silos to promote outcomes that draw on resources across agencies and rely on close coordination with local businesses, philanthropy, and Government.

The place-based approach also improves support for the innovative work happening in State and local government. For example, P3 gives State, local, and tribal governments an opportunity to test innovative new strategies to improve outcomes for disconnected youth ages 14 to 24, including youth who are low-income and in foster care, homeless, young parents, those involved in the justice system, unemployed, or who have dropped out, or are at risk of dropping out of school. A first round of nine pilots was launched in fall 2015. In 2016, P3 will expand to allow communities to take existing dollars that they already receive from seven different Federal agencies, propose better ways to improve outcomes for disconnected youth, and obtain flexibility from existing rules to move forward. In exchange for this flexibility, pilot communities agree to be accountable for concrete outcomes related to education, employment, and other key areas. The Budget supports a fourth round

of Performance Partnership Pilots that allows communities to draw on existing resources from across the Departments of Education, Labor, Health and Human Services (HHS), Justice, and Housing and Urban Development (HUD), as well as the Corporation for National and Community Service and the Institute for Museum and Library Services.

Many place-based initiatives add capacity for and deepen community engagement. These initiatives draw on new tools and methods through partnerships with local civic technology groups, as well as technology and data resources provided by the Federal Government. They recognize that building local capacity is more effective when we use all the tools available to us and that open, high-value data help communities make data-driven decisions, engage residents in new ways, and build trust. For example, after the New Orleans Police Department released 911 calls for service as its first open data set, the Department stepped forward in 2015 as a founding member of the White House Police Data Initiative, committing to opening even more data on policing. Inspired by the White House TechHire initiative, a multi-sector, community-based effort to increase access to high-paying tech jobs by empowering Americans with the skills they need, New Orleans partnered with a local code academy to teach software development skills to youth from low-opportunity neighborhoods. At an event with the New Orleans Police Chief, participating youth built prototype software on open policing data. The success of this initiative has inspired other cities from Indianapolis to Orlando to follow suit with their own local institutions, advocacy groups, and tech communities.

The 2017 Budget continues to institutionalize the Administration's place-based approach to coordinating programs that help create jobs and opportunity, promote resilience and sustainability, and implement local visions in communities across the Nation. At the Federal level, the success of this approach relies on both the staff with the skills and mandate to directly partner with communities as well as programs that provide direct funding and support to communities. In addition to investments in Federal staffing and training, the Budget supports key programs such as Choice Neighborhoods at HUD and Promise Neighborhoods at the Department of Education, providing increased funding for distressed communities to plan and implement comprehensive and community-driven approaches. As another example, the Budget helps communities adapt to the changing energy landscape and build a better future through the POWER Plus (POWER+) Plan. The POWER+ Plan invests in workers and jobs, addresses important legacy costs in coal country, and drives development of coal Carbon Capture and Storage (CCS) technology. Together, these investments and others equip the Federal Government to partner with communities and empower them to meet local needs in an efficient, effective, and integrated manner.

EFFICIENCY: INCREASING QUALITY AND VALUE IN CORE OPERATIONS

Over the years, duplicative administrative functions and back-office services have made the Government less effective and wasted taxpayer dollars. To address this issue, the President has focused on improving Government efficiency to maximize the value of Federal spending. For example, over a two-year period the Federal Government has reduced its domestic office and warehouse inventory by 21.4 million square feet. In an effort to reduce duplication of core administrative services, such as payroll, across Government agencies, large departments are also moving toward the use of shared services. For example, HUD has transitioned many of its core financial management functions to the Department of the Treasury (Treasury). In addition, in 2015, the Administration announced the launch of Category Management Government-wide, which enables the Government to save money by making purchases for common sets of goods and services as a single buyer.

The Budget invests in concentrating the delivery of administrative functions through shared services, simplifying Federal contracting, continued benchmarking to drive data-driven Federal management, implementing new transparency efforts, and shrinking the Federal real property footprint.

Expanding Shared Services to Increase Quality and Savings

Most Federal agencies have similar administrative functions. Human resources, financial management, and payroll, for example, are common administrative functions that all agencies need, but some agencies are better equipped to effectively manage them. By creating Shared Service Providers (SSPs), and concentrating the delivery of administrative services within a smaller number of agencies, we can reduce duplicative efforts. Further, by giving this task to agencies with the right expertise, we can unlock competition between agencies, free up resources for mission critical activities, and deliver cost-effective support to agencies.

The use of shared services has grown in recent years, with smaller agencies leading the charge. For example, the Securities and Exchange Commission and the Consumer Product Safety Commission both utilize shared service providers for multiple administrative functions. In 2015, cabinet-level agencies took steps to realize the benefit of shared service agreements. As noted above, HUD successfully transitioned many of its core financial management functions, as well as select administrative and human-resource functions, to Treasury—the Federal Government's largest financial management shared service arrangement to date. This transition will enable HUD to focus its workforce on serving the Nation's housing and community development needs. Other cabinet-level agencies, including the Department of Labor (DOL) and DHS, will soon follow, resulting in increased economies of scale for shared service providers.

With this increasing shift toward using SSPs, the Administration is taking steps to better manage this emerging practice. In the past, shared services were managed independently by various lines-of-business, such as financial management or human resources, resulting in inconsistent implementation across agencies. While each function operates in a unique environment with specific requirements and challenges, all lines of business would benefit from closer coordination and collaboration, supported by a more robust cross-functional governance model. To support an enterprise-wide approach to shared services, in October 2015 the Administration established a cross-function management and oversight structure comprised of an interagency Shared Services Governance Board (SSGB) and a Unified Shared Services Management (USSM) office within GSA. Led by the SSGB and USSM, stakeholders from across the Government will work together to manage and oversee mission-support shared services with an initial scope of acquisitions, financial management, human resources, travel and information technology. The Budget proposes $5 million to staff the USSM office to oversee SSPs and facilitate agency transitions to these more cost-effective services.

Buying as One through Category Management

The Federal Government is the single largest buyer in the world with annual spending on goods and services close to $450 billion. However, because agencies often purchase goods and services individually, the Federal Government is not able to fully leverage its size as a customer to save money. For this reason, in 2015, the Administration announced the launch of Category Management Government-wide. Category Management, an approach used extensively by the industry and other governments, enables the Federal Government to act more like the single enterprise it is. For example, just one month after OMB issued a new Category Management policy on laptops and desktops that prohibits contract duplication and drives agencies to standardize configurations, several vendors dropped their prices for these configurations by 50 percent. With the Federal Government spending $1.1 billion each year on these products

alone, the potential savings from this policy are large. To further support Category Management and the FITARA, GSA recently negotiated better prices, terms, and conditions for common geospatial software, and awarded a Government-wide agreement for common application development services. This agreement will allow agencies to share and reuse developed applications, code, and best practices, which could save between 50 and 80 percent on application development costs.

Through reinforcement of this management best practice, the Budget better leverages buying power, which leads to increased savings, more consistent practices across agencies, reduced duplication, and improved performance for the American taxpayers. The Administration is driving the adoption of Category Management through the implementation of a Category Management CAP Goal, which focuses on five areas: hardware; software; telecommunications; IT security; and IT professional services. The Federal Government spends over $50 billion per year on purchases in these areas alone. Implementation of this CAP Goal will save the Federal Government money, reduce duplication, increase the use of best-in-class solutions, and adopt Category Management principles. Specifically, by the end of 2019, the Administration aims to save at least $10.5 billion on IT in the areas of hardware, software, telecommunications, and outsourcing; and half of all IT spending should be under Government-wide management where agencies utilize best-in-class Government-wide solutions and adopt Category Management principles. Furthermore, through the implementation of the Category Management policy, described above, that prohibits the award of new contracts, mandates use of standard configurations, and implements demand management strategies for laptop and desktop purchases, the Administration aims to reduce the number of new and renewed contracts and cut administrative costs by 30 percent by the end of 2019. In the $1 billion laptop and desktop Federal market, 75 percent of spending should move through best-in-class acquisition solutions by 2019, an increase from 39 percent today.

The supporting backbone of Category Management is the Acquisition Gateway, a new online tool for the Federal acquisition workforce that contains key contract information and tools by categories of purchasing. Using this tool, over 5,000 Federal project managers, contracting specialists, and program officials are now able to search and compare existing contracts and prices paid under those contracts across hundreds of contracts and products. Sharing this information leverages Government purchasing power, reduces contract duplication, and streamlines delivery of goods and services in support of mission needs. Furthermore, businesses will spend less time responding to duplicate procurements and Federal program officials will have more time to concentrate on managing results.

Shrinking the Federal Real Property Footprint

The Federal Government is the largest property owner in the United States. The domestic building inventory contains almost 300,000 buildings requiring approximately $21 billion of annual operation and maintenance expenditures, including approximately $6.8 billion of annual lease costs. As a result, there are numerous opportunities to save by using Federal space more efficiently and disposing of unneeded buildings, land, and structures. The Administration has made significant progress on real property. In 2012, the Administration issued a "Freeze the Footprint" policy, which directed agencies to freeze the growth in their office and warehouse real estate inventory. While it only called for zero footprint growth, Freeze the Footprint policy actually led to a 10.2 million square foot reduction by the end of 2013. Also, by the end of 2014 the cumulative reduction reached 21.4 million square feet.

In March 2015, the Administration issued the National Strategy for the Efficient Use of Real Property (National Strategy) and its companion policy—the Reduce the Footprint (RTF) policy. Building on the Freeze the Footprint policy and agencies' successes in beginning to reduce their real property holdings, the five-year National

Strategy's primary objective is to formally adopt Government-wide requirements to reduce the size of the Government's domestic real property portfolio through efficiency improvement and property disposal. The RTF policy requires agencies to set annual reduction targets for office and warehouse space and annual disposal targets for all building types to improve efficiency and reduce costs. For the first time, the RTF policy requires that agencies reduce the size of their real property portfolios to improve program efficiency, and agencies have developed and finalized their first ever five-year RTF reduction plans to implement the policy. The agencies' RTF plans target an aggregate reduction of 60 million square feet between 2016 and 2020. Agencies will update their RTF plans and annual reduction targets annually with the goal of increasing the magnitude of targeted reductions over time. The Budget supports further efficiency improvement by providing funds for real property consolidation projects.

To support more ambitious reduction targets, GSA and OMB have developed a new management tool within the Federal Real Property Profile (FRPP) database that enables agencies to fully analyze their portfolios. The new management tool uses the real property performance metrics developed through the President's Management Agenda to measure the performance of agencies' portfolios and thereby identify and prioritize efficiency opportunities. The management tool, combined with FRPP's data quality improvements, will enhance agencies' ability to implement data-driven decision making to develop their annual RTF reduction targets. Focusing policy on reducing the portfolio, improving the quality of FRPP data through mandatory data validation and verification procedures, and the broad use of the new FRPP management tool will support higher RTF square foot reduction targets and efficiency gains in future years.

The Administration has fully deployed its administrative authority to reform real property management as evidenced by the National Strategy, its real property policies, and funding requests for the Consolidation Activities program. Achieving further progress on real property reform requires additional legislative authority, which should embody the core principles that framed the Administration's Civilian Property Realignment Act legislative proposal. These core principles include the creation of an independent Board to make real property disposition recommendations in the best interest of the Government, a Government-wide sale proceeds retention and reinvestment account, agency proceeds retention, and legislative relief from current program requirements. The Administration's proposal of another round of DOD Base Realignment and Closure (BRAC) to reduce unneeded facilities demonstrates its commitment to working with the Congress to develop authorities using these core principles that both improve the efficiency of Government-wide real property portfolio and reduce costs. (See Chapter 4 for more on the Budget's BRAC proposal.)

Benchmarking Agencies

Over the course of this Administration, we have used regular data-driven reviews—such as PortfolioStat and AqStat—to advance management priorities. Building on these efforts, in 2014 the Administration launched the Benchmarking initiative by establishing cost and quality benchmarks for core administrative operations across agencies to measure performance in key mission-support areas, including human resources, financial management, acquisition, IT, and real property. This initiative allows agencies to see how their bureaus compare against each other, how they perform peer-to-peer, and their individual agency impacts on Government-wide averages.

In 2015, OMB, in conjunction with GSA, launched the "FedStat" review with major agencies to have a holistic, data-driven discussion across all mission-support and mission-delivery areas. As part of this initiative, OMB met with agencies to identify potential areas for improvement, discuss shared challenges across the Government, and explore opportunities to pursue cross-agency solutions—including policies, processes, and leading practices of excellence for broader application across program administration and management. These data-driven reviews led to a number of tangible improvements—such as how agencies may benefit from shared services or strategies for addressing common hiring and recruitment challenges—that can improve the effectiveness and efficiency of individual agencies and the Government as a whole.

Reforming Federal Background Investigations

The Federal Government is responsible for issuing, handling, and storing much of America's most important data. The Government also performs key functions with these data, such as conducting background investigations to assess whether individuals may serve as Federal employees, members of the Armed Forces, or contractors, be granted access to its facilities and information systems, and be trusted with classified and other sensitive information. As the world's technologies continue to evolve and the economy becomes ever more digitally connected, the Federal Government's tools, systems, and processes for managing such sensitive information and conducting background investigations must keep pace with these advancements. This is necessary in order to better anticipate, detect, and counter malicious activities, as well as threats posed by trusted insiders, who may seek to do harm to the Government's personnel, property, and information systems.

Last year, in light of increasing cybersecurity threats, including the compromise of information housed at OPM, the Administration initiated a 90-Day Suitability and Security review to re-examine reforms to the Federal background investigations process, assess additional enhancements to further secure information networks and systems, and determine improvements that could be made to the way the Government conducts background investigations for suitability, security, and credentialing.

This review was conducted by the interagency Performance Accountability Council (PAC), which is chaired by OMB and comprised of the Director of National Intelligence, the Director of OPM, in their respective roles as Security and Suitability Executive Agents of the PAC, and the Departments of Defense, the Treasury, Homeland Security, State, Justice, Energy, the Federal Bureau of Investigation, and others. It also included consultation with outside experts.

The review resulted in a series of actions to modernize and strengthen the way the Federal Government conducts background investigations for Federal employees, members of the Armed services, and contractors, and protects sensitive data. These changes include the establishment of the National Background Investigations Bureau (NBIB), which will absorb OPM's existing Federal Investigative Services, and be headquartered in Washington, D.C. This new Government-wide service provider for background investigations will be housed within OPM. Its mission will be to provide effective, efficient, and secure background investigations for the Federal Government. Unlike the previous structure, DOD will assume the responsibility for the design, development, security, and operation of the background investigations IT systems for the NBIB. To support this work, the Budget includes $95 million in additional resources that will be dedicated to the development of these IT capabilities.

While these changes will take time to fully implement, the Administration has taken and will continue to take immediate action to move forward with strengthening the background investigations process. These include building on the security measures implemented in response to the calendar year 2015 OPM cyber incidents, the establishment of a NBIB transition team, and a focus on driving continuous performance improvements to address evolving threats.

These changes build upon the Administration's efforts to improve how the Federal Government performs security clearance determinations, and protect the safety of American citizens and of our Nation's most sensitive information and facilities.

Modernizing Infrastructure Permitting

Building a 21st Century infrastructure in a way that safeguards communities and the environment is a key component of the President's efforts to strengthen the economy and create new jobs. Over the last several years, the Administration has taken action to cut project review timelines for major infrastructure projects, while improving environmental and community outcomes.

In 2016, the Administration will work aggressively to implement the permitting provisions included in the recently enacted Fixing America's Surface Transportation Act, many of which align with ongoing Administration efforts. Among other things, the law establishes a new interagency governance structure to oversee the timely processing of permits and reviews; enables agencies to recover reasonable costs for such activities; and standardizes processes for resolving disputes. Implemented effectively, these reforms will facilitate more efficient, effective, and timely Federal permitting decisions.

Consistent with guidance issued from OMB and the Council for Environmental Quality in 2015, the law requires expanded use of an online dashboard to track major infrastructure projects under Federal review. Use of the Dashboard will improve agencies' communication with project sponsors, enhance interagency coordination, and increase the transparency and accountability of the permitting process.

Furthermore, the law outlines a comprehensive set of procedures that standardize Federal permitting and review processes for major infrastructure projects, such as requiring development of coordinated project plans to include a discussion of potential avoidance, minimization, and mitigation strategies. To this end, in November 2015, the President issued a memorandum to ensure that Federal mitigation policies are clear, work similarly across agencies, and are implemented consistently. By encouraging agencies to share and adopt a common set of best practices to mitigate harmful impacts to natural resources, the Federal Government can create a regulatory environment that allows us to build the economy faster and better while protecting healthy ecosystems that benefit this and future generations.

Increasing Federal Spending Transparency

On May 9, 2014, the President signed the Digital Accountability and Transparency Act (DATA Act), setting forth a new commitment to expand Federal spending transparency. When fully implemented, taxpayers will be able to access, search, and download Federal spending data on a publicly available website. This data includes obligations, outlays, unobligated balances, and other budgetary resources for each appropriations account. Taxpayers will also have access to more information about Federal awards as they will be linked with financial data for the first time. With increased access to this data, the public will see where, how, and on what their Government spends their tax dollars.

This level of Federal spending transparency is unprecedented and requires collaboration among the Federal and public stakeholders. OMB and Treasury are the lead agencies for Government-wide implementation of the DATA Act. During the first year of implementation, OMB and Treasury met the statutory deadline for finalizing financial data standards, in addition to data definition standards specific to procurement, and financial assistance award reporting under the Federal Funding Accountability and Transparency Act. Policy guidance was also issued to direct agencies on implementing the DATA Act and, in particular, the data standards by Federal agencies. Complementing these efforts, Treasury also re-launched *USAspending. gov* on a more stable and user-friendly platform. To drive these improvements and provide greater transparency in Federal spending, OMB and Treasury have leveraged real-time tools to gather feedback from the public, such as using GitHub in the development of the recent data standards. In 2017, OMB and Treasury will continue their work with Federal agencies to implement the *USAspending.gov* data standards. Further, Treasury will complete its efforts to not only redesign the current *USAspending.gov* to meet DATA Act publication needs, but ensure that reported financial and award data is publicly available and accurately represented on *USAspending.gov* (or its successor site) by May 2017.

The Budget invests in the ongoing work to implement the DATA Act's data standards across Federal agencies by the statutory deadline of May 2017. In particular, the Budget includes $15 million to support Treasury's Government-wide implementation efforts, including building a DATA Act-compliant *USAspending.gov*, and $9 million to fund the work of Federal SSPs to streamline implementation among several large and small agencies. With this funding, the Government will sustain its momentum on increasing Federal spending transparency.

Reducing the Administrative Reporting Burden for Federal Contractors and Grantees

In addition to expanding transparency, the DATA Act required a two-year pilot program on reducing the administrative reporting burden on grant recipients and contractors. OMB began the pilot in May 2015 with the release of a National Dialogue to solicit ideas from the public on their reporting burden and is collaborating with agencies and the grants and procurement communities to identify ways to reduce duplication, redundancy, and unnecessary costs in Federal reporting requirements. The dialogue is generating ideas that can be further explored for streamlined reporting and recommendations for Federal contractors and Federal grantees. OMB will complete its DATA Act pilot work in May 2017 and present its recommendations by August 2017.

While Federal awarding and reporting processes have similarities, there are unique burdens that could possibly be reduced. To accommodate those award-specific areas, two tracks are underway for Federal procurement and Federal grants. OMB has engaged HHS to be the executing agent of the grants-specific portion of the pilot. As the largest grant-issuing agency and owner of *Grants.gov* and the Payment Management System, HHS is uniquely positioned to provide tactical leadership and execution of grants-specific pilot efforts. OMB is leading the procurement-specific areas of the pilot with collaboration from GSA and the Chief Acquisition Officers Council.

In support of these pilot activities, the Budget provides necessary funding to complete testing of potential solutions to reduce grant and procurement related reporting burden, and supports the Administration's broad goals to maximize the impact of every taxpayer dollar.

ECONOMIC GROWTH: OPENING GOVERNMENT-FUNDED DATA AND RESEARCH TO THE PUBLIC TO SPUR INNOVATION, ENTREPRENEURSHIP, AND JOB GROWTH

The Budget continues to invest in efforts to open up Government-generated assets, including data and the results of federally funded research and development (R&D)—such as intellectual property and scientific knowledge—to the public. Through these efforts, the Government empowers citizens and businesses to increase the return on our investment with innovation, job creation, and economic prosperity gained through their use of open Government data and research results. The use of this data and scientific knowledge has impacted the private sector, including fueling innovative start-up companies and creating American jobs, increasing the transparency of retirement plans, helping consumers uncover fraudulent charges on their credit card bills, assisting potential homebuyers in making informed housing decisions, and creating new life-changing technologies, such as leading-edge vaccines.

Opening Data to Spark Innovation

The Administration continues to make progress toward its open data commitment and data governance. The data the Government collects has proven valuable well beyond the original purposes for which it was collected. For example, the U.S. Census Bureau, which collects data from citizens and businesses through surveys and other voluntary means, continues to encourage community innovators to create web tools and mobile applications by connecting local and national public data in one location and hosting challenges for their use. These challenges have led to a host of civic solutions including an application that helps people with disabilities find facility accessibility scores, helping local leaders and entrepreneurs find free meeting spaces, and aiding food truck vendors find urban areas with the highest social media activity. By the close of calendar year 2015, *Data.gov* featured over 188,000 datasets on topics such as education, public safety, health care, energy, and agriculture. To help assist agencies in their open data efforts and to support the Federal open data ecosystem, the Administration has built additional resources such as Project Open Data, which provides agencies with tools and best practices to make their data publicly available, and the Project Open Data Dashboard, which is used to provide the public a quarterly evaluation of agency open data progress. Eight Federal agencies co-hosted open data roundtables that connected agencies with the organizations that use their data to help identify high-value datasets and establish open data priorities.

Fueling the Economy by Bridging the Barriers from Lab-to-Market

The Budget invests $152 billion in R&D across Government in 2017, as discussed in Chapter 2. The Federal Government's investment in R&D has produced extraordinary long-term economic impact over the decades, through the creation of new knowledge, new jobs, and new industries. The Federal R&D enterprise will continue to support fundamental research that is motivated primarily by the interest in expanding the frontiers of human knowledge, and will continue to diffuse this knowledge through open data and publications. At the same time, there remains significant potential to increase the public's return on this investment through effective partnerships with academia, industry, and regional innovation networks. For example, the National Aeronautics and Space Administration has partnered with companies to make experimentation on the International Space Station more accessible to researchers, an approach that has played a significant role in jump-starting a new industry in very small satellites. In the case of the Department of Energy, industry partnerships can help broadly develop and deploy important next generation energy technologies and high-performance computers.

The Budget reflects the Administration's commitment to accelerating the transfer of the results of federally funded research to the commercial marketplace by prioritizing funding for Lab-to-Market programs at the National Institute of Standards and Technology ($8 million) and for NSF's public-private Innovation Corps (I-Corps) program ($30 million). Both of these programs are developing tools and best practices that are invigorating efforts to commercialize the results of federally funded R&D. For example, the I-Corps program at NSF has 10 agreements with other Federal agencies that are using its experiential entrepreneurial curriculum to train research scientists, graduate students, and other entrepreneurs in how to identify and mature discoveries ripe for commercialization. In addition, I-Corps has a growing number of partnerships with non-Federal entities, such as with the State of Ohio. The Budget also provides $50 million in mandatory funding for a new competitive grant program, building on the success of prior Economic Development Administration-led activities, to incentivize partnerships between Federal labs, academia, and regional economic development organizations to enable the transfer of knowledge and technologies from labs to private industry for commercialization. In addition, the Department of Energy is making the technologies and tools developed by its national labs more available to small businesses and entrepreneurs through innovative approaches designed to unlock new business or productive opportunities.

PEOPLE AND CULTURE: UNLOCKING THE FULL POTENTIAL OF TODAY'S FEDERAL WORKFORCE AND BUILDING THE WORKFORCE WE NEED FOR TOMORROW

In his December 2014 address to Federal Senior Executives, President Obama said, "[W]e need the best and brightest of the coming generations to serve. [T]hose of us who believe government can and must be a force for good...we've got to work hard to make sure that government works." Through the Management Agenda's focus on People and Culture, the Administration is committed to undertaking executive actions to attract and retain the best talent for the Federal workforce and foster a culture of excellence. The Budget supports efforts to strengthen the Senior Executive Service (SES) and improve employee engagement in order to fully capitalize on the talents in today's Federal workforce at all levels, and recruit and develop the talent needed to continue moving the Federal Government forward in the 21st Century.

White House Advisory Group

The White House Advisory Group on Senior Executive Service Reform, comprised of 24 leaders from across the Federal Government, was announced in December 2014 and charged with making recommendations for improving the way the Federal Government recruits, hires, develops, retains, manages, and holds accountable, top senior career leaders. The final reforms focus on three key areas: 1) hiring the best talent; 2) strengthening SES development; and 3) improving SES accountability, recognition, and rewards. On December 15, 2015, the President signed an Executive Order titled "Strengthening the Senior Executive Service" that included reforms to improve the hiring and selection processes and increase rotations to broaden experience and succession planning. In addition, the President's Management Council formed a subcommittee to oversee the implementation, and OPM and OMB will undertake a set of additional administrative actions.

The White House Leadership Development Fellows

Announced by the President in December 2014, the Administration launched the White House Leadership Development Program. Through this program, GS-15 (and equivalent) emerging leaders participate in rotational assignments to drive progress on CAP Goals and lead change across Departments and programs. Agencies nominated dozens of their top-performing employees, who then were assessed by panels comprised of existing executives across Government. The initial class of 17 Fellows entered the program in October 2015, and are now working on cross-agency priorities such as shared service centers, climate change, and human capital. Participants in the program will gain valuable experience by playing a key role in addressing critical management challenges facing the Federal Government and will build networks and best practices to bring back to their agencies. Many of the Fellows will be prepared to join the SES upon completing the program.

Hiring Excellence

The Hiring Excellence Initiative of the People and Culture CAP Goal is designed to enable agencies to hire the best talent from all backgrounds. In 2015, the Administration worked with agencies to understand their hiring challenges through the annual FedStat process while deploying OPM policy experts to provide sessions to identify and solve agency-based policy

barriers to successful Federal hiring. An interagency team consisting of OMB, the Presidential Personnel Office, and OPM also developed the Hiring Excellence Campaign, which will launch in calendar year 2016 as an educational outreach vehicle to enable agencies to attract highly qualified and diverse talent through engaged and empowered hiring managers, supported by highly skilled human resources staff. The team will also partner with the Office of the Federal CIO, DHS, and others on specific Cybersecurity Workforce initiatives as outlined in the 2015 Cybersecurity Implementation Plan.

Employee Engagement

In both the private and public sector, an employee's investment in the mission of their organization is closely related to the organization's overall performance. Engaged employees display greater dedication, persistence, and effort in their work, and better serve their customers—whether they are consumers or taxpayers. This makes employee engagement a critical performance measurement for Federal agencies. Starting in 2014, the Administration embarked on a campaign to improve employee engagement. Each agency named a senior level official to be accountable for determining the best method for improving employee engagement within their specific organizational culture. A team from OMB and OPM met with all 24 Chief Human Capital Officers Act agencies and hosted four conferences at the White House. As a result of these efforts, after years of steady declines, for the first time in the history of the survey the 2015 Federal Employee Viewpoint Survey showed either improvement or holding steady on all questions.

MEASURING RESULTS: SETTING GOALS AND TRACKING PERFORMANCE

Improving Performance and Accountability

Too often, multiple agencies work in isolation from one another to tackle a challenge, rather than delivering an integrated response

that better addresses the problem. The Administration uses CAP Goals to overcome this mismatch, helping break down organizational barriers to achieve better performance and results than one agency can achieve on its own.

For example, DOD and the Department of Veterans Affairs (VA) have partnered to improve veterans mental health. Through this collaboration, last year over 11,000 individuals participated in 144 VA medical center-hosted Mental Health Summits across the Nation in order to identify unmet needs and increase awareness of community-based programs and services for organizations supporting veterans and their families. Newly available data also shows that, for those service-members completing a Post-Deployment Health Reassessment in 2013, who screened positive for posttraumatic stress disorder (PTSD), depression, or alcohol abuse and received a referral to mental health specialty, or behavioral health in primary care, 55 percent received care at VAs or DOD (2013), up from 46 percent in 2011, and nearing the target of 56 percent by 2016.

Agencies have also used the Priority Goal process to drive performance improvements. For example, HUD and VA have reduced the total number of homeless veterans; the Department of Justice has improved the protection of the most vulnerable within society, including victims and survivors of human trafficking, and the Small Business Administration has helped increase small business access to capital by adding new lenders to its flagship lending program.

While there has been impressive progress made on CAP Goal priorities, from improving citizen interactions with Federal agencies—through the launch of the Feedback USA customer experience initiative within the Customer Service CAP Goal, to the establishment of the first-ever Government-wide shared services management and oversight operation model by the Shared Services CAP Goal team—overall performance delivery across agency boundaries remains a challenge, and in many cases significant management improvements require investments that cut across agencies and budget accounts. The Budget continues the enacted 2016 authority for the OMB Director, with prior notification to the Congress, to transfer up to $15 million to support these crosscutting management initiatives rather than handling them on a case-by-case basis.

More details about the Federal Government's specific performance framework can be found on *Performance.gov* and in the *Analytical Perspectives* volume of the Budget. The Government can, and should, be more effective and efficient, and this authority provides a powerful tool to turn management reform ideas into real and lasting results for the American people.

USING EVIDENCE AND EVALUATION TO DRIVE INNOVATION AND OUTCOMES

The President has made clear that policy decisions should be driven by evidence—evidence about what works and what does not, and evidence that identifies the greatest needs and opportunities to solve great challenges. Over the past seven years there has been growing momentum for evidence-based approaches at all levels of government, as well as among nonprofits, foundations, faith-based institutions, and community-based organizations. In addition, Members of Congress from both parties, visionary governors and State legislatures, action-oriented mayors, and the non-profit and research communities are promoting greater use of data and research in policymaking and program management.

As discussed in prior chapters, the Administration's embrace of this approach has resulted in important gains in areas ranging from reducing veteran homelessness, to improving educational outcomes, to enhancing the effectiveness of international development programs. In addition to continuing and expanding these effective strategies, the Budget proposes to invest in a broad variety of additional evidence-based approaches to tackle important challenges. For example, the Budget provides substantially more very low-income families with rental subsidies to move to higher-opportunity areas, which research has demonstrated can have large positive effects on children's—especially young children's—educational attainment and long-term earnings; proposes evidence-based strategies to end chronic and family homelessness; establishes an Apprenticeship Training Fund that would help meet the President's goal to double the number of apprentices across the United States to give more workers the opportunity to develop job-relevant skills while they are earning a paycheck; incentivizes States to adopt evidence-informed approaches to criminal justice reform; and encourages States to adopt evidence-based psychosocial interventions to address the behavioral and mental health needs of children in foster care and reduce reliance on psychotropic medications and improve overall health outcomes.

To enable future administrations and the Congress—as well as State and local leaders—to drive even more resources to policies backed by strong evidence, the Budget proposes a series of legislative changes and investments to accelerate learning about what programs work and why.

The Budget also expands the use of innovative, outcome-focused grant designs that focus Federal dollars on effective practices while also encouraging innovation in service delivery. The proposed Emergency Assistance and Service Connection Grants (discussed in Chapter 3), the Upward Mobility project (also discussed in Chapter 3), the expansion of Performance Partnership Pilots (discussed earlier in this chapter), funding for Education Innovation and Research, a new program that replaces and builds on the successes of Investing in Innovation (discussed in Chapter 3), First in the World, and the continued proposals to invest in Pay for Success are all examples of how the Administration is proposing to partner with States, communities, and consortia across the Nation to make it easier to test and validate promising evidence-based approaches. All of these models include strong validation and evaluation requirements and hold grantees accountable for achieving outcomes, while also granting flexibility on how

to best achieve those outcomes within their community.

Improving Capacity to Build and Use Evidence

Federal agencies, States, communities, and the nonprofit community have made notable progress in developing and implementing evidence-based practices and in learning which practices are more effective. As discussed in the *Analytic Perspectives* volume chapter, Building the Capacity to Produce and Use Evidence, the Administration is making progress in developing the Federal capacity to more routinely and reliably develop high-quality evidence to inform important policies. However, significant challenges remain, and in order to continue making progress, evidence-building must be cheaper and easier to do. One way to do this is by making better use of data the Government already collects through administering programs—also known as "administrative data"—to answer important questions about the effectiveness of Federal programs and policies.

Employment and earnings data are among the most valuable Federal administrative information. Because many Federal (as well as State and local) programs are intended, in whole or in part, to increase employment and earnings, accurate employment and earnings data are needed to measure performance or conduct rigorous evaluations across a range of programs. The National Directory of New Hires (NDNH) is a database of employment and Unemployment Insurance (UI) information administered by the Office of Child Support Enforcement within HHS. Access to this data is tightly controlled by statute, and HHS implements strong privacy, confidentiality, and security protections to safeguard the data from unauthorized use or disclosure—there has never been a breach of the national NDNH data. Currently several programs are successfully using this data for program integrity, implementation, and research purposes.

The Budget proposes to build on this strong history of data stewardship and protection to allow additional programs and agencies to access this valuable data to learn what works and improve program implementation, while continuing to protect the privacy, security, and confidentiality of that data. Specifically, the Budget supports a package of proposals designed to clearly specify the purpose for which the data may be used, require that the minimum data necessary be used to achieve the purpose, and include strong penalties for the unauthorized access, use, disclosure, or re-disclosure of the data. In order to streamline access to the data by authorized agencies for program integrity purposes, the package includes a proposal which would allow the authorized agencies access to the NDNH data through the Do Not Pay Business Center at Treasury. In addition, each component of the package is designed to satisfy the Administration's criteria for when authority to access NDNH data should be considered. The package also requires HHS to review each agency's data security before allowing that agency to access the data, prohibits HHS from granting access to the data for any purpose not authorized in statute, and requires HHS to publicly report on the use of NDNH data.

NDNH Access Proposals	
AGENCY	**PROPOSAL**
	PRIVACY AND CONFIDENTIALITY PROTECTIONS
HHS/ACF	The Package would: 1) require the Administration for Children and Families (ACF) to review an entity's data security prior to granting access to NDNH data; 2) prohibit ACF from granting access to NDNH data for any reason not authorized in statute; and 3) require ACF to generate public reporting on the use of records.
	PROGRAM INTEGRITY PROPOSALS
HHS/Centers for Medicare & Medicaid Services	Assist with income and employer verification and improve the Affordable Care Act advance premium tax credit payment accuracy to reduce improper payments.
Department of Agriculture/Rural Housing Service	Verify eligibility and validate the income source information provided by means-tested single family housing loan applicants and multifamily housing project-based tenants.
Railroad Retirement Board	Establish eligibility for processing disability benefits in a more efficient manner.
Department of Labor/UI	Require (rather than permit) states to cross-match with NDNH to identify improper payments.
	EVALUATION/STATISTICAL/PROGRAM ADMINISTRATION PROPOSALS
Multi/Statistical and Evaluation Access	Access to NDNH for Federal statistical agencies, units, and evaluation offices or their designees for statistical, research, evaluation, and performance measurement purposes associated with assessing positive labor market outcomes. Would reduce cost of the 2020 Census by several hundred million dollars.
Workforce Programs at Departments of Labor and Education	Provide access for program administration, including Federal oversight and evaluation, and authorize data exchanges between State child support and workforce agencies.

Reorganizing Government: Reforming to Win in the Global Economy

The Administration will also continue efforts to drive lasting change in how Government works through reorganizing or consolidating Federal programs to reduce duplication, and identify cost savings to allow the Government to invest more in productive activities. The President is again asking the Congress to revive an authority that Presidents had for almost the entire period from 1932 through 1984—the ability to submit proposals to reorganize the Executive Branch through a fast-track procedure. In effect, the President is asking that the next President have the same authority that any business owner has to reorganize or streamline operations to meet changing circumstances and customer demand. For example, consolidating business and trade promotion into a single department would enhance Government productivity and effectiveness. Bringing together the core tools to expand trade and investment, grow small businesses, and support innovation, would help American businesses compete in the global economy, expand exports, and create more jobs at home.

CUTS, CONSOLIDATIONS, AND SAVINGS

As part of the President's Management Agenda, the Administration has focused on improving Government efficiency to maximize the value of Federal spending. The Budget invests in concentrating the delivery of administrative functions through shared services, simplifying Federal contracting, continuing the use of benchmarking to inform data-driven Federal management, implementing new transparency efforts, and shrinking the Federal real property footprint. Further detail on all of these initiatives is provided in the chapter titled A Government of the Future.

The Budget continues efforts to reorganize or consolidate Federal programs to reduce duplication and identify cost savings to allow the Government to invest more in productive activities. The President is again asking the Congress to restore fast-track authority to the President to submit proposals to reorganize the Executive Branch. Previous Presidents have been granted this authority for almost the entire period from 1932 through 1984. In effect, the President is asking that the next President have the same authority that any business owner has to reorganize or streamline operations to meet changing circumstances and customer demand.

The Budget also continues to target unnecessary or lower priority programs for reduction or elimination. In the President's first seven Budgets,

the Administration identified, on average, more than 140 cuts, consolidations, and savings averaging more than $22 billion each year. Many of these proposals have now been implemented, and the Budget builds on this success. It includes 117 cuts, consolidations, and savings proposals, which are projected to save over $14 billion in 2017. Savings from discretionary proposals total $5.9 billion in 2017, reflecting the trade-offs and choices the Administration is making to adhere to the funding levels established in the Bipartisan Budget Act of 2015. Savings from mandatory and program integrity proposals total $8.2 billion in 2017 and $670 billion over 10 years; about 75 percent of these savings are from health reform proposals. The Budget shows that investments in growth and opportunity are compatible with putting the Nation's finances on a strong and sustainable path. Overall, the Budget achieves about $2.9 trillion in deficit reduction, primarily from reforms in health programs, the tax code, and immigration.

Discretionary and mandatory cuts, consolidations, and savings proposals in this year's Budget are detailed on the following tables. Savings from the Administration's program integrity proposals, totaling $119 billion through 2026, are detailed in the Budget Process chapter of the *Analytical Perspectives* volume.

DISCRETIONARY CUTS, CONSOLIDATIONS, AND SAVINGS

(Budget authority in millions of dollars)

	2016	2017	2017 Change from 2016
Cuts			
21st Century Community Learning Centers, Department of Education	1,167	1,000	−167
317 Immunization Program, Department of Health and Human Services	611	561	−50
Area Health Education Centers, Department of Health and Human Services	30	....	−30
Beaches Grants Program, Environmental Protection Agency	10	....	−10
Broadband Loans, Department of Agriculture [1]	5	....	−5
Centers for Disease Control and Prevention Direct Healthcare Screenings, Department of Health and Human Services	266	209	−57
Clean Water and Drinking Water State Revolving Loan Funds, Environmental Protection Agency	2,257	2,000	−257
Community Development Block Grant (Formula Funds), Department of Housing and Urban Development	3,000	2,800	−200
Community Economic Development, Department of Health and Human Services [1]	30	....	−30
Community Services Block Grant, Department of Health and Human Services	715	674	−41
Delta Regional Authority Grants, Department of Agriculture [1]	3	....	−3
Diesel Emissions Reduction Grant Program, Environmental Protection Agency [1]	50	10	−40
Economic Impact Grants, Department of Agriculture [1]	6	....	−6
Education Research Centers and Agricultural Research, Department of Health and Human Services [1]	54	....	−54
Environmental Health Outcome Tracking Network, Department of Health and Human Services	34	24	−10
FEMA Education, Training, and Exercises, Department of Homeland Security	233	157	−76
FEMA Pre-Disaster Mitigation Grants, Department of Homeland Security	100	54	−46
FEMA Preparedness Grants, Department of Homeland Security	1,317	857	−460
Foreign Military Financing, Department of State	6,026	5,714	−312
Global Agriculture and Food Security Program, Department of the Treasury	43	23	−20
Grants for Abstinence-Only Programs, Department of Health and Human Services	10	....	−10
Grants-In-Aid for Airports, Department of Transportation [1]	3,350	2,900	−450
Great Lakes Restoration Initiative, Environmental Protection Agency	300	250	−50
Harry S. Truman Scholarship Foundation	1	....	−1
Health Care Services Grant Program, Department of Agriculture [1]	3	....	−3
High Energy Cost Grants, Department of Agriculture [1]	10	....	−10
High Intensity Drug Trafficking Areas, Office of National Drug Control Policy [1]	250	196	−54
ICE Immigration Detention Beds, Department of Homeland Security	1,649	1,330	−319
Impact Aid - Payments for Federal Property, Department of Education [1]	67	....	−67
Integrated NSF Support Promoting Interdisciplinary Research and Education (INSPIRE), National Science Foundation [1]	25	....	−25
International Education (Overseas Programs), Department of Education [1]	7	2	−5
International Narcotics Control and Law Enforcement, Department of State	1,266	1,138	−128
LIHEAP, Department of Health and Human Services	3,390	3,000	−390
Littoral Combat Ships, Department of Defense	1,332	1,126	−206
Low Priority Studies and Construction, Corps of Engineers	1,983	1,175	−808
McGovern-Dole Food for Education Program, Department of Agriculture	202	182	−20
Mexico Border Targeted Water Infrastructure Grants, Environmental Protection Agency	10	5	−5
Mutual Self-Help Housing Grants, Department of Agriculture	28	18	−9
National Heritage Areas, Department of the Interior [1]	20	9	−11
National Priorities Research, Environmental Protection Agency [1]	14	....	−14
National Solar Observatory, National Science Foundation [1]	10	6	−4
National Wildlife Refuge Fund, Department of the Interior [1]	13	....	−13
Operation and Maintenance Work, Corps of Engineers	3,137	2,705	−432
Preventive Health and Health Services Block Grant, Department of Health and Human Services [1]	160	....	−160
PRIME Technical Assistance, Small Business Administration [1]	5	....	−5
REACH, Department of Health and Human Services	51	30	−21
Research, Education and Extension Grants, Department of Agriculture:			
Animal Health (Sec. 1433) [1]	4	....	−4

DISCRETIONARY CUTS, CONSOLIDATIONS, AND SAVINGS—Continued
(Budget authority in millions of dollars)

	2016	2017	2017 Change from 2016
Alfalfa Forage [1]	2	....	−2
Aquaculture Centers [1]	4	....	−4
Aquaculture Research [1]	1	....	−1
Capacity Building: Non-Land Grant Colleges [1]	5	....	−5
Farm Business Management and Benchmarking [1]	1	....	−1
Food Animal Residue Avoidance Database [1]	1	....	−1
Methyl Bromide Transition Program [1]	2	....	−2
New Technologies for Extension [1]	2	1	−1
Potato Breeding Research (Competitive) [1]	2	....	−2
Rural Health and Safety [1]	2	....	−2
Sungrants [1]	3	....	−3
Supplemental and Alternative Crops [1]	1	....	−1
Veterinary Services Grant Program [1]	3	....	−3
Rural Community Facilities, Department of Health and Human Services [1]	7	....	−7
Rural Energy Savings Program, Department of Agriculture [1]	8	....	−8
Rural Hospital Flexibility Grant Programs, Department of Health and Human Services	42	26	−16
Rural Multifamily Housing Preservation Grants, Department of Agriculture [1]	4	....	−4
State Criminal Alien Assistance Program, Department of Justice	210	....	−210
State Indoor Radon Grant Program, Environmental Protection Agency	8	....	−8
Sustainable and Healthy Communities Research, Environmental Protection Agency	155	147	−8
Targeted Airshed Grants, Environmental Protection Agency	20	....	−20
Urban and Community Forestry, Department of Agriculture	28	24	−4
Water and Wastewater and Community Facilities Loan Guarantees, Department of Agriculture [1]	4	....	−4
Water and Wastewater Grants and Direct Loans, Department of Agriculture	512	462	−50
Water Quality Research and Support Grants, Environmental Protection Agency [1]	13	....	−13
Women in Apprenticeship and Nontraditional Occupations, Department of Labor [1]	1	....	−1
Total, Discretionary Cuts	**34,290**	**28,815**	**−5,477**
Consolidations			
Chemical, Biological, Radiological, Nuclear, and Explosives Office, Department of Homeland Security	505	501	−4
Management Headquarters Reductions, Department of Defense	....	−154	−154
Section 4 and Rural Capacity Building, Department of Housing and Urban Development	40	35	−5
Self-Help Homeownership Opportunity Program, Department of Housing and Urban Development	10	10	....
Total, Discretionary Consolidations	**555**	**392**	**−163**
Savings			
Change in Plutonium Disposition Approach, Department of Energy	340	285	−55
Information Technology Consolidation, Business Process Improvements, and Other Efficiencies, Department of Defense	....	−243	−243
Senate Campaign Finance Reports Electronic Submission, Federal Election Commission	....	....	....
Total, Discretionary Savings	**340**	**42**	**−298**
Total, Discretionary Cuts, Consolidations, and Savings	**35,187**	**29,249**	**−5,938**

[1] This cut has been identified as a lower priority program activity for purposes of the GPRA Modernization Act, at 31 U.S.C. 1115(b)(10). Additional information regarding this proposed cut is included in the respective agency's Congressional Justification submission, where applicable.

MANDATORY CUTS, CONSOLIDATIONS, AND SAVINGS
(Outlays and receipts in millions of dollars)

	2017	2018	2019	2020	2021	2017-2021	2017-2026
Cuts							
Abstinence Education Program, Department of Health and Human Services[1]	−1	−50	−23	−1	....	−75	−75
Coal Tax Preferences, Department of Energy							
Domestic Manufacturing Deduction for Hard Mineral Fossil Fuels[1]	−11	−20	−21	−22	−23	−97	−227
Expensing of Exploration and Development Costs[1]	−20	−35	−35	−33	−32	−155	−285
Percent Depletion for Hard Mineral Fossil Fuels[1]	−113	−183	−177	−145	−114	−732	−1,121
Royalty Taxation[1]	−26	−52	−52	−52	−52	−234	−494
Crop Insurance Program, Department of Agriculture	−1,259	−1,575	−1,794	−1,843	−1,878	−8,351	−18,013
Geothermal Payments to Counties, Department of the Interior[2]	−4	−4	−4	−4	−4	−20	−41
Gulf of Mexico Energy Security Act (GOMESA) Payments to States, Department of the Interior[2]	....	−286	−310	−339	−376	−1,311	−3,254
Oil and Gas Company Tax Preferences, Department of Energy							
Increase Geological and Geophysical Amortization Period for Independent Producers to Seven Years[1]	−54	−197	−307	−296	−235	−1,089	−1,515
Repeal Credit for Oil and Gas Produced from Marginal Wells[1]	....	....	....	....	....	....	....
Repeal Deduction for Tertiary Injectants[1]	−5	−8	−8	−8	−8	−37	−77
Repeal Domestic Manufacturing Tax Deduction for Oil and Natural Gas Companies1	−470	−836	−869	−901	−932	−4,008	−9,149
Repeal Enhanced Oil Recovery Credit[1]	−235	−559	−792	−979	−1,070	−3,635	−8,803
Repeal Exception to Passive Loss Limitations for Working Interests in Oil and Natural Gas Properties[1]	−9	−12	−12	−12	−11	−56	−103
Repeal Expensing of Intangible Drilling Costs[1]	−966	−1,541	−1,439	−1,645	−1,526	−7,117	−10,050
Repeal Percentage Depletion for Oil and Natural Gas Wells[1]	−483	−770	−725	−666	−589	−3,233	−4,990
Unrestricted Abandoned Mine Lands Payments, Department of the Interior[2]	−6	−31	−63	−82	−90	−272	−520
Total, Mandatory Cuts	**−3,661**	**−6,109**	**−6,608**	**−7,027**	**−6,940**	**−30,347**	**−58,642**
Consolidations							
Reform Teacher Loan Forgiveness Benefits, Department of Education	....	....	....	....	....	....	....
Total, Mandatory Consolidations	....	....	....	....	....	....	....
Savings							
Federal Employee Health Benefits Program Reforms, Office of Personnel Management	....	−65	−141	−193	−239	−638	−2,889
Health Care (Medicaid Proposals), Department of Health and Human Services	−777	−1,037	−1,427	−3,443	−4,263	−10,947	−43,102
Health Care (Pharmaceuticals), Department of Health and Human Services[3]	−920	−1,010	−1,330	−1,800	−2,070	−7,130	−20,590
Medicare Provider Payment Modifications, Department of Health and Human Services[3, 4]	−3,431	−10,236	−20,292	−30,312	−38,429	−102,698	−425,572
Total, Mandatory Savings	**−5,128**	**−12,347**	**−23,190**	**−35,748**	**−45,000**	**−121,413**	**−492,153**
Total, Mandatory Cuts, Consolidations, and Savings	**−8,789**	**−18,457**	**−29,798**	**−42,775**	**−51,941**	**−151,760**	**−550,795**

[1] This cut has been identified as a lower priority program activity for purposes of the GPRA Modernization Act, at 31 U.S.C. 1115(b)(10). Additional information regarding this proposed cut is included in the Governmental Receipts chapter of the Analytical Perspectives volume.

[2] This cut has been identified as a lower priority program activity for purposes of the GPRA Modernization Act, at 31 U.S.C. 1115(b)(10). Additional information regarding this proposed cut is included in the respective agency's Congressional Justification submission, where applicable.

[3] Medicare savings estimates do not include interactions.

[4] In addition to the savings reported on this table, the Budget includes an additional $56.4 billion in 10-year savings for Medicare Structural Reforms, as detailed on table S-9.

Summary Tables

Table S–1. Budget Totals

(In billions of dollars and as a percent of GDP)

| | 2015 | 2016 | 2017 | 2018 | 2019 | 2020 | 2021 | 2022 | 2023 | 2024 | 2025 | 2026 | Totals | |
													2017–2021	2017–2026
Budget Totals in Billions of Dollars:														
Receipts	3,250	3,336	3,644	3,899	4,095	4,346	4,572	4,756	4,949	5,177	5,411	5,669	20,555	46,517
Outlays	3,688	3,951	4,147	4,352	4,644	4,880	5,124	5,415	5,626	5,827	6,152	6,462	23,148	52,630
Deficit	438	616	503	454	549	534	552	660	677	650	741	793	2,593	6,113
Debt held by the public	13,117	14,129	14,763	15,324	15,982	16,615	17,264	18,016	18,793	19,548	20,396	21,302		
Debt net of financial assets	11,882	12,498	13,001	13,454	14,003	14,537	15,089	15,748	16,424	17,074	17,814	18,607		
Gross domestic product (GDP)	17,803	18,472	19,303	20,130	21,013	21,921	22,875	23,872	24,912	25,995	27,123	28,301		
Budget Totals as a Percent of GDP:														
Receipts	18.3%	18.1%	18.9%	19.4%	19.5%	19.8%	20.0%	19.9%	19.9%	19.9%	20.0%	20.0%	19.5%	19.7%
Outlays	20.7%	21.4%	21.5%	21.6%	22.1%	22.3%	22.4%	22.7%	22.6%	22.4%	22.7%	22.8%	22.0%	22.3%
Deficit	2.5%	3.3%	2.6%	2.3%	2.6%	2.4%	2.4%	2.8%	2.7%	2.5%	2.7%	2.8%	2.5%	2.6%
Debt held by the public	73.7%	76.5%	76.5%	76.1%	76.1%	75.8%	75.5%	75.5%	75.4%	75.2%	75.2%	75.3%		
Debt net of financial assets	66.7%	67.7%	67.4%	66.8%	66.6%	66.3%	66.0%	66.0%	65.9%	65.7%	65.7%	65.7%		

Table S–2. Effect of Budget Proposals on Projected Deficits

(Deficit increases (+) or decreases (–) in billions of dollars)

	2016	2017	2018	2019	2020	2021	2022	2023	2024	2025	2026	Totals 2017-2021	Totals 2017-2026
Projected deficits in the adjusted baseline[1]	616	612	655	785	814	881	1,055	1,120	1,143	1,273	1,415	3,748	9,753
Percent of GDP	3.3%	3.2%	3.3%	3.7%	3.7%	3.9%	4.4%	4.5%	4.4%	4.7%	5.0%	3.5%	4.1%
Proposals in the 2017 Budget:[2]													
Tax reforms and investments in innovation, opportunity, and economic growth:													
Mission Innovation			*	1	2	3	4	4	5	5	5	6	29
Investments in a 21st Century infrastructure[3]		7	18	27	36	43	44	42	38	32	26	130	312
Impose an oil fee		-7	-14	-22	-28	-35	-41	-42	-43	-43	-43	-107	-319
Transition to a reformed business tax system		-36	-60	-60	-60	-60	-24					-275	-299
Elements of business tax reform[4]	*	-33	-61	-60	-56	-55	-55	-56	-56	-58	-59	-265	-549
Middle-class and pro-work tax reforms		6	25	24	25	26	26	27	28	29	30	105	246
Fund America's College Promise[5]		*	1	2	3	4	5	6	9	14	17	9	61
Child care for all low-and moderate-income families with young children		3	4	5	6	7	8	9	11	12	14	24	78
Capital gains tax reform		-15	-25	-21	-22	-23	-23	-25	-26	-27	-29	-105	-235
Focus retirement tax incentives on working and middle-class families		-2	-2	-2	-3	-3	-3	-3	-4	-4	-4	-12	-30
Financial fee		-6	-11	-11	-11	-11	-12	-12	-12	-13	-13	-50	-111
Investments in early education and children's health[6]		*	1	3	6	8	10	11	12	12	11	19	76
Tobacco tax financing		-10	-13	-13	-13	-12	-12	-11	-11	-10	-10	-61	-115
Replacement of mandatory sequestration		10	18	19	20	21	23	24	25	35	7	88	202
Additional discretionary proposals, including investments in education, infrastructure, innovation, and security		18	44	52	49	41	-19	-48	-62	-72	-80	204	-77
Additional mandatory and tax proposals	-1	4	-15	-20	-25	-31	-38	-41	-40	-42	-45	-86	-292
Debt service and indirect interest effects	*	-1	-3	-6	-10	-13	-17	-21	-26	-31	-37	-32	-164
Total, tax reforms and investments in innovation, opportunity, and economic growth	-1	-62	-93	-82	-81	-91	-124	-135	-151	-160	-209	-409	-1,189
Additional deficit reduction from health, tax, and immigration reform:													
Health savings		6	1	-6	-24	-33	-43	-54	-64	-71	-90	-56	-378
Curbing inefficient tax breaks for the wealthy and closing loopholes[7]		-56	-74	-81	-89	-95	-101	-106	-112	-118	-124	-394	-955
Immigration reform		4	3	-5	-10	-20	-20	-25	-29	-34	-34	-28	-170
Debt service		*	-2	-5	-10	-15	-21	-28	-36	-44	-54	-33	-216
Total, additional deficit reduction		-46	-71	-97	-132	-164	-185	-213	-241	-268	-301	-510	-1,719
Subtotal, tax reforms, investments, and additional deficit reduction	-1	-108	-165	-179	-213	-254	-309	-349	-392	-427	-511	-920	-2,908

Table S–2. Effect of Budget Proposals on Projected Deficits—Continued

(Deficit increases (+) or decreases (–) in billions of dollars)

	2016	2017	2018	2019	2020	2021	2022	2023	2024	2025	2026	Totals 2017-2021	Totals 2017-2026
Other changes to deficits:													
Reductions in Overseas Contingency Operations	....	*	–37	–55	–63	–67	–76	–81	–84	–86	–88	–221	–636
Debt service	....	*	*	–2	–4	–7	–10	–13	–16	–20	–23	–14	–96
Total, other changes to deficits	....	*	–37	–57	–67	–74	–86	–94	–100	–105	–111	–235	–732
Total proposals in the 2017 Budget	–1	–109	–202	–236	–280	–329	–395	–443	–492	–533	–622	–1,155	–3,640
Resulting deficits in 2017 Budget	616	503	454	549	534	552	660	677	650	741	793	2,593	6,113
Percent of GDP	3.3%	2.6%	2.3%	2.6%	2.4%	2.4%	2.8%	2.7%	2.5%	2.7%	2.8%	2.5%	2.6%
Memorandum:													
Debt held by the public in the adjusted baseline	14,129	14,869	15,620	16,502	17,399	18,360	19,490	20,690	21,917	23,278	24,788		
Percent of GDP	76.5%	77.0%	77.6%	78.5%	79.4%	80.3%	81.6%	83.1%	84.3%	85.8%	87.6%		
Debt held by the public in the 2017 Budget	14,129	14,763	15,324	15,982	16,615	17,264	18,016	18,793	19,548	20,396	21,302		
Percent of GDP	76.5%	76.5%	76.1%	76.1%	75.8%	75.5%	75.5%	75.4%	75.2%	75.2%	75.3%		

* $500 million or less.

[1] See Tables S-4 and S-8 for information on the adjusted baseline.

[2] For cumulative deficit reduction since January 2011, see Table S-3.

[3] Investments in a 21st Century Clean Transportation Plan and assistance to families with burdensome energy costs. These investments, and an existing $110 billion system through the 21st Century Clean Transportation Plan and assistance to families with burdensome energy costs. These investments, and an existing $110 billion Highway Trust Fund solvency gap, are fully paid for; including outlays outside the 10-year budget window, with $319 billion in net revenues from a new oil fee and $176 billion in transition revenues from business tax reform. The remaining $123 billion of transition revenues would be available for deficit reduction.

[4] The cost of business-related tax provisions enacted in December 2015 is projected to be nearly $500 billion over the 2016 to 2026 period.

[5] Including grants to Historically Black Colleges and Universities, Hispanic-Serving Institutions, and other Minority-Serving Institutions.

[6] Includes proposals to expand home visiting and enact Preschool for All.

[7] Includes proposals to implement the Buffett Rule by imposing a new "Fair Share Tax," rationalize Net Investment Income and Self-Employment Contributions Act (SECA) taxes, and reduce the value of certain tax expenditures.

Table S–3. Cumulative Deficit Reduction Since 2011

(Deficit reduction (–) or increase (+) in billions of dollars)

	2017–2026
Deficit reduction achieved through January 2016, excluding Overseas Contingency Operations (OCO):	
Enacted deficit reduction excluding pending Joint Committee enforcement:	
Discretionary savings [1]	–1,758
Mandatory savings	–157
Revenues	–814
Debt service	–1,061
Subtotal, enacted deficit reduction excluding pending Joint Committee enforcement	–3,790
Pending Joint Committee enforcement:[2]	
Discretionary cap reductions	–354
Mandatory sequestration	–202
Debt service	–125
Subtotal, pending Joint Committee enforcement	–680
Total, deficit reduction achieved, excluding OCO	–4,470
Tax reforms and investments in innovation, opportunity, and economic growth:[3]	
Mission Innovation	29
Investments in a 21st Century infrastructure	312
Impose an oil fee	–319
Transition to a reformed business tax system	–299
Elements of business tax reform [4]	–549
Middle-class and pro-work tax reforms	246
Fund America's College Promise	61
Child care for all low-and moderate-income families with young children	78
Capital gains tax reform	–235
Focus retirement tax incentives on working and middle-class families	–30
Financial fee	–111
Investments in early education and children's health	76
Tobacco tax financing	–115
Replacement of mandatory sequestration	202
Additional discretionary proposals, including investments in education, infrastructure, innovation, and security	–77
Additional mandatory and tax proposals	–292
Debt service and indirect interest effects	–164
Total, tax reforms and investments in innovation, opportunity, and economic growth	–1,189
Additional deficit reduction from health, tax, and immigration reform:[5]	
Health savings	–378
Curbing inefficient tax breaks for the wealthy and closing loopholes	–955
Immigration reform	–170
Debt service	–216
Total, additional deficit reduction	–1,719

Table S–3. Cumulative Deficit Reduction Since 2011—Continued

(Deficit reduction (–) or increase (+) in billions of dollars)

	2017–2026
Subtotal, tax reforms, investments, and additional deficit reduction	**–2,908**
Grand total, achieved and proposed deficit reduction excluding OCO	**–7,378**
Memoranda:	
Revenue and outlay effects of achieved and proposed deficit reduction:	
Enacted outlay reductions and 2017 Budget spending proposals	–3,760
Enacted receipt increases and 2017 Budget tax proposals	–3,448
Immigration reform	–170
Savings in Overseas Contingency Operations (OCO):	
Enacted reduction in OCO funding	–1,050
Proposed reductions in OCO	–636
Debt service	–401
Total, savings in overseas contingency operations (OCO)	–2,087

[1] Excludes savings from reductions in OCO.
[2] Consists of mandatory sequestration for 2017–2025 and discretionary cap reductions for 2018–2021.
[3] See Table S–2 for details on tax reform and investment proposals.
[4] The cost of business-related tax provisions enacted in December 2015 is projected to be nearly $500 billion over the 2016 to 2026 period.
[5] See Table S–2 for details on additional deficit reduction proposals.

Table S–4.　Adjusted Baseline by Category [1]

(In billions of dollars)

	2015	2016	2017	2018	2019	2020	2021	2022	2023	2024	2025	2026	Totals 2017–2021	Totals 2017–2026
Outlays:														
Appropriated ("discretionary") programs:														
Defense	583	595	601	638	666	683	696	702	719	736	753	771	3,275	6,954
Non-defense	581	627	614	626	638	648	660	674	689	705	721	738	3,186	6,713
Subtotal, appropriated programs	1,165	1,223	1,215	1,265	1,304	1,330	1,356	1,376	1,408	1,441	1,474	1,509	6,461	13,667
Mandatory programs:														
Social Security	882	924	967	1,025	1,089	1,157	1,224	1,297	1,373	1,454	1,538	1,626	5,463	12,750
Medicare	540	589	602	611	674	725	781	879	912	936	1,046	1,114	3,393	8,281
Medicaid	350	367	377	398	424	444	469	496	525	555	589	632	2,112	4,908
Other mandatory programs	529	608	629	647	692	712	742	786	791	794	828	878	3,422	7,497
Subtotal, mandatory programs	2,301	2,487	2,574	2,681	2,879	3,038	3,217	3,457	3,601	3,738	4,000	4,250	14,389	33,436
Net interest	223	240	304	390	473	547	609	669	729	783	838	901	2,323	6,243
Adjustments for disaster costs [2]	......	2	6	8	8	9	9	10	10	10	10	10	40	90
Joint Committee enforcement [3]	......	......	–9	–73	–96	–104	–107	–56	–36	–29	–36	–7	–390	–554
Total outlays	3,688	3,952	4,089	4,270	4,568	4,820	5,085	5,455	5,713	5,943	6,286	6,662	22,832	52,890
Receipts:														
Individual income taxes	1,541	1,628	1,724	1,793	1,878	1,988	2,095	2,205	2,319	2,437	2,559	2,688	9,478	21,686
Corporation income taxes	344	293	343	364	401	454	461	467	471	478	486	495	2,023	4,419
Social insurance and retirement receipts:														
Social Security payroll taxes	770	798	827	864	899	934	983	1,031	1,075	1,127	1,176	1,236	4,507	10,152
Medicare payroll taxes	234	244	253	264	276	287	302	317	331	347	362	381	1,383	3,122
Unemployment insurance	51	50	49	46	46	47	48	48	49	50	51	52	235	486
Other retirement	10	10	10	11	11	12	12	13	13	14	15	16	56	127
Excise taxes	98	97	86	105	106	108	114	117	120	124	128	134	520	1,142
Estate and gift taxes	19	21	22	24	25	26	28	30	31	33	36	38	126	294
Customs duties	35	37	40	42	44	46	48	49	51	53	54	56	219	483
Deposits of earnings, Federal Reserve System	96	116	65	44	38	42	48	55	60	65	69	74	237	560
Other miscellaneous receipts	51	43	58	57	59	62	65	68	71	74	75	78	302	667
Total receipts	3,250	3,336	3,477	3,615	3,783	4,006	4,204	4,400	4,593	4,801	5,012	5,247	19,084	43,137
Deficit	438	616	612	655	785	814	881	1,055	1,120	1,143	1,273	1,415	3,748	9,753
Net interest	223	240	304	390	473	547	609	669	729	783	838	901	2,323	6,243
Primary deficit	215	376	308	265	312	267	272	386	390	359	435	514	1,425	3,510

Table S–4. Adjusted Baseline by Category[1]—Continued

(In billions of dollars)

	2015	2016	2017	2018	2019	2020	2021	2022	2023	2024	2025	2026	Totals 2017–2021	Totals 2017–2026
On-budget deficit	466	623	608	634	741	737	788	939	972	966	1,064	1,179	3,508	8,628
Off-budget deficit / surplus (–)	–27	–7	4	21	45	77	93	116	148	176	210	236	239	1,125
Memorandum, budget authority for appropriated programs:[4]														
Defense	586	607	611	664	678	693	709	726	743	761	780	798	3,346	7,154
Non-defense	527	556	531	566	579	591	603	618	633	649	665	681	2,871	6,116
Total, appropriated funding	1,113	1,163	1,142	1,230	1,257	1,285	1,312	1,344	1,376	1,410	1,444	1,479	6,216	13,270

[1] See Table S–8 for information on adjustments to the Balanced Budget and Emergency Deficit Control Act (BBEDCA) baseline.
[2] These amounts represent a placeholder for major disasters requiring Federal assistance for relief and reconstruction. Such assistance might be provided in the form of discretionary or mandatory outlays or tax relief. These amounts are included as outlays for convenience.
[3] Consists of mandatory sequestration for 2017–2025 and discretionary cap reductions for 2018–2021.
[4] Excludes discretionary cap reductions for Joint Committee enforcement.

Table S–5. Proposed Budget by Category

(In billions of dollars)

	2015	2016	2017	2018	2019	2020	2021	2022	2023	2024	2025	2026	Totals 2017–2021	Totals 2017–2026
Outlays:														
Appropriated ("discretionary") programs:														
Defense	583	595	608	589	591	597	603	602	614	626	638	650	2,987	6,117
Non-defense	581	627	625	629	635	639	646	651	660	671	684	698	3,175	6,538
Subtotal, appropriated programs	1,165	1,223	1,233	1,219	1,226	1,236	1,249	1,253	1,274	1,297	1,322	1,348	6,162	12,655
Mandatory programs:														
Social Security	882	924	967	1,025	1,089	1,156	1,223	1,295	1,375	1,452	1,536	1,624	5,461	12,740
Medicare	540	589	598	601	656	695	744	833	857	870	974	1,030	3,294	7,858
Medicaid	350	367	386	405	426	450	474	501	528	559	593	631	2,140	4,952
Other mandatory programs	529	607	651	700	764	790	831	878	887	897	934	983	3,737	8,315
Allowance for immigration reform	......	......	5	10	15	20	20	25	30	35	40	50	70	250
Subtotal, mandatory programs	2,301	2,487	2,606	2,741	2,950	3,112	3,292	3,532	3,675	3,813	4,077	4,318	14,702	34,116
Net interest	223	240	303	385	460	523	574	621	668	706	744	787	2,244	5,769
Adjustments for disaster costs[1]	......	2	6	8	8	9	9	10	10	10	10	10	40	90
Total outlays	3,688	3,951	4,147	4,352	4,644	4,880	5,124	5,415	5,626	5,827	6,152	6,462	23,148	52,630
Receipts:														
Individual income taxes	1,541	1,628	1,788	1,891	1,985	2,106	2,222	2,339	2,461	2,586	2,716	2,853	9,992	22,948
Corporation income taxes	344	293	419	493	525	575	582	554	537	546	556	568	2,594	5,355
Social insurance and retirement receipts:														
Social Security payroll taxes	770	798	827	863	898	932	980	1,028	1,072	1,124	1,173	1,232	4,500	10,129
Medicare payroll taxes	234	244	254	265	278	289	304	319	333	349	364	383	1,389	3,137
Unemployment insurance	51	50	50	52	53	54	56	57	60	60	61	64	265	568
Other retirement	10	10	10	11	11	12	12	13	13	14	15	16	56	127
Excise taxes	98	97	110	143	153	165	178	189	193	196	201	206	748	1,734
Estate and gift taxes	19	21	22	32	34	37	40	43	47	51	55	60	164	421
Customs duties	35	37	40	40	41	42	44	45	47	48	49	50	207	445
Deposits of earnings, Federal Reserve System	96	116	65	44	38	42	48	55	60	65	69	74	237	560
Other miscellaneous receipts	51	43	58	58	60	63	66	69	71	74	76	78	304	673
Allowance for immigration reform	......	......	1	7	20	30	40	45	55	64	74	84	98	420
Total receipts	3,250	3,336	3,644	3,899	4,095	4,346	4,572	4,756	4,949	5,177	5,411	5,669	20,555	46,517
Deficit	**438**	**616**	**503**	**454**	**549**	**534**	**552**	**660**	**677**	**650**	**741**	**793**	**2,593**	**6,113**
Net interest	223	240	303	385	460	523	574	621	668	706	744	787	2,244	5,769
Primary deficit / surplus (–)	**215**	**376**	**201**	**69**	**90**	**11**	**–22**	**39**	**9**	**–56**	**–3**	**6**	**349**	**344**
On-budget deficit	466	624	502	433	506	458	460	544	529	475	532	558	2,358	4,997
Off-budget deficit / surplus (–)	–27	–8	2	21	44	76	92	115	147	175	209	235	235	1,116

Table S–5. Proposed Budget by Category—Continued

(In billions of dollars)

	2015	2016	2017	2018	2019	2020	2021	2022	2023	2024	2025	2026	Totals 2017–2021	Totals 2017–2026
Memorandum, budget authority for appropriated programs:														
Defense	586	607	610	584	593	599	614	624	636	648	661	674	3,000	6,243
Non-defense	527	556	540	561	570	575	590	589	601	613	626	639	2,836	5,904
Total, appropriated funding	1,113	1,163	1,149	1,145	1,163	1,174	1,205	1,213	1,237	1,261	1,287	1,313	5,836	12,147

[1] These amounts represent a placeholder for major disasters requiring Federal assistance for relief and reconstruction. Such assistance might be provided in the form of discretionary or mandatory outlays or tax relief. These amounts are included as outlays for convenience.

Table S–6.　Proposed Budget by Category as a Percent of GDP

(As a percent of GDP)

	2015	2016	2017	2018	2019	2020	2021	2022	2023	2024	2025	2026	Averages 2017–2021	Averages 2017–2026
Outlays:														
Appropriated ("discretionary") programs:														
Defense	3.3	3.2	3.1	2.9	2.8	2.7	2.6	2.5	2.5	2.4	2.4	2.3	2.8	2.6
Non-defense	3.3	3.4	3.2	3.1	3.0	2.9	2.8	2.7	2.6	2.6	2.5	2.5	3.0	2.8
Subtotal, appropriated programs	6.5	6.6	6.4	6.1	5.8	5.6	5.5	5.2	5.1	5.0	4.9	4.8	5.9	5.4
Mandatory programs:														
Social Security	5.0	5.0	5.0	5.1	5.2	5.3	5.3	5.4	5.5	5.6	5.7	5.7	5.2	5.4
Medicare	3.0	3.2	3.1	3.0	3.1	3.2	3.3	3.5	3.4	3.3	3.6	3.6	3.1	3.3
Medicaid	2.0	2.0	2.0	2.0	2.0	2.1	2.1	2.1	2.1	2.2	2.2	2.2	2.0	2.1
Other mandatory programs	3.0	3.3	3.4	3.5	3.6	3.6	3.6	3.7	3.6	3.4	3.4	3.5	3.5	3.5
Allowance for immigration reform	......	*	*	*	0.1	0.1	0.1	0.1	0.1	0.1	0.1	0.2	0.1	0.1
Subtotal, mandatory programs	12.9	13.5	13.5	13.6	14.0	14.2	14.4	14.8	14.8	14.7	15.0	15.3	13.9	14.4
Net interest	1.3	1.3	1.6	1.9	2.2	2.4	2.5	2.6	2.7	2.7	2.7	2.8	2.1	2.4
Adjustments for disaster costs[1]	......	*	*	*	*	*	*	*	*	*	*	*	*	*
Total outlays	20.7	21.4	21.5	21.6	22.1	22.3	22.4	22.7	22.6	22.4	22.7	22.8	22.0	22.3
Receipts:														
Individual income taxes	8.7	8.8	9.3	9.4	9.4	9.6	9.7	9.8	9.9	9.9	10.0	10.1	9.5	9.7
Corporation income taxes	1.9	1.6	2.2	2.4	2.5	2.6	2.5	2.3	2.2	2.1	2.1	2.0	2.5	2.3
Social insurance and retirement receipts:														
Social Security payroll taxes	4.3	4.3	4.3	4.3	4.3	4.3	4.3	4.3	4.3	4.3	4.3	4.4	4.3	4.3
Medicare payroll taxes	1.3	1.3	1.3	1.3	1.3	1.3	1.3	1.3	1.3	1.3	1.3	1.4	1.3	1.3
Unemployment insurance	0.3	0.3	0.3	0.3	0.3	0.2	0.2	0.2	0.2	0.2	0.2	0.2	0.3	0.2
Other retirement	0.1	0.1	0.1	0.1	0.1	0.1	0.1	0.1	0.1	0.1	0.1	0.1	0.1	0.1
Excise taxes	0.6	0.5	0.6	0.7	0.7	0.8	0.8	0.8	0.8	0.8	0.7	0.7	0.7	0.7
Estate and gift taxes	0.1	0.1	0.1	0.2	0.2	0.2	0.2	0.2	0.2	0.2	0.2	0.2	0.2	0.2
Customs duties	0.2	0.2	0.2	0.2	0.2	0.2	0.2	0.2	0.2	0.2	0.2	0.2	0.2	0.2
Deposits of earnings, Federal Reserve System	0.5	0.6	0.3	0.2	0.2	0.2	0.2	0.2	0.2	0.2	0.3	0.3	0.2	0.2
Other miscellaneous receipts	0.3	0.2	0.3	0.3	0.3	0.3	0.3	0.3	0.2	0.3	0.3	0.3	0.2	0.3
Allowance for immigration reform	......	*	*	*	0.1	0.1	0.2	0.2	0.2	0.2	0.3	0.3	0.1	0.2
Total receipts	18.3	18.1	18.9	19.4	19.5	19.8	20.0	19.9	19.9	19.9	20.0	20.0	19.5	19.7
Deficit	2.5	3.3	2.6	2.3	2.6	2.4	2.4	2.8	2.7	2.5	2.7	2.8	2.5	2.6
Net interest	1.3	1.3	1.6	1.9	2.2	2.4	2.5	2.6	2.7	2.7	2.7	2.8	2.1	2.4
Primary deficit / surplus (–)	1.2	2.0	1.0	0.4	0.4	0.1	–0.1	0.2	*	–0.2	–*	*	0.4	0.2
On-budget deficit	2.6	3.4	2.6	2.1	2.4	2.1	2.0	2.3	2.1	1.8	2.0	2.0	2.3	2.1
Off-budget deficit / surplus (–)	–0.2	–*	*	0.1	0.2	0.3	0.4	0.5	0.6	0.7	0.8	0.8	0.2	0.4

Table S–6. Proposed Budget by Category as a Percent of GDP—Continued

(As a percent of GDP)

	2015	2016	2017	2018	2019	2020	2021	2022	2023	2024	2025	2026	Averages 2017–2021	Averages 2017–2026
Memorandum, budget authority for appropriated programs:														
Defense	3.3	3.3	3.2	2.9	2.8	2.7	2.7	2.6	2.6	2.5	2.4	2.4	2.9	2.7
Non-defense	3.0	3.0	2.8	2.8	2.7	2.6	2.6	2.5	2.4	2.4	2.3	2.3	2.7	2.5
Total, appropriated funding	6.2	6.3	6.0	5.7	5.5	5.4	5.3	5.1	5.0	4.9	4.7	4.6	5.6	5.2

*0.05 percent of GDP or less.

[1] These amounts represent a placeholder for major disasters requiring Federal assistance for relief and reconstruction. Such assistance might be provided in the form of discretionary or mandatory outlays or tax relief. These amounts are included as outlays for convenience.

Table S-7.   Proposed Budget in Population- and Inflation-Adjusted Dollars

(In billions of constant dollars, adjusted for population growth)

	2017	2018	2019	2020	2021	2022	2023	2024	2025	2026
Outlays:										
Appropriated ("discretionary") programs:										
Defense	608	572	556	544	533	515	509	504	498	492
Non-defense	625	611	598	583	571	557	547	540	534	528
Subtotal, appropriated programs	1,233	1,183	1,153	1,127	1,103	1,072	1,056	1,044	1,031	1,020
Mandatory programs:										
Social Security	967	996	1,025	1,054	1,082	1,108	1,138	1,168	1,199	1,230
Medicare	598	583	617	634	657	713	711	700	760	779
Medicaid	386	393	400	410	419	429	438	450	463	478
Other mandatory programs	651	680	719	721	734	752	736	721	728	744
Allowance for immigration reform	5	10	14	18	18	21	25	28	31	38
Subtotal, mandatory programs	2,606	2,662	2,776	2,837	2,907	3,023	3,048	3,067	3,181	3,268
Net interest	303	373	432	477	507	531	554	568	580	596
Adjustments for disaster costs[1]	6	7	8	8	8	8	8	8	8	8
Total outlays	4,147	4,226	4,370	4,449	4,526	4,635	4,667	4,687	4,800	4,892
Receipts:										
Individual income taxes	1,788	1,836	1,868	1,920	1,963	2,002	2,041	2,080	2,119	2,160
Corporation income taxes	419	478	494	524	514	474	445	439	434	430
Social insurance and retirement receipts										
Social Security payroll taxes	827	838	845	850	866	879	889	904	915	933
Medicare payroll taxes	254	258	261	263	268	273	276	281	284	290
Unemployment insurance	50	50	50	50	49	49	50	48	48	48
Other retirement	10	10	10	11	11	11	11	11	12	12
Excise taxes	110	139	144	150	157	162	160	158	157	156
Estate and gift taxes	22	31	32	33	35	37	39	41	43	46
Customs duties	40	39	39	39	39	39	39	38	38	38
Deposits of earnings, Federal Reserve System	65	43	36	38	42	47	50	52	54	56
Other miscellaneous receipts	58	56	56	57	58	59	59	60	59	59
Allowance for immigration reform	1	7	19	27	35	39	46	51	58	64
Total receipts	3,644	3,786	3,853	3,962	4,038	4,070	4,105	4,164	4,222	4,292
Deficit	**503**	**440**	**517**	**487**	**488**	**565**	**562**	**523**	**578**	**600**
Net interest	303	373	432	477	507	531	554	568	580	596
Primary deficit / surplus (–)	**201**	**67**	**84**	**10**	**-19**	**33**	**8**	**-45**	**-2**	**5**
On-budget deficit	502	420	476	417	407	466	439	382	415	423
Off-budget deficit / surplus (–)	2	20	41	70	81	99	122	141	163	178

Table S–7. Proposed Budget in Population– and Inflation–Adjusted Dollars—Continued

(In billions of constant dollars, adjusted for population growth)

	2017	2018	2019	2020	2021	2022	2023	2024	2025	2026
Memorandum, budget authority for appropriated programs:										
Defense	610	568	558	546	543	534	528	521	516	510
Non-defense	540	544	536	525	521	504	499	493	488	484
Subtotal, appropriated programs	1,149	1,112	1,094	1,070	1,064	1,038	1,026	1,014	1,004	994
Memorandum, population and inflation indexes:										
Population	1.00	1.01	1.02	1.03	1.04	1.05	1.06	1.07	1.07	1.08
Inflation	1.00	1.02	1.04	1.07	1.09	1.12	1.14	1.17	1.19	1.22
Population and Inflation	1.00	1.03	1.06	1.10	1.13	1.17	1.21	1.24	1.28	1.32

[1] These amounts represent a placeholder for major disasters requiring Federal assistance for relief and reconstruction. Such assistance might be provided in the form of discretionary or mandatory outlays or tax relief. These amounts are included as outlays for convenience.

Table S–8. Bridge from Balanced Budget and Emergency Deficit Control Act (BBEDCA) Baseline to Adjusted Baseline

(Deficit increases (+) or decreases (–) in billions of dollars)

	2015	2016	2017	2018	2019	2020	2021	2022	2023	2024	2025	2026	Totals 2016–2020	Totals 2016–2025
BBEDCA baseline deficit	438	615	636	719	875	917	994	1,121	1,167	1,185	1,325	1,440	4,141	10,380
Adjustments for provisions contained in the Budget Control Act:														
Set discretionary budget authority at cap levels[1]	....	....	–27	–3	7	7	5	4	4	3	3	2	–11	5
Reflect Joint Committee enforcement[2]	....	....	....	–64	–96	–104	–107	–56	–36	–29	–36	–7	–371	–535
Subtotal	....	....	–27	–67	–89	–97	–102	–52	–32	–26	–33	–5	–381	–530
Adjustments for emergency and disaster costs:														
Remove non-recurring emergency costs	....	....	–2	–3	–6	–8	–8	–8	–8	–9	–9	–9	–26	–70
Add placeholder for future emergency costs[3]	....	2	6	8	8	9	9	10	10	10	10	10	40	90
Reclassify surface transportation outlays:														
Remove outlays from appropriated category	–4	–4	–4	–5	–5	–5	–5	–5	–5	–5	–5	–5	–24	–48
Add outlays to mandatory category	4	4	4	5	5	5	5	5	5	5	5	5	24	48
Subtotal	....	....	....	....	....	....	....	....	....	....	....	....	....	....
Total program adjustments	....	2	–24	–62	–86	–95	–101	–51	–30	–24	–32	–4	–368	–510
Debt service on adjustments	....	*	–*	–1	–4	–8	–12	–15	–17	–18	–20	–21	–26	–117
Total adjustments	....	2	–24	–64	–90	–103	–113	–66	–47	–43	–52	–25	–394	–627
Adjusted baseline deficit	438	616	612	655	785	814	881	1,055	1,120	1,143	1,273	1,415	3,748	9,753

*$500 million or less.

[1] Includes adjustments for discretionary and mandatory program integrity.

[2] Consists of mandatory sequestration for 2018–2021 and discretionary cap reductions for 2018–2025.

[3] These amounts represent a placeholder for major disasters requiring Federal assistance for relief and reconstruction.

Table S–9. Mandatory and Receipt Proposals

(Deficit increases (+) or decreases (–) in millions of dollars)

	2016	2017	2018	2019	2020	2021	2022	2023	2024	2025	2026	Totals 2017–2021	Totals 2017–2026
Mandatory Initiatives and Savings:													
Legislative Branch:													
Provide additional funding for the World War I Centennial Commission		6	7	6								19	19
Agriculture:													
Reduce premium subsidies for harvest price revenue protection and improve prevented planting coverage		–1,259	–1,575	–1,794	–1,843	–1,878	–1,891	–1,910	–1,937	–1,961	–1,963	–8,349	–18,011
Reauthorize Secure Rural Schools		178	188	105	63	40	7					574	581
Enact Food Safety and Inspection Service (FSIS) fee		–4	–4	–4	–5	–5	–5	–5	–5	–5	–5	–22	–47
Enact biobased labeling fee													
Enact Grain Inspection, Packers, and Stockyards Administration (GIPSA) fee		–30	–30	–30	–30	–30	–30	–30	–30	–30	–30	–150	–300
Enact Animal Plant and Health Inspection Service (APHIS) fee		–20	–27	–27	–28	–29	–30	–31	–32	–33	–34	–131	–291
Enact Natural Resource and Conservation Service (NRCS) Conservation User Fee													
Establish Rural Housing Service Guaranteed Underwriting System Fee													
Fund the Agriculture and Food Research Initiative at the authorized level of $700 million		16	114	114	81							325	325
Create State option to improve Supplemental Nutrition Assistance Program (SNAP) access for elderly		10	23	36	44	50	57	64	71	77	85	163	517
Establish a summer Electronic Benefits Transfer program		127	214	326	462	625	1,053	1,521	2,038	2,595	3,209	1,754	12,170
Increase The Emergency Food Assistance Program funding to equal 2015 levels		30	35	50	50	50	50	50	50	50	50	215	465
Modify SNAP simplified reporting requirements to include out-of-State moves													
Total, Agriculture		–952	–1,062	–1,224	–1,206	–1,177	–789	–341	155	693	1,312	–5,621	–4,591
Commerce:													
Enact Scale-Up Manufacturing Investment Initiative [1]			155	365	365	365						1,250	1,250
Create National Network for Manufacturing Innovation			100	200	300	350	350	300	200	90		950	1,890
Recapitalize National Oceanic and Atmospheric Administration research fleet		70	25	5								100	100
Renovate lab facilities at the National Institute of Standards and Technology (NIST)		12	14	16	32	16	10					90	100
Support Lab to Market efforts in the Economic Development Administration		30	15	5								50	50
Total, Commerce		112	309	591	697	731	360	300	200	90		2,440	3,390

Table S–9. Mandatory and Receipt Proposals—Continued

(Deficit increases (+) or decreases (−) in millions of dollars)

	2016	2017	2018	2019	2020	2021	2022	2023	2024	2025	2026	Totals 2017–2021	Totals 2017–2026
Education:													
Support Preschool for All	......	130	1,235	3,110	5,456	7,360	8,773	9,787	10,560	10,275	9,356	17,291	66,042
Enact RESPECT: Best Job in the World	......	50	200	300	300	150	......	......	......	......	......	1,000	1,000
Create Computer Science for All	......	40	720	1,070	1,200	660	280	30	......	......	......	3,690	4,000
Fund America's College Promise, including grants to Historically Black Colleges and Universities, Hispanic-Serving Institutions, and other Minority-Serving Institutions	......	38	847	1,616	2,887	3,911	5,249	6,033	9,189	14,362	16,669	9,299	60,801
Enact Pell completion and reform policies	......	65	248	238	235	255	277	307	325	336	349	1,041	2,635
Shift mandatory funds to support Pell policies	......	−65	−248	−238	−235	−255	−277	−307	−325	−336	−349	−1,041	−2,635
Extend Pell CPI increase	......	......	186	920	1,721	2,600	3,528	4,492	5,522	6,609	7,746	5,427	33,324
Implement College Opportunity and Graduation Bonus Program	......	104	307	420	600	635	668	699	731	765	801	2,066	5,730
Reform student loan Income-Based Repayment plans [2]	......	−1,151	−2,220	−3,294	−4,294	−5,083	−5,668	−6,149	−6,713	−7,058	−7,234	−16,042	−48,864
Reform teacher loan forgiveness benefits	......	......	......	......	......	112	249	301	322	337	358	112	1,679
Limit Federal revenue to 85 percent of total revenue at for-profit universities (loan effects)	......	......	......	......	−1	−4	1	−4	−2	3	−7	−5	−14
Reform and expand Perkins loan program	......	−305	−795	−595	−497	−431	−404	−408	−409	−392	−339	−2,623	−4,575
Total, Education	......	−1,094	480	3,547	7,372	9,910	12,676	14,781	19,200	24,901	27,350	20,215	119,123
Energy:													
Enact nuclear waste management program	......	......	56	94	107	169	267	233	317	1,115	−1,656	426	702
Reauthorize special assessment from domestic nuclear utilities [3]	......	−208	−212	−217	−222	−227	−232	−237	−243	−248	−254	−1,086	−2,300
Allow the United States Enrichment Corporation Fund to use balances to support Uranium Enrichment Decontamination and Decommissioning	......	472	674	394	82	......	......	......	......	......	......	1,622	1,622
Provide additional research and development (R&D) funding for Advanced Research Project Agency-Energy Trust	......	8	39	102	186	304	384	371	276	174	6	639	1,850
Provide additional R&D funding for Office of Science	......	45	45	7	3	......	......	......	......	......	......	100	100
Establish Southwestern Power Administration Purchase Power Drought Fund [4]	......	−15	−15	5	−15	−2	......	......	24	......	−15	−42	−33
Total, Energy	......	302	587	385	141	244	419	367	350	1,065	−1,919	1,659	1,941
Health and Human Services:													
HHS health savings:													
Medicare providers:													
Encourage delivery system reform:													
Allow the Secretary to introduce primary care payments under the Physician Fee Schedule in a budget neutral manner	......											......	......

Table S–9. Mandatory and Receipt Proposals—Continued

(Deficit increases (+) or decreases (–) in millions of dollars)

	2016	2017	2018	2019	2020	2021	2022	2023	2024	2025	2026	Totals 2017–2021	Totals 2017–2026
Allow Accountable Care Organizations (ACOs) to pay beneficiaries for primary care visits up to the applicable Medicare cost sharing amount	......	......	–10	–10	–10	–10	–10	–10	–10	–10	–10	–40	–70
Allow Centers for Medicare and Medicaid Services (CMS) to assign beneficiaries to Federally Qualified Health Centers (FQHCs) and Rural Health Centers (RHCs) participating in the Medicare Shared Savings Program	......	......	......	......	–10	–10	–10	–10	–10	–10	–20	–20	–80
Expand basis for beneficiary assignment for ACOs to include Nurse Practitioners, Physician Assistants, and Clinical Nurse Specialists	......	......	......	–10	–10	–20	–20	–20	–20	–20	–30	–40	–150
Establish quality bonus payments for high-performing Part D plans	......	......	......	......	......	......	......	......	......	......	......	......	......
Implement bundled payment for post-acute care	......	......	......	......	......	–470	–1,080	–1,790	–2,010	–2,170	–2,330	–470	–9,850
Implement value-based purchasing for skilled nursing facilities (SNFs), home health agencies (HHAs), ambulatory surgical centers (ASCs), hospital outpatient departments (HOPDs), and community mental health centers	......	......	......	......	......	......	......	......	......	......	......	......	......
Establish a hospital-wide readmissions reduction measure	......	......	......	......	......	......	......	......	......	......	......	......	......
Extend accountability for hospital-acquired conditions	......	......	......	......	......	......	......	......	......	......	......	......	......
Encourage workforce development through targeted and more accurate indirect medical education payments	......	......	......	......	......	......	......	......	......	......	......	......	......
Allow the Secretary to determine Hospital-Acquired Condition Reduction Program penalty amounts and distribution	......	–1,170	–1,400	–1,490	–1,590	–1,700	–1,830	–1,960	–2,090	–2,220	–2,350	–7,350	–17,800
Establish a bonus payment for hospitals cooperating with certain alternative payment models (APMs)	......	......	......	......	......	......	......	......	......	......	......	......	......
Enhance competition in Medicare Advantage (MA): Reform MA payments to increase the efficiency and sustainability of the program	......	......	–960	–2,620	–7,160	–9,170	–9,910	–10,580	–11,350	–12,130	–13,360	–19,910	–77,240
Improve beneficiary access: Eliminate the 190-day lifetime limit on inpatient psychiatric facility services	......	110	140	150	150	160	170	180	190	190	210	710	1,650

Table S–9. Mandatory and Receipt Proposals—Continued

(Deficit increases (+) or decreases (–) in millions of dollars)

	2016	2017	2018	2019	2020	2021	2022	2023	2024	2025	2026	Totals 2017–2021	Totals 2017–2026
Repeal the rental cap for oxygen equipment	......	......	......	......	......	......	......	......	......	......	......	......	......
Eliminate beneficiary coinsurance for screening colonoscopies with polyp removal	......	160	170	190	200	230	250	270	290	320	350	950	2,430
Expand the ability of Medicare Advantage organizations to pay for services delivered via telehealth ...	......	......	......	–20	–20	–20	–20	–20	–20	–20	–20	–60	–160
Establish RHC and FQHC telehealth services	......	......	......	......	......	......	......	......	......	......	......	......	......
Cut waste, fraud, and improper payments in Medicare:													
Suspend coverage and payment for questionable Part D prescriptions and incomplete clinical information	......	......	–70	–60	–70	–80	–80	–90	–100	–110	–120	–280	–780
Retain a portion of Medicare Recovery Audit Contractor (RAC) recoveries to implement actions that prevent fraud and abuse	......	110	130	70	–20	–120	–150	–180	–200	–210	–230	170	–800
Allow prior authorization for Medicare fee-for-service items	......	–5	–5	–5	–5	–5	–10	–10	–10	–10	–10	–25	–75
Permit exclusion from Federal Health Care Programs if affiliated with sanctioned entities	......	......	......	......	–10	–10	–10	–10	–10	–10	–10	–20	–70
Protect program integrity algorithms from disclosure	......	–9	–9	–9	–9	–9	–9	–9	–9	–9	–9	–45	–90
Allow the Secretary to reject claims for new providers and suppliers located outside moratorium areas ..	......	–5	–5	–5	–5	–5	–5	–5	–5	–5	–5	–25	–50
Allow civil monetary penalties for providers and suppliers who fail to update enrollment records	......	–2	–2	–3	–3	–3	–3	–4	–4	–4	–4	–13	–32
Allow collection of application fees from individual providers and suppliers	......	......	......	......	......	......	......	......	......	......	......	......	......
Assess a fee on physicians and practitioners who order services or supplies without proper documentation	......	......	......	......	......	......	......	......	......	......	......	......	......
Establish gifting authority for the Healthcare Fraud Prevention Partnership	......	......	......	......	......	......	......	......	......	......	......	......	......
Establish registration process for clearinghouses and billing agents ..	......	......	......	......	......	......	......	......	......	......	......	......	......
Pay recovery auditor after a Qualified Independent Contractor (QIC) decision on appealed claims	......	......	......	......	......	......	......	......	......	......	......	......	......
Publish the National Provider Identifier for covered recipients in the Open Payments Program	......	......	......	......	......	......	......	......	......	......	......	......	......

Table S-9. Mandatory and Receipt Proposals—Continued

(Deficit increases (+) or decreases (−) in millions of dollars)

	2016	2017	2018	2019	2020	2021	2022	2023	2024	2025	2026	Totals 2017-2021	Totals 2017-2026
Require a surety bond or escrow account to cover overturned recovery auditor decisions	......	......	......	......	......	......	......	......	......	......	......	......	......
Address the rising cost of pharmaceuticals:													
Align Medicare drug payment policies with Medicaid policies for low-income beneficiaries	......	......	−2,930	−7,040	−8,800	−10,740	−12,420	−15,150	−18,450	−20,920	−24,800	−29,510	−121,250
Accelerate manufacturer discounts for brand drugs to provide relief to Medicare beneficiaries in the coverage gap	......	......	−250	−640	−1,100	−1,270	−1,390	−1,330	−1,250	−1,460	−1,520	−3,260	−10,210
Require mandatory reporting of other prescription drug coverage	......	−10	−30	−40	−40	−50	−50	−60	−60	−70	−70	−170	−480
Establish authority for a program to prevent prescription drug abuse in Medicare Part D	......	......	......	......	......	......	......	......	......	......	......	......	......
Allow the Secretary to negotiate prices for biologics and high cost prescription drugs	......	......	......	......	......	......	......	......	......	......	......	......	......
Modify reimbursement of Part B drugs	......	......	−380	−680	−740	−800	−870	−950	−1,020	−1,110	−1,200	−2,600	−7,750
Require evidence development for coverage of high cost drugs	......	......	......	......	......	......	......	......	......	......	......	......	......
Increase Part D plan sponsors' risk for catastrophic drug costs	......	......	......	......	......	......	......	......	......	......	......	......	......
Change the Part D coverage gap discount program agreements from annually to quarterly	......	......	......	......	......	......	......	......	......	......	......	......	......
Enhance efficiency in the Medicare program:													
Reduce Medicare coverage of bad debts	......	−410	−1,370	−2,620	−3,330	−3,590	−3,820	−4,060	−4,310	−4,570	−4,840	−11,320	−32,920
Adjust payment updates for certain post-acute care providers	......	−1,600	−2,100	−3,490	−5,120	−6,850	−9,120	−11,250	−13,420	−15,760	−17,870	−19,160	−86,580
Encourage appropriate use of inpatient rehabilitation hospitals by requiring that 75 percent of inpatient rehabilitation facility (IRF) patients require intensive rehabilitation services	......	−160	−190	−200	−200	−210	−220	−230	−240	−250	−250	−960	−2,150
Exclude certain services from the in-office ancillary services exception	......	......	−280	−440	−500	−530	−570	−610	−650	−680	−720	−1,750	−4,980
Reform Medicare hospice payments ..	......	......	−170	−510	−910	−1,000	−1,100	−1,210	−1,340	−1,430	−1,580	−2,590	−9,250
Recoup initial Clinical Laboratory Fee Schedule payments for advanced diagnostic laboratory tests in excess of 100 percent of the final payment amount	......	......	......	......	......	......	......	......	......	......	......	......	......

Table S-9. Mandatory and Receipt Proposals—Continued

(Deficit increases (+) or decreases (−) in millions of dollars)

	2016	2017	2018	2019	2020	2021	2022	2023	2024	2025	2026	Totals 2017–2021	Totals 2017–2026
Provide authority to expand competitive bidding for certain durable medical equipment	....	....	....	....	....	....	....	....	....	....	....	....	....
Reduce Critical Access Hospital (CAH) payments from 101 percent of reasonable costs to 100 percent of reasonable costs	....	....	....	−240	−400	−430	−460	−500	−530	−570	−620	−1,070	−3,750
Prohibit CAH designation for facilities that are less than 10 miles from the nearest hospital	....	−110	−130	−140	−150	−160	−170	−180	−190	−210	−230	−690	−1,670
Other Medicare:													
Strengthen the Independent Payment Advisory Board (IPAB) to reduce long-term drivers of Medicare cost growth	....	....	....	....	....	−1,067	−1,417	−6,940	−6,021	−10,127	−10,822	−1,067	−36,394
Clarify the calculation of the late enrollment penalty for Medicare Part B premiums	....	−60	−70	−70	−80	−80	−90	−90	−100	−110	−130	−360	−880
Clarify the Medicare Fraction in the Medicare Disproportional Share Hospital (DSH) statute	....	....	....	....	....	....	....	....	....	....	....	....	....
Update Medicare Disproportionate Share formula for hospitals in Puerto Rico	....	....	....	....	....	....	....	....	....	....	....	....	....
Allow beneficiaries to pay a sum certain to Medicare for future medical items and services	....	....	....	....	10	10	10	10	10	10	10	20	70
Modernize funding for End Stage Renal Disease Networks	....	....	−5	−20	−20	−20	....	....	....	....	....	−65	−65
Total, Medicare providers	....	−3,161	−9,926	−19,952	−29,952	−38,029	−44,414	−56,798	−62,929	−73,675	−82,590	−101,020	−421,426
Medicare structural reforms:													
Increase income-related premiums under Medicare Parts B and D	....	....	....	....	−1,870	−3,390	−4,660	−6,240	−8,040	−7,840	−9,190	−5,260	−41,230
Modify the Part B deductible for new beneficiaries	....	....	....	....	−60	−80	−320	−450	−970	−1,130	−1,220	−140	−4,230
Introduce home health copayments for new beneficiaries	....	....	....	....	−30	−70	−120	−170	−230	−300	−380	−100	−1,300
Encourage the use of generic drugs by low-income beneficiaries	....	....	−580	−830	−920	−1,000	−1,080	−1,170	−1,260	−1,340	−1,450	−3,330	−9,630
Total, Medicare structural reforms	....	....	−580	−830	−2,880	−4,540	−6,180	−8,030	−10,500	−10,610	−12,240	−8,830	−56,390
Interactions	....	33	1,171	3,511	4,583	6,362	6,268	11,969	10,317	14,410	12,704	15,660	71,328
Medicaid and Children's Health Insurance Program (CHIP):													
Improve access to coverage and services: Ensure access to enhanced Federal match for all Medicaid Expansion States	....	430	470	500	540	360	250	60	....	....	....	2,300	2,610

Table S-9. Mandatory and Receipt Proposals—Continued

(Deficit increases (+) or decreases (−) in millions of dollars)

	2016	2017	2018	2019	2020	2021	2022	2023	2024	2025	2026	Totals 2017–2021	Totals 2017–2026
Strengthen Medicaid in Puerto Rico and other U.S. Territories	......	320	1,433	1,771	2,791	3,000	3,219	3,468	3,998	4,297	5,347	9,315	29,644
Permanently extend Express Lane Eligibility (ELE) for children		......	30	50	70	85	100	115	125	140	155	235	870
Require full coverage of preventive health and tobacco cessation services for adults in traditional Medicaid		99	95	91	85	80	75	70	67	64	63	450	789
Require coverage of Early and Periodic Screening, Diagnostic, and Treatment program for children in inpatient psychiatric treatment facilities		35	40	45	45	50	50	55	60	60	65	215	505
Create State option to provide 12-month continuous Medicaid eligibility for adults [3]		467	851	1,300	973	1,140	1,097	1,156	1,305	1,351	1,495	4,731	11,135
Extend 100 percent Federal match to all Indian health programs		6	6	7	7	8	8	9	9	10	10	34	80
Provide full Medicaid coverage to pregnant and post-partum beneficiaries		30	30	35	35	35	40	40	40	45	45	165	375
Create demonstration to address over-prescription of psychotropic medications for children in foster care		119	216	221	228	235	88	−14	−11	−9	−6	1,019	1,067
Streamline certain Medicaid appeals processes		......	......	......	......	......	......	......	......	......	......	......	......
Expand State flexibility to provide benchmark benefit packages		......	......	......	......	......	......	......	......	......	......	......	......
Preserve coverage in CHIP:													
Extend CHIP funding through 2019 [3]		......	514	2,158	−1,002	......	......	......	......	......	......	1,670	1,670
Extend the performance bonus fund		180	350	350	350	170	......	......	......	......	......	1,400	1,400
Extend the child enrollment contingency fund		......	......	......	......	......	......	......	......	......	......	......	......
Strengthen the integrity of the Medicaid program:													
Expand funding for the Medicaid Integrity Program		−60	−60	−65	−65	−65	−65	−70	−70	−75	−80	−315	−675
Expand Medicaid Fraud Control Unit (MFCU) authority review to additional care settings		−6	−6	−6	−7	−7	−7	−8	−8	−8	−9	−32	−72
Require States to suspend Medicaid payments when there is a significant risk of fraud		......	......	......	......	......	......	......	......	......	......	......	......
Track high prescribers and utilizers of prescription drugs in Medicaid		......	......	......	......	......	......	......	......	......	......	......	......
Prevent use of Federal funds to pay State share of Medicaid or CHIP		−30	−50	−80	−80	−80	−90	−90	−90	−90	−90	−320	−770
Consolidate redundant error rate measurement programs		......	......	......	......	......	......	......	......	......	......	......	......

Table S–9. Mandatory and Receipt Proposals—Continued

(Deficit increases (+) or decreases (–) in millions of dollars)

	2016	2017	2018	2019	2020	2021	2022	2023	2024	2025	2026	Totals 2017–2021	Totals 2017–2026
Require manufacturers that improperly report items for Medicaid drug coverage to fully repay States	.....	.....	.....	.....	.....	.....	.....	.....	.....	.....	.....	.....	.....
Increase penalties on drug manufacturers for fraudulent noncompliance with Medicaid drug rebate agreements	.....	.....	.....	.....	.....	.....	.....	.....	.....	.....	.....	.....	.....
Require drugs be properly listed with the Food and Drug Administration (FDA) to receive Medicaid coverage	.....	.....	.....	.....	.....	.....	.....	.....	.....	.....	.....	.....	.....
Require drug wholesalers to report wholesale acquisition costs to CMS	.....	.....	.....	.....	.....	.....	.....	.....	.....	.....	.....	.....	.....
Enforce manufacturer compliance with drug rebate requirements	.....	.....	.....	.....	.....	.....	.....	.....	.....	.....	.....	.....	.....
Strengthen CMS compliance tools in Medicaid managed care	.....	.....	.....	.....	.....	.....	.....	.....	.....	.....	.....	.....	.....
Improve quality and cost-effectiveness: Rebase future Medicaid Disproportionate Share Hospital (DSH) allotments	.....	.....	.....	.....	.....	.....	.....	.....	.....	.....	–6,640	.....	–6,640
Require remittances for medical loss ratios for Medicaid and CHIP managed care	.....	.....	.....	–100	–2,100	–2,900	–3,100	–3,400	–3,600	–4,000	–4,300	–5,100	–23,500
Extend funding for the Adult Health Quality Measures Program	.....	14	14	14	14	14	.....	.....	.....	.....	.....	70	70
Encourage delivery system reform: Reestablish the Medicaid primary care payment increase through CY 2017 and include additional providers	.....	7,610	1,900	.....	.....	.....	.....	.....	.....	.....	.....	9,510	9,510
Allow States to develop age-specific health home programs	.....	210	210	90	90	90	90	80	80	80	80	690	1,100
Provide home and community-based services (HCBS) to children eligible for psychiatric residential treatment facilities	.....	.....	78	161	169	177	185	194	204	215	226	585	1,609
Allow full Medicaid benefits for individuals in a HCBS State plan option	.....	.....	1	1	1	1	1	1	1	1	1	4	9
Expand eligibility for the 1915(i) HCBS State plan option	.....	7	15	24	34	44	46	48	50	52	54	124	374
Expand eligibility under the Community First Choice option	.....	255	296	319	343	368	395	424	455	488	523	1,581	3,866
Pilot comprehensive long-term care State plan option	.....	.....	753	779	809	840	872	.....	.....	.....	.....	3,181	4,053
Strengthen Medicaid drug coverage and reimbursement: Create a Federal-State Medicaid negotiating pool for high-cost drugs	.....	–200	–410	–630	–630	–640	–650	–660	–660	–670	–680	–2,510	–5,830

Table S–9. Mandatory and Receipt Proposals—Continued

(Deficit increases (+) or decreases (–) in millions of dollars)

	2016	2017	2018	2019	2020	2021	2022	2023	2024	2025	2026	Totals 2017–2021	Totals 2017–2026
Correct Affordable Care Act (ACA)													
Medicaid rebate formula for new drug formulations and exempt abuse deterrent formulations	....	–410	–410	–415	–425	–425	–435	–440	–440	–440	–445	–2,085	–4,285
Exclude authorized generics from Medicaid brand-name rebate calculations	....	–20	–20	–20	–20	–20	–20	–20	–20	–20	–20	–100	–200
Exclude brand-name and authorized generic drug prices from Medicaid Federal upper limit (FUL)	....	–30	–60	–90	–90	–100	–100	–100	–100	–100	–100	–370	–870
Clarify the Medicaid definition of brand drugs to prevent inappropriately low rebates	....	–21	–21	–21	–26	–26	–26	–26	–31	–31	–31	–115	–260
Additional improvements to the Medicaid drug rebate program	....	....	....	....	....	....	....	....	....	....	....	....	....
Total, Medicaid and Children's Health Insurance Program	....	9,005	6,265	6,489	2,139	2,434	2,023	892	1,364	1,360	–4,337	26,332	27,634
Other health:													
Medicare-Medicaid enrollees:													
Ensure retroactive Part D coverage of newly-eligible low-income beneficiaries	....	....	....	....	10	10	10	10	20	20	20	20	100
Establish integrated appeals process for Medicare-Medicaid enrollees	....	....	....	....	....	....	....	....	....	....	....	....	....
Allow for Federal/State coordinated review of Duals Special Need Plan marketing materials	....	....	....	....	....	....	....	....	....	....	....	....	....
Align Medicare Savings Program income and asset definitions with Part D low-income subsidy definitions	....	31	32	32	35	38	40	42	45	48	51	170	396
Total, Medicare-Medicaid enrollees	....	31	32	34	45	48	50	52	65	68	71	190	496
Pharmaceutical savings:													
Prohibit brand and generic drug companies from delaying the availability of new generic drugs and biologics	....	–920	–1,010	–1,100	–1,210	–1,290	–1,400	–1,500	–1,610	–1,730	–1,860	–5,530	–13,630
Modify length of exclusivity to facilitate faster development of generic biologics	....	....	....	–230	–590	–780	–870	–1,020	–1,080	–1,140	–1,250	–1,600	–6,960
Establish transparency and reporting requirements in pharmaceutical drug pricing	....	....	....	....	....	....	....	....	....	....	....	....	....
Total, pharmaceutical savings	....	–920	–1,010	–1,330	–1,800	–2,070	–2,270	–2,520	–2,690	–2,870	–3,110	–7,130	–20,590
Public health and workforce investments:													
Support Teaching Health Centers Graduate Medical Education (GME)	....	....	74	214	141	99	....	....	....	....	....	528	528
Support Children's Hospital GME	....	130	269	286	292	295	165	27	9	2	....	1,272	1,475

Table S–9. Mandatory and Receipt Proposals—Continued

(Deficit increases (+) or decreases (−) in millions of dollars)

	2016	2017	2018	2019	2020	2021	2022	2023	2024	2025	2026	Totals 2017–2021	Totals 2017–2026
Invest in the National Health Service Corps	......	......	227	729	770	575	81	40	8	......	......	2,301	2,430
Extend Health Centers	......	75	1,867	3,388	1,695	181	108	36	......	......	......	7,206	7,350
Extend special diabetes program at National Institutes of Health (NIH) and the Indian Health Service (IHS) permanently	......	......	180	266	291	296	298	300	300	300	300	1,033	2,531
Fund a dedicated Mental Health Initiative	......	87	218	150	37	8	......	......	......	......	......	500	500
Expand access to treatment for prescription drug abuse and heroin use	......	154	426	321	68	25	6	......	......	......	......	994	1,000
Total, public health and workforce investments	......	446	3,261	5,354	3,294	1,479	658	403	317	302	300	13,834	15,814
Medicare appeals:													
Provide Office of Medicare Hearings and Appeals and Department Appeals Board authority to use RAC collections	......	127	127	127	127	127	127	127	127	127	127	635	1,270
Establish Medicare appeals refundable filing fee	......	......	......	......	......	......	......	......	......	......	......	......	......
Remand appeals to the redetermination level with the introduction of new evidence	......	......	......	......	......	......	......	......	......	......	......	......	......
Sample and consolidate similar claims for administrative efficiency	......	......	......	......	......	......	......	......	......	......	......	......	......
Increase minimum amount in controversy for administrative law judge (ALJ) adjudication of claims to equal amount required for judicial review	......	......	......	......	......	......	......	......	......	......	......	......	......
Establish magistrate adjudication for claims with amount in controversy below new ALJ amount in controversy threshold	......	......	......	......	......	......	......	......	......	......	......	......	......
Expedite procedures for claims with no material fact in dispute	......	......	......	......	......	......	......	......	......	......	......	......	......
Total, Medicare appeals	......	127	127	127	127	127	127	127	127	127	127	635	1,270
Health information technology (IT):													
Add certain behavioral health providers to the Electronic Health Record (EHR) Incentive Programs	......	......	1,710	910	910	920	490	270	−10	......	......	4,450	5,200
Establish health IT governance certification	......	......	......	......	......	......	......	......	......	......	......	......	......
Prohibit information blocking and associated business practices	......	......	......	......	......	......	......	......	......	......	......	......	......
Require health IT transparency	......	......	......	......	......	......	......	......	......	......	......	......	......

Table S-9. Mandatory and Receipt Proposals—Continued

(Deficit increases (+) or decreases (–) in millions of dollars)

	2016	2017	2018	2019	2020	2021	2022	2023	2024	2025	2026	Totals 2017–2021	Totals 2017–2026
Provide the Office of the National Coordinator for Health IT (ONC) authority to use contracts, grants, or cooperative agreements to establish a Health IT Safety Collaborative and provide adequate confidentiality protections	....	....	....	....	....	....	....	....	....	....	....		
Total, Health information technology	....	....	1,710	910	910	920	490	270	–10	....	....	4,450	5,200
Program implementation investments:													
Provide CMS Program Management implementation funding	....	25	300	75	....	....	....	....	....	....	....	400	400
Allow CMS to reinvest civil monetary penalties recovered from home health agencies	....	1	1	1	1	1	1	1	1	1	1	5	10
Allow CMS to assess a fee on Medicare providers for payments subject to the Federal Payment Levy Program	....	....	....	....	....	....	....	....	....	....	....		
Total, program implementation investments	....	26	301	76	1	1	1	1	1	1	1	405	410
Private health insurance:													
Standardize definition of American Indian and Alaska Native in the ACA	....	30	40	50	50	50	50	60	60	60	70	220	520
Increase access to consumer protections in non-Federal governmental self-insured health plans	....	....	....	....	....	....	....	....	....	....	....		
Eliminate surprise out-of-network health care charges for privately insured patients	....	....	....	....	....	....	....	....	....	....	....		
Develop uniform and transparent consumer health care bills	....	....	....	....	....	....	....	....	....	....	....		
Total, private health insurance	....	30	40	50	50	50	50	60	60	60	70	220	520
Total, HHS health savings [5]	....	5,617	1,391	–5,561	–23,483	–33,218	–43,197	–53,574	–63,878	–70,827	–89,004	–55,254	–375,734
Provide mandatory funding for tribal contract support costs:													
PAYGO effects			111	269	453	....	....	....	....	....	....	833	833
Nonscoreable reclassification			814	831	847	864	882	899	917	935	954	3,356	7,943
Total, provide mandatory funding for tribal contract support costs			925	1,100	1,300	864	882	899	917	935	954	4,189	8,776
Annual reduction to discretionary spending limits (non-add)			*–814*	*–831*	*–847*	*–864*	*–882*	*–899*	*–917*	*–935*	*–954*	*–3,356*	*–7,943*
Support medical research and development at the National Institutes of Health and the FDA		562	1,004	252	48	26	8	....	....	....	....	1,892	1,900
Promote family based care		76	45	20	7	–9	–23	–36	–44	–52	–52	139	–68
Enhance support for tribal child welfare programs		37	34	38	32	27	14	14	16	16	14	168	242

Table S-9. Mandatory and Receipt Proposals—Continued

(Deficit increases (+) or decreases (−) in millions of dollars)

	2016	2017	2018	2019	2020	2021	2022	2023	2024	2025	2026	Totals 2017–2021	Totals 2017–2026
Extend and Expand the Maternal, Infant, and Early Childhood Home Visiting (MIECHV) Program	......	......	20	135	450	745	1,340	1,585	1,910	1,995	2,135	1,350	10,315
Establish Title IV-E funding for prevention and permanency services	......	29	40	41	52	59	61	59	65	91	119	221	616
Expand eligibility through age 23 for Chafee Foster Care Independence Program	......	1	4	4	4	4	3	......	......	......	......	17	20
Reauthorize Family Connection Grants	......	1	10	14	15	15	14	5	1	......	......	55	75
Reauthorize the Personal Responsibility Education Program (PREP)	......	......	2	24	57	74	75	73	51	18	1	157	375
Reauthorize Health Profession and Opportunity Grants	......	......	4	46	78	85	85	81	39	7	1	213	425
Support demonstration to address over-prescription of psychotropic drugs for children in foster care	......	1	20	55	71	52	28	16	6	1	1	199	251
Expand access to high-quality, affordable care for young children	......	2,969	3,889	4,632	5,599	6,639	7,709	9,205	10,787	12,476	14,422	23,728	78,327
Establish Low Income Home Energy Assistance Program (LIHEAP) contingency fund	......	560	377	63	......	......	......	......	......	......	......	1,000	1,000
Fund Upward Mobility Project	......	300	300	300	300	300	......	......	......	......	......	1,500	1,500
Apply Child Care and Development Fund health and safety standards to Temporary Assistance for Needy Families- (TANF) and Social Services Block Grant-funded child care	......	......	......	......	......	......	......	......	......	......	......	......	......
Apply set-asides in the Child Care and Development Block Grant to the Child Care Entitlement funding	......	......	......	......	......	......	......	......	......	......	......	......	......
Enhance Title IV-E administrative costs for IT systems updates	......	13	13	14	13	13	13	13	13	13	13	66	131
Invest in child welfare workforce development	......	50	59	64	70	80	141	162	193	222	799	323	1,840
Promote responsible parenthood by modernizing Child Support	......	54	75	179	203	274	313	354	355	352	228	785	2,387
Strengthen Child Support enforcement	......	−22	−35	−53	−68	−85	−86	−87	−90	−90	−91	−263	−707
Establish a Child Support Technology Fund	......	−78	−89	−85	−86	−100	−6	−10	−16	4	−1	−438	−467
Establish a Child Support Research Fund	......	100	100	100	100	100	100	100	100	100	100	500	1,000
Eliminate Abstinence Education Program	......	−1	−50	−23	−1	......	......	......	......	......	......	−75	−75
Expand Child Welfare Regional Partnership Grants and the Tribal Court Improvement Program	......	1	25	38	41	42	43	43	43	43	43	147	362
Repurpose TANF contingency fund to support Pathways to Jobs initiative	......	......	......	......	......	......	......	......	......	......	......	......	......
Increase TANF Block Grant	......	585	1,087	1,567	1,862	2,130	445	132	102	65	22	7,231	7,997
Establish TANF Economic Response Fund	......	29	96	148	168	195	......	......	......	......	......	636	636
Fund Emergency Aid and Service Connection Grants	......	1	40	388	454	486	480	108	39	5	......	1,369	2,001

Table S–9. Mandatory and Receipt Proposals—Continued

(Deficit increases (+) or decreases (–) in millions of dollars)

	2016	2017	2018	2019	2020	2021	2022	2023	2024	2025	2026	Totals 2017–2021	Totals 2017–2026
Provide grants for Statewide Human Services Data Systems	....	5	25	37	45	50	45	25	12	5	....	162	249
Total, Health and Human Services	....	10,890	9,411	3,537	–12,669	–21,152	–31,513	–40,833	–49,379	–54,621	–70,297	–9,983	–256,626
Homeland Security:													
Reform the aviation passenger security user fee to more accurately reflect the costs of aviation security		....	–410	–490	–550	–410	–400	–390	–380	–370	–2,000	–1,860	–5,400
Increase customs user fees[6]		–86	–93	–102	–112	–125	–135	–146	–158	–170	....	–518	–1,127
Increase immigration inspection user fees[6]		–6	–6	–7	–7	–9	–9	–10	–10	–10	....	–35	–74
Increase Express Consignment Courier fees[6]		....	....	....	....	....	....	....	....	....	....	....	....
Establish user fee for Electronic Visa Update System[3]		....	....	....	....	....	....	....	....	....	....	....	....
Total, Homeland Security		–92	–509	–599	–669	–544	–544	–546	–548	–550	–2,000	–2,413	–6,601
Housing and Urban Development:													
Provide funding for grants to reduce local barriers to housing development		6	30	45	81	81	51	6	....	....	....	243	300
End family homelessness		79	359	616	813	998	1,204	1,410	1,618	1,829	2,041	2,865	10,967
Total, Housing and Urban Development		85	389	661	894	1,079	1,255	1,416	1,618	1,829	2,041	3,108	11,267
Interior:													
Provide a fair return to taxpayers for the use of public resources:													
Enact Federal oil and gas management reforms		–20	–70	–90	–110	–120	–140	–150	–170	–180	–190	–410	–1,240
Reform hardrock mining on public lands		....	–2	–4	–5	–5	–6	–6	–11	–17	–24	–16	–80
Repeal geothermal payments to counties		–4	–4	–4	–4	–4	–4	–4	–4	–4	–5	–20	–41
Enact offshore energy revenue reform		....	–286	–310	–339	–376	–376	–380	–384	–393	–410	–1,311	–3,254
Total, provide a fair return to taxpayers for the use of public resources		–24	–362	–408	–458	–505	–526	–540	–569	–594	–629	–1,757	–4,615
Ensure industry is held responsible for legacy pollution and risks to safety:													
Establish an Abandoned Mine Lands (AML) hardrock reclamation fund[3]		....	–200	–150	–100	–50	....	....	....	....	....	–500	–500
Increase coal AML fee to pre–2006 levels[3]		–49	–38	–25	–15	–8	52	40	23	13	5	–135	–2
Terminate AML payments to certified States		–6	–31	–63	–82	–90	–92	–73	–41	–28	–14	–272	–520
Fund abandoned mine lands reclamation and economic revitalization		50	112	152	182	200	150	88	48	18	....	696	1,000
Total, ensure industry is held responsible for legacy pollution and risks to safety		–5	–157	–86	–15	52	110	55	30	3	–9	–211	–22
Conserve natural resources for future generations and provide recreation access to the public:													
Establish dedicated funding for Land and Water Conservation Fund (LWCF) programs		129	474	988	977	918	900	900	900	900	900	3,486	7,986

Table S–9. Mandatory and Receipt Proposals—Continued

(Deficit increases (+) or decreases (−) in millions of dollars)

	2016	2017	2018	2019	2020	2021	2022	2023	2024	2025	2026	Totals 2017–2021	Totals 2017–2026
Establish a dedicated Coastal Climate Resilience Fund from offshore energy revenues	....	40	100	140	170	200	200	200	200	200	200	650	1,650
Reauthorize the Federal Land Transaction Facilitation Act of 2000 (FLTFA)	....	−5	−6	−10	−12	−3						−36	−36
Permanently reauthorize the Federal Lands Recreation Enhancement Act (FLREA)	....	....	....	....	....	....	....	....	....	....	....	....	....
Provide funding for a National Park Service Centennial Initiative	....	28	275	473	431	177	−1	−9	−9	−8	−4	1,384	1,353
Total, conserve natural resources for future generations and provide recreation access to the public	....	192	843	1,591	1,566	1,292	1,099	1,091	1,091	1,092	1,096	5,484	10,953
Maintain commitments to communities and insular territories:													
Provide mandatory funding for tribal contract support costs:													
PAYGO effects	....	....	19	32	43	11	....	....	....	....	....	105	105
Noncoreable reclassification	....	....	212	287	293	299	305	311	317	324	329	1,091	2,677
Total, provide mandatory funding for tribal contract support costs	....	....	231	319	336	310	305	311	317	324	329	1,196	2,782
Annual reduction to discretionary spending limits (non-add)	....	....	−212	−287	−293	−299	−305	−311	−317	−324	−329	−1,091	−2,677
Extend the Palau Compact of Free Association	....	46	26	20	17	15	14	6	5	....	....	124	149
Extend funding for Payments in Lieu of Taxes (PILT)	....	480	....	....	....	....	....	....	....	....	....	480	480
Improve coal miner retiree health and pension benefits	....	375	394	407	414	418	428	430	431	434	436	2,008	4,167
Total, maintain commitments to communities and insular territories	....	901	651	746	767	743	747	747	753	758	765	3,808	7,578
Total, Interior	....	1,064	975	1,843	1,860	1,582	1,430	1,353	1,305	1,259	1,223	7,324	13,894
Justice:													
Provide funding for 21st Century Justice grants to incentivize justice reform	....	110	300	475	500	500	500	500	500	500	500	1,885	4,385
Labor:													
Establish an American Talent Compact	....	600	600	600	600	600	....	....	....	....	....	3,000	3,000
Create Career Navigators program	....	400	400	400	400	400	....	....	....	....	....	2,000	2,000
Create Opening Doors for Youth program	....	2,035	2,035	715	715	....	....	....	....	....	....	5,500	5,500
Create an Apprenticeship Training Fund	....	400	400	400	400	400	....	....	....	....	....	2,000	2,000
Establish Paid Leave Partnership Initiative	....	221	664	664	664	....	....	....	....	....	....	2,213	2,213
Improve Pension Benefit Guaranty Corporation (PBGC) solvency	....	−1,060	−1,109	−1,172	−1,295	−1,418	−1,615	−1,763	−1,942	−3,322	−953	−6,054	−15,649
Unemployment Insurance Modernization and Reform:[7]													
Strengthen Unemployment Insurance (UI) system solvency[3,8]	....	....	−3,128	−3,185	−3,922	−4,303	−5,425	−6,802	−6,068	−6,346	−7,114	−14,538	−46,293

Table S–9. Mandatory and Receipt Proposals—Continued

(Deficit increases (+) or decreases (–) in millions of dollars)

	2016	2017	2018	2019	2020	2021	2022	2023	2024	2025	2026	Totals 2017–2021	Totals 2017–2026
Improve UI Extended Benefits	....	741	2,033	2,533	2,989	3,477	3,933	4,136	5,381	5,828	5,602	11,773	36,653
Modernize UI [3,8]	....	2,057	2,587	1,224	1,185	950	854	1,340	1,267	1,299	1,348	8,003	14,111
Expand Short-Time Compensation	....	177	178	178	179	179	180	180	180	184	187	891	1,802
Create a wage insurance program	....	....	302	935	1,293	1,338	1,382	1,422	1,467	1,504	1,541	3,868	11,184
Improve UI program integrity [3]	....	–69	–108	–141	–184	–178	–171	–166	–136	–178	–154	–680	–1,485
Implement cap adjustments for UI program integrity [3,8]	....	–76	–56	8	13	14	13	11	10	8	6	–97	–49
Outlays from reduction to discretionary spending limits (non-add)	....	....	–154	–157	–160	–163	–166	–170	–173	–177	–180	–634	–1,500
Outlays from program integrity discretionary cap adjustment (non-add)	....	30	5	....	....	....	....	....	....	....	....	35	35
Create mandatory Reemployment Services and Eligibility Assessment program [3]	....	....	–28	–322	–326	–308	–229	–228	–233	–210	–211	–984	–2,095
Pilot models for providing multiple-employer benefits	....	25	50	25	....	....	....	....	....	....	....	100	100
Expand Foreign Labor Certification fees	....	....	....	....	....	....	....	....	....	....	....	....	....
Total, Labor	....	5,451	4,820	2,862	2,711	1,151	–1,078	–1,870	–74	–1,233	252	16,995	12,992
Treasury:													
Establish a Pay for Success Incentive Fund	....	29	21	10	24	40	56	46	42	27	5	124	300
Authorize Treasury to locate and recover assets of the United States and to retain a portion of amounts collected to pay for the costs of recovery	....	–8	–8	–8	–8	–8	–9	–9	–9	–9	–9	–40	–85
Increase delinquent Federal non-tax debt collections by authorizing administrative bank garnishment for non-tax debts	....	–32	–32	–32	–32	–32	–32	–32	–32	–32	–32	–160	–320
Allow offset of Federal income tax refunds to collect delinquent State income taxes for out-of-State residents	....	....	....	....	....	....	....	....	....	....	....	....	....
Reduce costs for States collecting delinquent income tax obligations	....	....	....	....	....	....	....	....	....	....	....	....	....
Reauthorize the State Small Business Credit Initiative	....	212	571	235	312	130	....	....	....	....	....	1,460	1,460
Implement tax enforcement program integrity cap adjustment [3]	....	–278	–1,585	–3,263	–5,008	–6,763	–8,327	–9,264	–9,590	–9,737	–9,814	–16,897	–63,629
Outlays from discretionary cap adjustment (non-add)	....	458	890	1,255	1,622	1,996	2,125	2,153	2,180	2,206	2,231	6,221	17,116
Create a Financing America's Infrastructure Renewal (FAIR) program	....	2	2	2	2	2	2	2	2	2	2	10	20
Establish Financial Innovation for Working Families Challenge and Demonstration Grants	....	15	45	40	....	....	....	....	....	....	....	100	100
Provide allotment for Puerto Rico earned income tax credit (EITC) payments	....	601	613	626	640	655	670	685	701	717	734	3,135	6,642
Total, Treasury	....	541	–373	–2,390	–4,070	–5,976	–7,640	–8,572	–8,886	–9,032	–9,114	–12,268	–55,512

Table S–9. Mandatory and Receipt Proposals—Continued

(Deficit increases (+) or decreases (–) in millions of dollars)

	2016	2017	2018	2019	2020	2021	2022	2023	2024	2025	2026	Totals 2017–2021	Totals 2017–2026
Veterans Affairs (VA):													
Extend round-down of cost of living adjustments (compensation)	....	–21	–64	–120	–169	–225	–246	–258	–272	–286	–291	–599	–1,952
Extend round-down of cost of living adjustments (education)	....	–1	–1	–1	–2	–2	–2	–2	–2	–3	–2	–7	–18
Provide burial receptacles for certain new casketed gravesites	....	2	3	1	2	3	2	4	2	7	1	11	27
Improve housing grant program	....	1	1	1	1	1	1	1	1	1	1	5	10
Increase cap on vocational rehabilitation contract counseling	....	1	1	1	1	1	1	1	1	1	1	5	10
Extend supplemental service disabled veterans insurance coverage	....	....	....	....	....	1	....	....	1	1	1	1	4
Clarify evidentiary threshold at which VA is required to provide medical examination	....	–120	–125	–130	–135	–140	–146	–152	–158	–164	–171	–650	–1,441
Cap Post–9/11 GI Bill benefits for flight training	....	–44	–45	–47	–50	–52	–54	–57	–59	–62	–65	–238	–535
Expand eligibility for Montgomery GI Bill refund	....	2	2	2	2	1	2	3	2	2	2	9	20
Extend authorization of work-study activities	....	1	1	1	1	1	1	1	2	1	1	5	11
Pro-rate GI Bill benefit usage for certification tests	....	2	1	1	1	1	1	1	1	2	2	6	13
Modernize the definition of Automobile Adaptive Equipment (AAE)	....	–3	–3	–2	–1	–2	–2	–2	–1	–1	–1	–11	–18
Eliminate reductions of special monthly compensation for hospitalized veterans	....	....	1	1	1	....	1	1	1	1	1	3	8
Restore the eligibility of certain veterans for special aid and attendance allowance	....	2	2	2	2	3	3	3	3	3	3	11	26
Reissue VA benefit payments to all victims of fiduciary misuse	....	2	2	2	2	2	2	2	2	2	2	10	20
Increase Burial Benefit Allowances with increases in CPI	....	1	2	3	5	7	9	11	13	15	18	18	84
Remove annual income from net worth calculation	....	....	....	....	....	1	....	....	1	1	1	1	4
Restore program entitlement when approval is withdrawn during enrollment	....	....	....	....	....	1	....	....	....	1	1	1	3
Add Section 12304b of Title 10 as qualification for active duty for GI Bill eligibility	....	....	17	32	36	38	40	42	43	45	47	123	340
Move home modifications under a rehabilitation program to the Specially Adapted Housing (SAH) Program	....	–1	–1	–1	–1	....	....	–1	–1	–1	–1	–4	–8
Expand eligibility for Medal of Honor marker	....	....	....	....	....	....	....	....	....	....	....	....	....
Eliminate sunset date for vocational rehabilitation for servicemembers	....	11	–2	–2	–2	–1	–1	–1	–1	–1	–1	4	–1
Allow extension of a period of employment services	....	1	....	....	....	....	....	1	....	....	....	1	2
Sunset Montgomery GI Bill Active Duty program	....	....	....	....	....	....	....	19	69	45	34	....	167

Table S–9. Mandatory and Receipt Proposals—Continued

(Deficit increases (+) or decreases (–) in millions of dollars)

	2016	2017	2018	2019	2020	2021	2022	2023	2024	2025	2026	Totals 2017–2021	Totals 2017–2026
Expansion of eligibility for medallion or other device to signify status of deceased veteran	......	......	1	1	1	1	1	1	1	1	1	4	9
Expansion of Specially Adapted Housing Assistance for certain veterans with disabilities	......	2	3	3	3	2	......	......	......	......	......	13	13
Authorize the Secretary to establish debts for breaching 38 U.S.C. Section 2101 (Specially Adapted Housing) contractual obligation	......	......	......	......	......	......	......	......	......	......	......		
Total, Veterans Affairs	......	–162	–204	–252	–302	–358	–387	–382	–351	–389	–415	–1,278	–3,202
Corps of Engineers:													
Reform inland waterways financing[3]	......	–3	–78	–118	–156	–156	–156	–156	–156	–155	–155	–511	–1,289
Environmental Protection Agency (EPA):													
Eliminate statutory cap on pre-manufacture notice fee	......	–4	–8	–8	–8	–8	–8	–8	–8	–8	–8	–36	–76
Enact confidential business information management fee	......	......	–2	–2	......	......	......	......	......	......	......	–4	–4
Lift restrictions on EPA spending of Federal Insecticide, Fungicide, and Rodenticide Act (FIFRA) pesticide fees	......	6	6	6	1	1	......	......	......	......	......	14	14
Total, Environmental Protection Agency	......	2	–4	–9	–7	–8	–8	–8	–8	–8	–8	–26	–66
General Services Administration:													
Establish an Information Technology Modernization Fund	......	1,500	600	750	......	......	......	......	......	......	......	2,850	2,850
National Aeronautics and Space Administration (NASA):													
Provide additional R&D funding for NASA	......	325	283	56	......	......	......	......	......	......	......	664	664
National Science Foundation (NSF):													
Provide additional R&D funding for NSF	......	77	157	88	34	13	4	4	23	......	......	369	400
Other Defense–Civil Programs:													
Increase TRICARE pharmacy copayments	......	–35	–54	–93	–351	–394	–433	–507	–601	–724	–767	–927	–3,959
Increase annual premiums for TRICARE-For-Life (TFL) enrollment	......	–3	–16	–44	–85	–117	–153	–192	–235	–281	–332	–265	–1,458
Increase TRICARE pharmacy copayments (accrual effects)	......	322	338	355	374	394	415	438	463	487	514	1,783	4,100
Increase annual premiums for TFL enrollment (accrual effects)	......	281	286	294	303	311	328	346	366	385	408	1,475	3,308
Enact changes to the military retirement reform enacted in the 2016 National Defense Authorization Act[3]	......	–394	–408	–388	–380	–315	–308	–299	–298	–292	–291	–1,885	–3,373
Total, Other Defense–Civil Programs	......	171	146	124	–139	–121	–151	–214	–305	–425	–468	181	–1,382
Office of Personnel Management:													
Streamline Federal Employee Health Benefit Plan (FEHBP) pharmacy benefit contracting	......	......	–69	–127	–141	–151	–161	–173	–184	–198	–212	–488	–1,416

Table S–9. Mandatory and Receipt Proposals—Continued

(Deficit increases (+) or decreases (–) in millions of dollars)

	2016	2017	2018	2019	2020	2021	2022	2023	2024	2025	2026	Totals 2017–2021	Totals 2017–2026
Expand FEHBP plan types			–1	–3	–5	–7	–8	–12	–15	–18	–19	–16	–88
Adjust FEHBP premiums for wellness			5	–11	–47	–81	–119	–164	–233	–315	–421	–134	–1,386
Extend FEHBP to infants born to daughters of FEHBP enrollees for 30 days			11	31	36	37	39	43	45	52	51	115	345
Add FEHBP to the Federal Anti-Kickback Statute													
Total, Office of Personnel Management			–54	–110	–157	–202	–249	–306	–387	–479	–601	–523	–2,545
Social Security Administration (SSA):													
Hold fraud facilitators liable for overpayments[9]				–1	–1	–1	–1	–1	–1	–1	–1	–3	–8
Allow Government-wide use of Customs and Border Protection (CBP) entry/exit data to prevent improper payments				–1	–5	–11	–20	–26	–31	–40	–43	–17	–177
Lower electronic wage reporting threshold to five employees													
Move from annual to quarterly wage reporting		20	30	90	–119	–126	–148	–178	–203	–225	–270	–105	–1,129
Improve collection of pension information and transition to an alternative approach based on years of non-covered earnings after 10 years		18	28	24	–433	–1,002	–1,350	–1,421	–1,318	–1,246	–1,142	–1,365	–7,842
Establish workers compensation information reporting		5	5									10	10
Extend Supplemental Security Income (SSI) time limits for qualified refugees		48	57									105	105
Conform treatment of State and local government EITC and child tax credit (CTC for SSI[10]													
Terminate step-child benefits in the same month as step-parent[11]								–1	–1	–1	–1		–4
Use the Death Master File to prevent Federal improper payments													
Modernize SSA information technology			80	80	80							240	240
Authorize SSA to conduct a new continuing disability review (CDR) when fraud was involved in a prior CDR													
Authorize SSA to use all collection tools to recover funds in certain scenarios, such as when someone improperly cashes a beneficiary's check or removes a benefit from a joint account			–2	–2	–3	–4	–4	–5	–5	–5	–5	–11	–35
Allow SSA to use commercial databases to verify real property data in the SSI program		–12	–28	–44	–53	–60	–69	–70	–68	–76	–79	–197	–559
Increase the minimum monthly Old-Age Survivors and Disability Insurance (OASDI) overpayment collection from $10 a month to 10 percent		–8	–26	–43	–59	–77	–93	–107	–135	–144	–156	–213	–848

Table S-9. Mandatory and Receipt Proposals—Continued

(Deficit increases (+) or decreases (−) in millions of dollars)

	2016	2017	2018	2019	2020	2021	2022	2023	2024	2025	2026	Totals 2017–2021	Totals 2017–2026
Exclude SSA debts from discharge in bankruptcy		−9	−18	−23	−29	−34	−36	−38	−40	−43	−45	−113	−315
Eliminate SSI dedicated accounts		5	3									8	8
Modify the treatment of certain debt referrals to the Treasury Offset Program			6	5	6	5	6	5	6	5	6	22	50
Total, Social Security Administration		67	135	85	−616	−1,310	−1,715	−1,842	−1,796	−1,776	−1,736	−1,639	−10,504
Other Independent Agencies:													
Federal Communications Commission (FCC):													
Enact Spectrum License User Fee and allow the FCC to auction predominantly domestic satellite services		−225	−325	−425	−550	−550	−550	−550	−550	−550	−550	−2,075	−4,825
Postal Service:													
Enact Postal Service financial relief and reform	−625	−1,514	−2,132	−4,219	−4,192	−4,359	−4,428	−4,457	−4,384	−4,312	−4,291	−16,416	−38,288
Railroad Retirement Board (RRB):													
Amend Railroad Retirement Act and the Railroad Unemployment Insurance Act to include a felony charge for fraud													
Promote RRB program integrity		4	4	4	4	4	4	4	5	5	5	20	43
Total, Railroad Retirement Board		4	4	4	4	4	4	4	5	5	5	20	43
National Infrastructure Bank:													
Create infrastructure bank		33	153	373	595	831	1,058	1,158	1,233	1,207	1,062	1,985	7,703
Total, Other Independent Agencies	−625	−1,702	−2,300	−4,267	−4,143	−4,074	−3,916	−3,845	−3,696	−3,650	−3,774	−16,486	−35,367
Multi-Agency:													
Enact immigration reform [3]		4,000	3,000	−5,000	−10,000	−20,000	−20,000	−25,000	−29,000	−34,000	−34,000	−28,000	−170,000
Establish hold harmless for Federal poverty guidelines													
Expand access to the National Directory of New Hires (NDNH)													
Auction or assign via fee 1675–1680 megahertz				−150	−150							−300	−300
Establish a consolidated TRICARE program (mandatory effects in Coast Guard, Public Health Service, and National Oceanic and Atmospheric Administration)													
Establish Interagency Coordinating Council on Workforce Attachment		51	51	51	51							204	204
Index the $750 offset of SSA benefits to inflation (Student Aid Bill of Rights proposal)		1,890	9	14	21	27	33	40	46	53	60	1,961	2,193
Enact 21st Century Clean Transportation Plan		5,392	14,616	22,470	30,463	35,485	35,877	33,848	29,479	22,730	16,669	108,426	247,029
Establish Family Energy Assistance Fund		1,445	2,903	4,343	5,770	7,157	8,465	8,624	8,766	8,892	9,022	21,618	65,387
Mandatory effects of proposal to authorize additional Afghan Special Immigrant Visas			18	18	16	15	16	16	15	15	16	67	145
Total, Multi-Agency		12,779	20,591	21,735	26,159	22,671	24,376	17,511	9,288	−2,330	−8,255	103,935	144,525
Total, mandatory initiatives and savings	−625	29,477	34,606	27,776	16,234	2,803	−7,126	−22,683	−32,947	−44,311	−66,064	110,896	−62,235

Table S-9. Mandatory and Receipt Proposals—Continued

(Deficit increases (+) or decreases (–) in millions of dollars)

	2016	2017	2018	2019	2020	2021	2022	2023	2024	2025	2026	Totals 2017–2021	Totals 2017–2026
Tax proposals:													
Elements of business tax reform:													
Reform the U.S. international tax system:													
Restrict deductions for excessive interest of members of financial reporting groups	....	–2,822	–4,986	–5,485	–6,033	–6,637	–7,300	–8,030	–8,833	–9,717	–10,688	–25,963	–70,531
Provide tax incentives for locating jobs and business activity in the United States and remove tax deductions for shipping jobs overseas	....	11	18	20	20	21	22	23	24	26	26	90	211
Repeal delay in the implementation of worldwide interest allocation	....	1,406	2,400	2,496	2,596	1,055	....	....	....	....	....	9,953	9,953
Impose a 19-percent minimum tax on foreign income	....	–24,201	–38,418	–35,969	–33,192	–32,831	–34,211	–35,651	–37,117	–38,635	–40,166	–164,611	–350,391
Limit shifting of income through intangible property transfers	....	–88	–167	–201	–237	–275	–315	–361	–413	–473	–542	–968	–3,072
Disallow the deduction for excess non-taxed reinsurance premiums paid to affiliates	....	–411	–657	–697	–731	–771	–815	–848	–882	–918	–958	–3,267	–7,688
Modify tax rules for dual capacity taxpayers	....	–465	–814	–878	–930	–970	–992	–1,032	–1,074	–1,121	–1,359	–4,057	–9,635
Tax gain from the sale of a partnership interest on look-through basis	....	–146	–251	–264	–277	–291	–305	–321	–337	–354	–371	–1,229	–2,917
Modify sections 338(h)(16) and 902 to limit credits when non-double taxation exists	....	–59	–102	–105	–105	–105	–105	–105	–106	–106	–107	–476	–1,005
Close loopholes under subpart F	....	–1,517	–2,635	–2,821	–3,019	–3,230	–3,453	–3,692	–3,945	–4,215	–4,501	–13,222	–33,028
Restrict the use of hybrid arrangements that create stateless income	....	–115	–201	–215	–230	–247	–264	–283	–304	–326	–350	–1,008	–2,535
Limit the ability of domestic entities to expatriate	....	–118	–327	–556	–807	–1,083	–1,383	–1,711	–2,068	–2,457	–2,880	–2,891	–13,390
Total, reform the U.S. international tax system	....	–28,525	–46,140	–44,675	–42,945	–45,364	–49,121	–52,011	–55,055	–58,296	–61,896	–207,649	–484,028
Simplification and tax relief for small business:													
Expand expensing for small business	....	2,101	2,863	2,072	1,625	1,335	1,132	1,009	961	971	997	9,996	15,066
Expand simplified accounting for small business and establish a uniform definition of small business for accounting methods	....	6,248	4,874	2,819	1,975	1,814	1,745	1,724	1,819	1,839	1,845	17,730	26,702
Increase the limitations for deductible new business expenditures and consolidate provisions for start-up and organizational expenditures	....	490	484	477	473	471	469	465	461	456	452	2,395	4,698
Expand and simplify the tax credit provided to qualified small employers for non-elective contributions to employee health insurance[12]	10	170	163	146	131	100	118	80	60	27	14	710	1,009

Table S–9. Mandatory and Receipt Proposals—Continued

(Deficit increases (+) or decreases (–) in millions of dollars)

	2016	2017	2018	2019	2020	2021	2022	2023	2024	2025	2026	Totals 2017–2021	Totals 2017–2026
Total, simplification and tax relief for small business	10	9,009	8,384	5,514	4,204	3,720	3,464	3,278	3,301	3,293	3,308	30,831	47,475
Incentives for job creation, manufacturing, research, and clean energy:													
Enhance and simplify research incentives	....	959	1,896	2,154	2,409	2,660	2,913	3,166	3,426	3,690	3,964	10,078	27,237
Extend and modify certain employment tax credits, including incentives for hiring veterans	....	2	7	9	511	1,062	1,194	1,308	1,406	1,492	1,573	1,591	8,564
Provide new Manufacturing Communities tax credit	....	97	277	483	619	693	751	788	677	417	107	2,169	4,909
Provide Community College Partnership Tax Credit	....	109	277	380	406	405	273	124	96	79	64	1,577	2,213
Designate Promise Zones [12]	....	301	610	681	829	902	836	786	752	730	723	3,323	7,150
Modify and permanently extend renewable electricity production tax credit and investment tax credit [12]	....	122	230	345	587	1,041	1,359	1,633	3,990	6,549	8,287	2,325	24,143
Modify and permanently extend the deduction for energy-efficient commercial building property	....	159	268	281	285	283	279	277	273	270	272	1,276	2,647
Provide a carbon dioxide investment and sequestration tax credit [12]	....	9	34	47	48	388	709	409	791	677	338	526	3,450
Provide additional tax credits for investment in qualified property used in a qualifying advanced energy manufacturing project	....	74	194	1,118	787	111	4	–34	–28	–14	–3	2,284	2,209
Extend the tax credit for second generation biofuel production	....	87	157	172	175	175	175	153	118	83	48	766	1,343
Provide a tax credit for the production of advanced technology vehicles	....	505	503	497	469	386	220	83	–161	–296	–267	2,360	1,939
Provide a tax credit for medium- and heavy-duty alternative-fuel commercial vehicles	....	44	78	85	89	93	61	15	....	....	....	389	465
Modify and extend the tax credit for the construction of energy-efficient new homes	....	82	182	238	268	288	306	323	351	382	405	1,058	2,825
Total, incentives for job creation, manufacturing, research, and clean energy	....	2,550	4,713	6,490	7,482	8,487	9,080	9,031	11,691	14,059	15,511	29,722	89,094
Incentives to promote regional growth:													
Modify and permanently extend the New Markets tax credit	....	....	....	....	97	278	483	716	970	1,235	1,505	375	5,284
Reform and expand the Low-Income Housing tax credit	1	19	99	272	512	769	1,031	1,300	1,576	1,860	2,152	1,671	9,590
Total, incentives to promote regional growth	1	19	99	272	609	1,047	1,514	2,016	2,546	3,095	3,657	2,046	14,874
Incentives for investment in infrastructure: Provide America Fast Forward Bonds and expand eligible uses [12]	....	....	....	....	–1	1	....	....	–1	....	....	*	–1

Table S–9. Mandatory and Receipt Proposals—Continued

(Deficit increases (+) or decreases (−) in millions of dollars)

	2016	2017	2018	2019	2020	2021	2022	2023	2024	2025	2026	Totals 2017–2021	Totals 2017–2026
Allow eligible uses of America Fast Forward Bonds to include financing all qualified private activity bond program categories [12]	....	1	4	10	15	20	26	32	38	44	48	50	238
Allow current refundings of State and local governmental bonds	....	1	5	5	5	5	5	5	5	5	5	21	46
Repeal the $150 million non-hospital bond limitation on all qualified 501(c)(3) bonds	....	....	1	3	5	7	9	11	13	16	17	16	82
Increase national limitation amount for qualified highway or surface freight transfer facility bonds	6	28	60	93	125	153	167	163	136	96	55	459	1,076
Provide a new category of qualified private activity bonds for infrastructure projects referred to as "qualified public infrastructure bonds"	....	27	121	258	397	534	646	698	714	728	741	1,337	4,864
Modify qualified private activity bonds for public education facilities	....	....	....	....	....	....	....	....	....	....	....	....	....
Modify treatment of banks investing in tax-exempt bonds	....	5	38	131	225	317	405	493	574	630	616	716	3,434
Repeal tax-exempt bond financing of professional sports facilities	....	–3	–11	–23	–35	–47	–60	–72	–85	–97	–109	–119	–542
Allow more flexible research arrangements for purposes of private business use limits	....	....	....	....	1	1	1	3	3	3	4	2	16
Modify tax-exempt bonds for Indian tribal governments	....	4	12	12	12	12	12	12	12	12	12	52	112
Total, incentives for investment in infrastructure	6	63	230	489	749	1,003	1,211	1,345	1,409	1,437	1,389	2,534	9,325
Eliminate fossil fuel tax preferences:													
Treat publicly-traded partnerships for fossil fuels as C corporations	....	....	....	....	....	....	–201	–280	–295	–309	–323	....	–1,408
Eliminate oil and natural gas preferences:													
Repeal enhanced oil recovery credit	....	–235	–559	–792	–979	–1,070	–1,049	–1,011	–1,010	–1,038	–1,060	–3,635	–8,803
Repeal credit for oil and natural gas produced from marginal wells	....	....	....	....	....	....	....	....	....	....	....	....	....
Repeal expensing of intangible drilling costs	....	–966	–1,541	–1,439	–1,645	–1,526	–1,100	–733	–472	–340	–288	–7,117	–10,050
Repeal deduction for tertiary injectants	....	–5	–8	–8	–8	–8	–8	–8	–8	–8	–8	–37	–77
Repeal exception to passive loss limitations for working interests in oil and natural gas properties	....	–9	–12	–12	–12	–11	–10	–10	–9	–9	–9	–56	–103
Repeal percentage depletion for oil and natural gas wells	....	–483	–770	–725	–666	–589	–509	–429	–350	–270	–199	–3,233	–4,990
Repeal domestic manufacturing deduction for oil and natural gas production	....	–470	–836	–869	–901	–932	–962	–993	–1,026	–1,062	–1,098	–4,008	–9,149

Table S–9. Mandatory and Receipt Proposals—Continued

(Deficit increases (+) or decreases (−) in millions of dollars)

	2016	2017	2018	2019	2020	2021	2022	2023	2024	2025	2026	Totals 2017-2021	Totals 2017-2026
Increase geological and geophysical amortization period for independent producers to seven years	....	−54	−197	−307	−296	−235	−170	−103	−58	−47	−48	−1,089	−1,515
Subtotal, eliminate oil and natural gas preferences	....	−2,222	−3,923	−4,152	−4,507	−4,371	−3,808	−3,287	−2,933	−2,774	−2,710	−19,175	−34,687
Eliminate coal preferences:													
Repeal expensing of exploration and development costs	....	−20	−35	−35	−33	−32	−30	−27	−25	−24	−24	−155	−285
Repeal percentage depletion for hard mineral fuels	....	−113	−183	−177	−145	−114	−99	−87	−75	−66	−62	−732	−1,121
Repeal capital gains treatment for royalties	....	−26	−52	−52	−52	−52	−52	−52	−52	−52	−52	−234	−494
Repeal domestic manufacturing deduction for the production of coal and other hard mineral fossil fuels	....	−11	−20	−21	−22	−23	−24	−25	−26	−27	−28	−97	−227
Subtotal, eliminate coal preferences	....	−170	−290	−285	−252	−221	−205	−191	−178	−169	−166	−1,218	−2,127
Total, eliminate fossil fuel tax preferences	....	−2,392	−4,213	−4,437	−4,759	−4,592	−4,214	−3,758	−3,406	−3,252	−3,199	−20,393	−38,222
Reform the treatment of financial and insurance industry products:													
Require that derivative contracts be marked to market with resulting gain or loss treated as ordinary	....	−3,674	−5,415	−4,347	−2,743	−1,665	−1,124	−679	−466	−434	−405	−17,844	−20,952
Modify rules that apply to sales of life insurance contracts	....	−26	−44	−46	−48	−50	−54	−56	−58	−61	−63	−214	−506
Modify proration rules for life insurance company general and separate accounts	....	−345	−527	−534	−551	−579	−609	−628	−642	−658	−681	−2,536	−5,754
Expand pro rata interest expense disallowance for corporate-owned life insurance	....	−116	−232	−337	−457	−597	−753	−910	−1,075	−1,245	−1,422	−1,739	−7,144
Conform net operating loss (NOL) rules of life insurance companies to those of other corporations	....	−18	−28	−30	−31	−33	−35	−36	−38	−39	−41	−140	−329
Total, reform the treatment of financial and insurance industry products	....	−4,179	−6,246	−5,294	−3,830	−2,924	−2,575	−2,309	−2,279	−2,437	−2,612	−22,473	−34,685
Other business revenue changes and loop-hole closers:													
Repeal LIFO method of accounting for inventories	....	−5,369	−7,647	−8,307	−8,394	−8,611	−8,082	−8,032	−8,455	−9,475	−8,963	−38,328	−81,335
Repeal lower-of-cost-or-market inventory accounting method	....	−878	−1,321	−1,381	−1,390	−521	−240	−250	−260	−271	−283	−5,491	−6,795
Modify like-kind exchange rules	....	−2,684	−7,828	−6,889	−5,903	−4,870	−3,986	−3,668	−3,748	−3,831	−3,916	−28,174	−47,323
Modify depreciation rules for purchases of general aviation passenger aircraft	....	−48	−159	−260	−345	−460	−511	−434	−346	−286	−208	−1,272	−3,057
Expand the definition of substantial built-in loss for purposes of partnership loss transfers	....	−7	−8	−8	−8	−9	−9	−10	−10	−10	−10	−40	−89
Extend partnership basis limitation rules to nondeductible expenditures	....	−89	−122	−126	−129	−132	−134	−136	−139	−141	−144	−598	−1,292

Table S–9. Mandatory and Receipt Proposals—Continued

(Deficit increases (+) or decreases (−) in millions of dollars)

												Totals	
	2016	2017	2018	2019	2020	2021	2022	2023	2024	2025	2026	2017–2021	2017–2026
Deny deduction for punitive damages	......	−48	−70	−72	−73	−76	−77	−79	−80	−82	−84	−339	−741
Conform corporate ownership standards	......	−1	−16	−31	−32	−33	−34	−35	−36	−38	−40	−113	−296
Tax corporate distributions as dividends	......	−48	−82	−87	−91	−95	−99	−104	−109	−114	−119	−403	−948
Repeal FICA tip credit	......	−729	−883	−921	−961	−1,004	−1,047	−1,092	−1,140	−1,189	−1,241	−4,498	−10,207
Repeal the excise tax credit for distilled spirits with flavor and wine additives [13]	......	−82	−109	−109	−109	−109	−109	−109	−109	−109	−109	−518	−1,063
Total, other revenue changes and loophole closers		−9,983	−18,245	−18,191	−17,435	−15,920	−14,328	−13,949	−14,432	−15,546	−15,117	−79,774	−153,146
Total, elements of business tax reform	17	−33,438	−61,418	−59,832	−55,925	−54,543	−54,969	−56,357	−56,225	−57,647	−58,959	−265,156	−549,313
Transition to a reformed business tax system:													
Impose a 14-percent one-time tax on previously untaxed foreign income	......	−35,930	−59,883	−59,883	−59,883	−59,883	−23,953	......	......	......	......	−275,462	−299,415
Middle-class and pro-work tax reforms:													
Reform child care tax incentives [12]	......	684	3,539	3,720	3,909	4,081	4,277	4,459	4,652	5,009	5,492	15,933	39,822
Simplify and better target tax benefits for education [12]	......	19	4,518	4,622	4,561	5,089	5,375	5,778	6,090	6,465	6,272	18,809	48,789
Expand the EITC for workers without qualifying children [12]	......	468	6,255	6,387	6,495	6,628	6,756	6,894	7,028	7,176	7,322	26,233	61,409
Simplify the rules for claiming the EITC for workers without qualifying children [12]	......	41	550	540	547	560	572	587	601	615	629	2,238	5,242
Provide a second-earner tax credit [12]	......	2,037	8,926	9,065	9,160	9,281	9,429	9,563	9,703	9,841	10,016	38,469	87,021
Extend exclusion from income for cancellation of certain home mortgage debt	......	2,467	822	......	......	......	......	......	......	......	......	3,289	3,289
Total, middle-class and pro-work tax reforms	......	5,716	24,610	24,334	24,672	25,639	26,409	27,281	28,074	29,106	29,731	104,971	245,572
Reforms to retirement and health benefit plans:													
Provide for automatic enrollment in IRAs, including a small employer tax credit, increase the tax credit for small employer plan start-up costs, and provide an additional tax credit for small employer plans newly offering auto-enrollment [12]	......	......	959	1,556	1,672	1,722	1,779	1,885	1,989	2,119	2,221	5,909	15,902
Expand penalty-free withdrawals for long-term unemployed	......	226	231	235	240	245	250	255	260	265	270	1,177	2,477
Require retirement plans to allow long-term part-time workers to participate	......	46	47	49	50	51	52	53	55	56	57	243	516
Facilitate annuity portability	......	......	......	......	......	......	......	......	......	......	......		
Simplify minimum required distribution rules	......	......	......	......	......	......	......	......	......	......	......		
Allow all inherited plan and IRA balances to be rolled over within 60 days	......	5	6	2	−4	−19	−37	−61	−91	−127	−172	−10	−498
Permit unaffiliated employers to maintain a single multi-employer defined contribution plan	......	97	137	147	155	169	181	196	209	230	246	705	1,767
Improve the excise tax on high cost employer-sponsored health coverage	......	......	......	......	66	112	138	172	209	254	314	178	1,265

Table S–9. Mandatory and Receipt Proposals—Continued

(Deficit increases (+) or decreases (–) in millions of dollars)

	2016	2017	2018	2019	2020	2021	2022	2023	2024	2025	2026	Totals 2017–2021	Totals 2017–2026
Total, reforms to retirement and health benefit plans	....	374	1,380	1,989	2,179	2,280	2,363	2,500	2,631	2,797	2,936	8,202	21,429
Reforms to capital gains taxation, upper-income tax benefits, and the taxation of financial institutions:													
Reduce the value of certain tax expenditures	....	–31,092	–50,403	–54,946	–59,515	–63,910	–68,322	–72,776	–77,183	–81,525	–85,866	–259,866	–645,538
Reform the taxation of capital income	....	–14,757	–24,669	–20,639	–22,015	–23,211	–23,426	–24,696	–25,976	–27,254	–28,565	–105,291	–235,208
Implement the Buffett Rule by imposing a new "Fair Share Tax"	....	–7,848	62	–1,317	–3,102	–4,035	–4,136	–4,170	–4,240	–4,334	–4,388	–16,240	–37,508
Impose a financial fee	....	–5,653	–11,084	–10,949	–11,163	–11,420	–11,683	–11,952	–12,226	–12,508	–12,795	–50,269	–111,433
Total, reforms to capital gains taxation, upper-income tax benefits, and the taxation of financial institutions	....	–59,350	–86,094	–87,851	–95,795	–102,576	–107,567	–113,594	–119,625	–125,621	–131,614	–431,666	–1,029,687
Loophole closers:													
Require current inclusion in income of accrued market discount and limit the accrual amount for distressed debt	....	–4	–12	–20	–28	–34	–42	–50	–58	–69	–79	–98	–396
Require that the cost basis of stock that is a covered security must be determined using an average cost basis method	....	....	–74	–223	–377	–539	–634	–657	–684	–713	–744	–1,213	–4,645
Tax carried (profits) interests as ordinary income	....	–2,619	–2,633	–2,520	–2,420	–2,351	–1,932	–1,472	–1,213	–1,121	–1,029	–12,543	–19,310
Require non-spouse beneficiaries of deceased IRA owners and retirement plan participants to take inherited distributions over no more than five years	....	–111	–285	–471	–660	–853	–891	–841	–780	–718	–654	–2,380	–6,264
Limit the total accrual of tax-favored retirement benefits	....	–1,616	–2,302	–2,406	–2,639	–2,947	–3,084	–3,465	–3,606	–3,828	–4,085	–11,910	–29,978
Rationalize Net Investment Income and SECA taxes	....	–16,660	–23,276	–24,773	–25,913	–26,943	–28,124	–29,421	–30,816	–32,163	–33,570	–117,565	–271,659
Limit Roth conversions to pre-tax dollars	....	....	–5	–10	–16	–20	–20	–21	–28	–32	–99	–51	–251
Eliminate deduction for dividends on stock of publicly-traded corporations held in ESOPs	....	–702	–945	–962	–978	–995	–1,011	–1,028	–1,044	–1,062	–1,079	–4,582	–9,806
Repeal exclusion of net unrealized appreciation in employer securities	....	–16	–27	–28	–13	–4	–4	12	23	23	24	–88	–10
Disallow the deduction for charitable contributions that are a prerequisite for purchasing tickets to college sporting events	....	–150	–237	–255	–272	–290	–308	–327	–348	–369	–391	–1,204	–2,947
Total, loophole closers	....	–21,878	–29,796	–31,668	–33,316	–34,976	–36,050	–37,270	–38,554	–40,052	–41,706	–151,634	–345,266
Modify estate and gift tax provisions:													
Restore the estate, gift, and generation-skipping transfer (GST) tax parameters in effect in 2009	....	....	–15,717	–17,102	–18,415	–20,027	–21,695	–23,660	–25,815	–28,303	–31,020	–71,261	–201,754
Expand requirement of consistency in value for transfer and income tax purposes	....	....	–142	–143	–169	–174	–185	–198	–211	–228	–243	–628	–1,693

Table S–9. Mandatory and Receipt Proposals—Continued

(Deficit increases (+) or decreases (−) in millions of dollars)

												Totals	
	2016	2017	2018	2019	2020	2021	2022	2023	2024	2025	2026	2017–2021	2017–2026
Modify transfer tax rules for grantor retained annuity trusts (GRATs) and other grantor trusts	....	....	−1,123	−1,241	−1,478	−1,622	−1,969	−2,374	−2,743	−3,194	−3,405	−5,464	−19,149
Limit duration of GST tax exemption	....	....	....	....	....	....	....	....	....	....	....	....	....
Extend the lien on estate tax deferrals where estate consists largely of interest in closely held business	....	....	....	....	....	....	....	....	....	....	....	....	....
Modify GST tax treatment of Health and Education Exclusion Trusts	....	....	−24	−25	−26	−27	−28	−29	−31	−34	−36	−102	−260
Simplify gift tax exclusion for annual gifts	....	....	35	33	30	29	27	26	24	23	20	127	247
Expand applicability of definition of executor	....	....	−84	−160	−259	−336	−413	−453	−548	−657	−770	−839	−3,680
Total, modify estate and gift tax provisions	....	....	−17,055	−18,638	−20,317	−22,157	−24,263	−26,688	−29,324	−32,393	−35,454	−78,167	−226,289
Other revenue raisers:													
Impose an oil fee [13]	....	−7,221	−14,439	−21,505	−28,450	−35,135	−41,377	−41,989	−42,521	−42,977	−43,456	−106,750	−319,070
Increase and modify Oil Spill Liability Trust Fund financing [13]	....	−94	−133	−135	−138	−138	−139	−141	−143	−144	−147	−638	−1,352
Reinstate Superfund taxes [13]	....	−1,596	−2,087	−2,163	−2,202	−2,276	−2,300	−2,359	−2,445	−2,445	−2,492	−10,324	−22,319
Increase tobacco taxes and index for inflation [13]	....	−9,982	−12,910	−12,715	−12,719	−12,329	−11,880	−11,436	−10,877	−10,399	−9,902	−60,655	−115,149
Make unemployment insurance surtax permanent [13]	....	−1,172	−1,604	−1,624	−1,645	−1,667	−1,690	−1,712	−1,737	−1,762	−1,789	−7,712	−16,402
Total, other revenue raisers	....	−20,065	−31,173	−38,142	−45,154	−51,545	−57,386	−57,637	−57,677	−57,727	−57,786	−186,079	−474,292
Reduce the tax gap and make reforms:													
Expand information reporting:													
Improve information reporting for certain businesses and contractors	....	−15	−36	−60	−82	−85	−89	−93	−97	−102	−106	−278	−765
Provide an exception to the limitation on disclosing tax return information to expand TIN matching beyond forms where payments are subject to backup withholding	....	....	....	....	....	....	....	....	....	....	....	....	....
Provide for reciprocal reporting of information in connection with the implementation of FATCA	....	....	....	....	....	....	....	....	....	....	....	....	....
Require Form W–2 reporting for employer contributions to defined contribution plans	....	....	....	....	....	....	....	....	....	....	....	....	....
Improve compliance by businesses:													
Increase certainty with respect to worker classification	−5	−93	−451	−871	−1,038	−1,127	−1,220	−1,321	−1,428	−1,544	−1,668	−3,580	−10,761
Increase information sharing to administer excise taxes [13]	....	−4	−9	−13	−14	−16	−17	−17	−18	−18	−19	−56	−145
Provide authority to readily share information about beneficial ownership information of U.S. companies with law enforcement	....	....	−1	−2	−9	−6	−4	−3	−3	−3	−3	−18	−34
Strengthen tax administration:													

Table S–9. Mandatory and Receipt Proposals—Continued

(Deficit increases (+) or decreases (−) in millions of dollars)

	2016	2017	2018	2019	2020	2021	2022	2023	2024	2025	2026	Totals 2017–2021	Totals 2017–2026
Modify the conservation easement deduction and pilot a conservation credit	....	−6	−22	−46	−63	−72	−79	−83	−89	−94	−101	−209	−655
Impose liability on shareholders to collect unpaid income taxes of applicable corporations	....	−395	−423	−442	−461	−481	−502	−524	−546	−570	−595	−2,202	−4,939
Revise offer-in-compromise application rules	....	−1	−2	−2	−2	−2	−2	−2	−2	−2	−2	−9	−19
Make repeated willful failure to file a tax return a felony	....	....	....	....	−1	−1	−1	−1	−2	−2	−2	−2	−10
Facilitate tax compliance with local jurisdictions	....	−1	−1	−1	−2	−2	−2	−2	−2	−2	−2	−7	−17
Improve investigative disclosure statute	....	−1	....	....	....	−1	−1	−1	−2	−2	−2	−2	−10
Allow the IRS to absorb credit and debit card processing fees for certain tax payments	....	−2	−2	−2	−2	−2	−2	−2	−2	−2	−2	−10	−20
Provide the IRS with greater flexibility to address correctable errors [12]	....	−31	−62	−62	−63	−65	−66	−68	−70	−72	−74	−283	−633
Enhance electronic filing of returns	....	....	....	....	....	....	....	....	....	....	....	....	−10
Improve the whistleblower program	....	....	....	....	....	....	....	....	....	....	....	....	....
Index all civil tax penalties for inflation	....	....	....	....	....	....	....	....	....	....	....	....	....
Combat tax-related identity theft	....	....	....	....	....	....	....	....	....	....	....	....	....
Allow States to send notices of intent to collect State tax refunds to offset Federal tax obligations by regular first-class mail instead of certified mail	....	....	....	....	....	....	....	....	....	....	....	....	....
Accelerate information return filing due dates [12]	....	−3	−5	−11	−12	−12	−13	−13	−13	−13	−14	−43	−109
Increase oversight of tax return preparers [12]	....	−14	−31	−34	−37	−41	−45	−49	−54	−57	−62	−157	−424
Enhance administrability of the appraiser penalty	....	....	....	....	....	....	....	....	....	....	....	....	....
Request a program integrity cap adjustment for the reemployment services and eligibility assessment (RESEA) program [13]	....	....	2	7	10	11	10	9	9	7	5	30	70
Total, reduce the tax gap and make reforms	−5	−565	−1,043	−1,539	−1,778	−1,903	−2,034	−2,171	−2,321	−2,478	−2,649	−6,828	−18,481
Simplify the tax system:													
Modify adoption credit to allow tribal determination of special needs	....	....	....	....	1	1	1	1	1	1	1	2	7
Repeal non-qualified preferred stock designation	....	−33	−55	−55	−53	−50	−46	−41	−36	−32	−29	−246	−430
Reform excise tax based on investment income of private foundations	....	5	5	6	6	6	6	6	7	7	7	28	61
Simplify arbitrage investment restrictions	....	....	2	10	18	28	38	46	58	68	76	58	344
Simplify single-family housing mortgage bond targeting requirements	....	....	1	3	5	7	10	12	17	20	22	16	97

Table S–9. Mandatory and Receipt Proposals—Continued

(Deficit increases (+) or decreases (–) in millions of dollars)

	2016	2017	2018	2019	2020	2021	2022	2023	2024	2025	2026	Totals 2017–2021	Totals 2017–2026
Streamline private activity limits on governmental bonds	......	......	1	3	5	7	9	11	13	15	17	16	81
Repeal technical terminations of partnerships	......	–13	–19	–21	–23	–25	–27	–29	–30	–32	–33	–101	–252
Repeal anti-churning rules of section 197	......	24	99	198	281	338	370	378	378	378	378	940	2,822
Repeal special estimated tax payment provision for certain insurance companies	......	......	......	......	......	......	......	......	......	......	......	......	......
Repeal the telephone excise tax [3]	......	368	327	287	248	209	170	132	94	57	44	1,439	1,936
Increase the standard mileage rate for automobile use by volunteers	......	20	62	65	68	69	71	72	74	76	79	284	656
Consolidate contribution limitations for charitable deductions and extend the carryforward period for excess charitable contribution deduction amounts	......	......	93	51	6	6	6	491	1,188	1,830	2,416	156	6,087
Exclude from gross income subsidies from public utilities for purchase of water run-off management	......	......	......	......	......	......	......	......	......	......	......	......	......
Provide relief for certain accidental dual citizens	......	63	108	58	23	25	26	28	29	30	32	277	422
Total, simplify the tax system	......	434	624	605	585	621	634	1,107	1,793	2,418	3,010	2,869	11,831
Trade initiatives:													
Enact the Trans-Pacific Partnership Trade Agreement [3]	......	......	1,690	2,343	2,586	2,858	3,147	3,445	3,724	4,003	4,318	9,477	28,114
Other initiatives:													
Allow offset of Federal income tax refunds to collect delinquent State income taxes for out-of-State residents	......	......	......	......	......	......	......	......	......	......	......	......	......
Improve disclosure for child support enforcement	......	......	......	......	......	......	......	......	......	......	......	......	......
Authorize the limited sharing of business tax return information to improve the accuracy of important measures of the economy	......	......	......	......	......	......	......	......	......	......	......	......	......
Eliminate certain reviews conducted by the U.S. Treasury Inspector General for Tax Administration (TIGTA)	......	......	......	......	......	......	......	......	......	......	......	......	......
Modify indexing to prevent deflationary adjustments	......	......	......	......	......	......	......	......	......	......	......	......	......
Total, other initiatives	......	......	......	......	......	......	......	......	......	......	......	......	......
Total, tax proposals	12	–164,702	–258,158	–268,282	–282,146	–296,185	–273,669	–259,384	–267,504	–277,594	–288,173	–1,269,473	–2,635,797
Grand total, mandatory and receipt proposals	–613	–135,225	–223,552	–240,506	–265,912	–293,382	–280,795	–282,067	–300,451	–321,905	–354,237	–1,158,577	–2,698,032

Note: For receipt effects, positive figures indicate lower receipts. For outlay effects, positive figures indicate higher outlays. For net costs, positive figures indicate higher deficits.

[1] Based on placeholder credit subsidy rate. Actual approvals would be evaluated and estimated for each fund application individually.

[2] In the Fall of 2015, the President took action within his existing authority to implement eligibility expansions to income-based repayment plans proposed in the 2015 Budget. However, the Administration continues to seek to work with the Congress to create a unified, simple, and better targeted PAYE program.

[3] The estimates for this proposal include effects on receipts. The receipt effects included in the totals above are as follows:

Table S–9. Mandatory and Receipt Proposals—Continued

(Deficit increases (+) or decreases (–) in millions of dollars)

	2016	2017	2018	2019	2020	2021	2022	2023	2024	2025	2026	Totals 2017–2021	Totals 2017–2026
Reauthorize special assessment from domestic nuclear utilities	....	–208	–212	–217	–222	–227	–232	–237	–243	–248	–254	–1,086	–2,300
Create State option to provide 12-month continuous Medicaid eligibility for adults	....	....	–37	–77	–158	–165	–174	–181	–191	–200	–209	–437	–1,392
Extend CHIP funding through 2019	....	....	–66	–454	–528	....	....	....	....	....	....	–1,048	–1,048
Establish user fee for Electronic Visa Update System	....	–31	–25	–27	–31	–27	–31	–29	–34	–24	–28	–141	–287
Establish an AML hardrock reclamation fund	....	....	–200	–200	–200	–200	–200	–200	–200	–200	–200	–800	–1,800
Increase coal AML fee to pre–2006 levels	....	–49	–50	–52	–53	–54	....	....	....	....	....	–258	–258
Strengthen Unemployment Insurance (UI) system solvency	....	....	–3,128	–3,185	–3,922	–4,303	–5,425	–6,802	–6,068	–6,346	–7,114	–14,538	–46,293
Modernize UI	....	....	....	–514	–468	–415	–429	–410	–560	–585	–604	–1,397	–3,985
Improve UI program integrity	....	....	1	7	16	29	43	60	96	61	99	53	412
Implement cap adjustments for UI program integrity	....	....	2	8	13	14	13	11	10	8	6	37	85
Create mandatory Reemployment Services and Eligibility Assessment program	....	....	....	4	24	65	168	195	216	267	293	93	1,232
Implement tax enforcement program integrity cap adjustment	....	–278	–1,585	–3,263	–5,008	–6,763	–8,327	–9,264	–9,590	–9,737	–9,814	–16,897	–63,629
Reform inland waterways financing	....	–3	–78	–118	–156	–156	–156	–156	–156	–155	–155	–511	–1,289
Enact changes to the military retirement reform enacted in the 2016 National Defense Authorization Act	....	....	53	85	94	110	126	144	154	169	180	342	1,115
Enact immigration reform	....	–1,000	–7,000	–20,000	–30,000	–40,000	–45,000	–55,000	–64,000	–74,000	–84,000	–98,000	–420,000
Total receipt effects of mandatory proposals	....	–1,569	–12,325	–28,003	–40,599	–52,092	–59,624	–71,869	–80,566	–90,990	–101,800	–134,588	–539,437

[4] Makes assumptions regarding the timing and magnitudes of future droughts in the SWPA region.
[5] Health savings in Table S–2 includes all HHS health savings and OPM FEHBP savings.
[6] Authorization expires in 2025.
[7] Unemployment insurance reform also includes the proposal to make the unemployment insurance surtax permanent. On net, the package increases the deficit by $1.1 billion over 10 years.
[8] Revenues are net of the 20 percent Treasury offset.
[9] This proposal also saves less than $500,000 in SSI over 10 years.
[10] This proposals costs less than $500,000 in each year and over five and 10 years.
[11] Savings of $1 million over five years and $4 million over 10 years.
[12] The estimates for this proposal include effects on outlays. The outlay effects included in the totals above are as follows:

	2016	2017	2018	2019	2020	2021	2022	2023	2024	2025	2026	Totals 2017–2021	Totals 2017–2026
Expand and simplify the tax credit provided to qualified small employers for non-elective contributions to employee health insurance	....	21	23	19	17	12	14	10	7	4	2	92	129
Designate Promise Zones	....	27	29	29	31	31	33	35	37	37	39	147	328
Modify and permanently extend renewable electricity production tax credit and investment tax credit	....	58	155	281	453	695	973	1,300	1,695	2,117	2,629	1,642	10,356

Table S–9. Mandatory and Receipt Proposals—Continued

(Deficit increases (+) or decreases (−) in millions of dollars)

	2016	2017	2018	2019	2020	2021	2022	2023	2024	2025	2026	Totals 2017–2021	Totals 2017–2026
Provide a carbon dioxide investment and sequestration tax credit	....	....	....	....	....	142	280	123	338	226	....	142	1,109
Provide America Fast Forward Bonds and expand eligible uses	....	239	1,085	2,328	3,635	5,002	6,407	7,836	9,282	10,743	12,217	12,289	58,774
Allow eligible uses of America Fast Forward Bonds to include financing all qualified private activity bond program categories	....	49	221	475	742	1,020	1,307	1,599	1,894	2,192	2,492	2,507	11,991
Reform child care tax incentives	....	....	962	1,009	1,051	1,091	1,147	1,182	1,227	1,264	1,268	4,113	10,201
Simplify and better target tax benefits for education	....	....	4,377	4,521	4,479	4,663	5,079	5,255	5,679	5,870	5,833	18,040	45,756
Expand the EITC for workers without qualifying children	....	273	5,468	5,577	5,677	5,796	5,906	6,020	6,134	6,262	6,383	22,791	53,496
Simplify the rules for claiming the EITC for workers without qualifying children	....	24	484	475	481	492	503	516	528	541	553	1,956	4,597
Provide a second-earner tax credit	....	....	739	735	735	740	754	758	760	759	754	2,949	6,734
Provide for automatic enrollment in IRAs, including a small employer tax credit, increase the tax credit for small employer plan start-up costs, and provide an additional tax credit for small employer plans newly offering auto-enrollment	....	....	126	198	203	207	215	222	228	230	236	734	1,865
Provide the IRS with greater flexibility to address correctable errors	....	−26	−53	−52	−53	−54	−55	−56	−58	−59	−61	−238	−527
Accelerate information return filing due dates	....	−1	−3	−6	−7	−7	−8	−8	−8	−8	−8	−24	−64
Increase oversight of tax return preparers	....	−2	−14	−15	−16	−18	−19	−21	−23	−24	−26	−65	−178
Total, outlay effects of receipt proposals	....	662	13,599	15,574	17,428	19,812	22,536	24,771	27,720	30,154	32,311	67,075	204,567

[13] Net of income offsets.

Table S-10. Funding Levels for Appropriated ("Discretionary") Programs by Category

(Budget authority in billions of dollars)

	Actual	Enacted	Request	Outyears									Totals	
	2015	2016	2017	2018	2019	2020	2021	2022	2023	2024	2025	2026	2017-2021	2017-2026
Discretionary Adjusted Baseline by Category:[1]														
Defense Category	521	548	551	549	562	576	590	660	676	692	709	727	2,828	6,292
Non-Defense Category	508	536	519	516	530	543	556	604	619	634	650	666	2,662	5,836
Total, Base Discretionary Funding	1,030	1,085	1,070	1,065	1,092	1,119	1,146	1,264	1,295	1,327	1,359	1,392	5,490	12,128
Discretionary Policy Changes to Baseline Caps:														
Proposed Cap Changes:[2]														
Defense Category	......	......	......	+35	+31	+23	+24	–36	–40	–44	–48	–53	+113	–108
Non-Defense Category	......	......	......	+36	+31	+23	+25	–14	–17	–20	–23	–26	+114	+14
Non-Defense Category Reclassifications:														
Surface Transportation Programs	–4	–4	–4	–4	–5	–5	–5	–5	–5	–5	–5	–5	–23	–48
Program Integrity	......	......	......	–*	–*	–*	–*	–*	–*	–*	–*	–*	–1	–2
Contract Support Costs	......	......	......	–1	–1	–1	–1	–1	–1	–1	–1	–1	–5	–11
Proposed Discretionary Policy by Category:														
Defense Category	521	548	551	584	593	599	614	624	636	648	661	674	2,941	6,184
Non-Defense Category	504	532	514	546	555	560	574	584	596	608	620	633	2,748	5,789
Total, Base Discretionary Funding	1,025	1,080	1,065	1,130	1,147	1,158	1,188	1,208	1,232	1,256	1,281	1,307	5,690	11,973
Discretionary Cap Adjustments and Other Funding (not included above):[3]														
Overseas Contingency Operations[4]	74	74	74	11	11	11	11	......	......	......	......	......	118	118
Disaster Relief	7	7	7	......	......	......	......	......	......	......	......	......	7	7
Program Integrity	1	2	3	3	3	3	4	4	4	4	4	4	16	37
Wildfire Suppression	......	......	1	1	1	1	1	1	1	1	1	1	6	13
Other Emergency/Supplemental Funding	5	*	......	......	......	......	......	......	......	......	......	......	.....	.....
Total, Cap Adjustments and Other	87	83	84	15	15	16	16	5	5	5	6	6	146	174
Grand Total, Discretionary Budget Authority	1,113	1,163	1,149	1,145	1,163	1,174	1,205	1,213	1,237	1,261	1,287	1,313	5,836	12,147

Memorandum: Current Law and Proposed Changes to Existing BBEDCA Caps[5]	2017	2018	2019	2020	2021	2018-2021
Joint Committee Reductions	N/A	–91	–90	–89	–88	–359
2017 Budget Proposed Addback to caps	N/A	+71	+61	+46	+49	+227

Table S–10. Funding Levels for Appropriated ("Discretionary") Programs by Category

(Budget authority in billions of dollars)

* $500 million or less.

[1] The discretionary funding levels from OMB's adjusted baseline are consistent with the caps in the Balanced Budget and Emergency Deficit Control Act of 1985 (BBEDCA) with separate categories of funding for "defense" (or Function 050) and "non-defense" for 2016–2021. These baseline levels assume Joint Committee enforcement cap reductions in effect through 2021. For 2022 through 2026, programs are assumed to grow at current services growth rates with Joint Committee enforcement no longer in effect, consistent with current law. The levels shown here for the non-defense category do not include the reclassification of surface transportation programs shown later in the table.

[2] The 2017 Budget provides a detailed request for 2017 at the cap levels enacted in the Bipartisan Budget Act of 2015 and, after 2017, continues the framework of previous President's Budgets by providing additional investments in both defense and non-defense programs above the baseline levels that include Joint Committee enforcement.

[3] Where applicable, amounts in 2015 through 2026 are existing or proposed cap adjustments designated pursuant to Section 251(b)(2) of BBEDCA. The 2017 Budget proposes new cap adjustments for program integrity and wildfire suppression activities. For 2018 through 2026, the cap adjustment levels for wildfire suppression are a placeholder that increase at the policy growth rates in the President's Budget. The existing disaster relief cap adjustment ceiling (which is determined one year at a time) would be reduced by the amount provided for wildfire suppression activities under the cap adjustment for the preceding fiscal year. The amounts will be refined in subsequent Budgets as data on the average costs for wildfire suppression are updated annually.

[4] The 2017 Budget includes placeholder amounts of nearly $11 billion per year for Government-wide OCO funding from 2018 to 2021. The placeholder amounts continue to reflect a total OCO budget authority cap from 2013 to 2021 of $450 billion, in line with previous years' policy, but do not reflect any specific decisions or assumptions about OCO funding in any particular year.

[5] Under Joint Committee enforcement, the current law defense and non-defense discretionary caps specified in BBEDCA are estimated to be reduced by a combined $359 billion over 2018 through 2021. The 2017 Budget proposes to restore more than three-fifths of those reductions.

Table S–11. Funding Levels for Appropriated ("Discretionary") Programs by Agency

(Budget authority in billions of dollars)

	Actual 2015	Enacted 2016	Request 2017	Outyears 2018	2019	2020	2021	2022	2023	2024	2025	2026	Totals 2017-2021	2017-2026
Base Discretionary Funding by Agency:[1]														
Agriculture	24.9	25.2	23.4	24.9	25.2	25.8	26.2	26.8	27.3	27.9	28.5	29.1	125.4	265.0
Commerce	8.6	9.4	9.7	10.1	11.4	15.7	10.4	10.2	10.4	10.6	11.1	11.4	57.3	111.0
Census Bureau	*1.1*	*1.4*	*1.6*	*1.8*	*2.9*	*7.1*	*1.6*	*1.2*	*1.3*	*1.3*	*1.5*	*1.7*	*15.1*	*22.1*
Defense[2]	496.1	521.7	523.9	556.7	564.8	570.4	585.2	597.2	609.4	621.9	634.7	647.7	2,801.1	5,912.1
Education	66.9	68.3	69.4	70.3	71.3	72.3	73.2	74.3	75.3	76.3	77.4	78.5	356.5	738.3
Energy	27.4	29.6	30.2	30.1	32.2	34.0	35.8	36.5	37.2	38.0	38.7	39.5	162.4	352.3
National Nuclear Security Administration[2]	*11.4*	*12.5*	*12.9*	*11.9*	*12.4*	*12.6*	*13.0*	*13.3*	*13.5*	*13.8*	*14.1*	*14.4*	*62.8*	*131.9*
Health & Human Services[3]	80.3	84.6	77.9	87.2	88.9	90.7	92.5	94.3	96.2	98.2	100.1	102.1	437.2	928.1
Homeland Security	39.9	41.1	40.6	41.8	42.5	43.3	44.0	44.9	45.8	46.7	47.6	48.5	212.2	445.7
Housing and Urban Development	30.4	37.5	38.0	39.0	39.7	40.5	41.2	42.0	42.7	43.5	44.3	45.1	198.4	416.0
Interior	12.2	13.2	12.9	13.0	13.2	13.5	13.7	14.0	14.3	14.6	14.9	15.2	66.3	139.3
Justice	26.3	28.7	18.1	30.0	30.6	31.2	31.8	32.4	33.1	33.7	34.4	35.1	141.6	310.4
Labor	11.9	12.2	12.8	12.8	13.1	13.3	13.5	13.7	14.0	14.2	14.5	14.7	65.4	136.6
State and Other International Programs	40.9	37.9	37.8	46.5	47.4	48.3	49.2	50.2	51.2	52.2	53.3	54.3	229.1	490.3
Transportation	13.8	14.3	12.0	14.7	15.0	15.3	15.6	15.9	16.2	16.6	16.9	17.2	72.6	155.5
Treasury	12.2	12.6	12.6	13.6	13.9	14.2	14.5	14.8	15.1	15.5	15.8	16.2	68.7	146.1
Veterans Affairs	65.1	71.6	75.1	78.5	79.4	81.0	82.6	84.3	86.0	87.7	89.4	91.2	396.7	835.2
Corps of Engineers	5.6	6.0	4.6	4.7	4.8	4.9	5.0	5.1	5.2	5.3	5.4	5.5	24.0	50.5
Environmental Protection Agency	8.1	8.1	8.3	8.4	8.6	8.8	8.9	9.1	9.3	9.5	9.7	9.9	43.0	90.5
General Services Administration	-0.4	0.6	0.4	0.4	0.4	0.4	0.4	0.4	0.4	0.4	0.4	0.4	1.9	4.0
National Aeronautics & Space Administration	18.0	19.3	18.3	18.6	19.0	19.4	19.8	20.2	20.6	21.0	21.4	21.8	95.0	200.0
National Science Foundation	7.3	7.5	7.6	8.1	8.3	8.5	8.6	8.8	9.0	9.1	9.3	9.5	41.0	86.8
Small Business Administration	0.9	0.9	0.7	0.7	0.7	0.8	0.8	0.8	0.8	0.8	0.8	0.9	3.7	7.8
Social Security Administration[3]	9.0	9.3	9.6	9.8	10.1	10.5	10.7	10.9	11.1	11.3	11.5	11.7	50.7	107.0
Corporation for National & Community Service	1.1	1.1	1.1	1.1	1.1	1.2	1.2	1.2	1.2	1.2	1.3	1.3	5.7	12.0
Other Agencies	18.9	19.5	20.3	20.5	21.2	21.9	22.7	23.2	23.6	24.1	24.5	25.0	106.6	227.0
Allowances[4]				-11.5	-15.4	-26.9	-19.1	-23.3	-23.9	-24.8	-24.6	-24.6	-73.0	-194.2
Subtotal, Base Discretionary Funding	**1,025.4**	**1,080.2**	**1,065.2**	**1,130.2**	**1,147.4**	**1,158.4**	**1,184.4**	**1,207.8**	**1,231.7**	**1,255.5**	**1,281.4**	**1,307.3**	**5,689.6**	**11,973.2**
Discretionary Cap Adjustments and Other Funding (not included above):[5]														
Overseas Contingency Operations	**73.7**	**73.7**	**73.7**	11.0	11.0	11.0	11.0						**117.6**	**117.6**
Defense	64.2	58.6	58.8										58.8	58.8
Homeland Security	0.2	0.2												
State and Other International Programs	9.3	14.9	14.9	11.0	11.0	11.0	11.0						14.9	14.9
Overseas Contingency Operations Outyears[6]													43.9	43.9

Table S–11. Funding Levels for Appropriated ("Discretionary") Programs by Agency—Continued

(Budget authority in billions of dollars)

	Actual 2015	Enacted 2016	Request 2017	Outyears									Totals	
				2018	2019	2020	2021	2022	2023	2024	2025	2026	2017-2021	2017-2026
Program Integrity	**1.5**	**1.5**	**2.5**	**2.8**	**3.2**	**3.5**	**3.8**	**4.0**	**4.1**	**4.2**	**4.3**	**4.4**	**15.8**	**36.7**
Health & Human Services	0.4	0.4	0.4	0.4	0.5	0.5	0.5	0.5	0.5	0.6	0.6	0.6	2.3	5.1
Labor	......	......	*	......	......	......	......	......	......	......	......	......	*	*
Treasury	......	......	0.5	0.9	1.3	1.7	2.0	2.1	2.2	2.2	2.2	2.2	6.5	17.4
SSA	1.1	1.2	1.5	1.5	1.4	1.3	1.3	1.3	1.4	1.4	1.5	1.5	7.0	14.2
Disaster Relief	**6.5**	**7.1**	**6.9**	......	......	......	......	......	......	......	......	......	**6.9**	**6.9**
Agriculture	0.1	0.1												
Homeland Security	6.4	6.7	6.7	......									6.7	6.7
Housing and Urban Development	......	0.3												
Small Business Administration	......	......	0.2	......									0.2	0.2
Wildfire Suppression [7]	......	......	**1.2**	**1.2**	**1.2**	**1.2**	**1.2**	**1.3**	**1.3**	**1.3**	**1.4**	**1.4**	**6.0**	**12.6**
Agriculture	......	......	0.9	0.9	0.9	0.9	0.9	1.0	1.0	1.0	1.0	1.0	4.5	9.5
Interior	......	......	0.3	0.3	0.3	0.3	0.3	0.3	0.3	0.3	0.3	0.3	1.5	3.2
Other Emergency Funding	**5.4**	**0.4**	......	......	......	......	......	......	......	......	......	......	......	......
Agriculture	......	0.3												
Defense	0.1	......												
Health & Human Services	2.8	......												
State and Other International Programs	2.5	0.1												
Grand Total, Discretionary Funding	**1,112.5**	**1,163.0**	**1,149.4**	**1,145.2**	**1,162.7**	**1,174.0**	**1,204.5**	**1,213.1**	**1,237.0**	**1,261.0**	**1,287.0**	**1,313.0**	**5,835.9**	**12,147.0**

* $50 million or less.

1 Amounts in the actual and enacted years of 2015 and 2016 exclude changes in mandatory programs enacted in appropriations bills since those amounts have been rebased as mandatory, whereas amounts in 2017 are net of these proposals.

2 The Department of Defense (DOD) levels in 2018–2026 include funding that will be allocated, in annual increments, to the National Nuclear Security Administration (NNSA). Current estimates by which DOD's budget authority will decrease and NNSA's will increase are, in millions of dollars: 2018: $1,665; 2019: $1,698; 2020: $1,735; 2021: $1,770; 2018–2026: $16,263. DOD and NNSA are reviewing NNSA's outyear requirements and these will be included in future reports to the Congress.

3 Funding from the Hospital Insurance and Supplementary Medical Insurance trust funds for administrative expenses incurred by the Social Security Administration that support the Medicare program are included in the Health and Human Services total and not in the Social Security Administration total.

4 The 2017 Budget includes allowances, similar to the Function 920 allowances used in Budget Resolutions, to represent amounts to be allocated among the respective agencies to reach the proposed defense and non-defense caps for 2018 and beyond. These levels are determined for illustrative purposes but do not reflect specific policy decisions.

5 Where applicable, amounts in 2015 through 2026 are existing or proposed cap adjustments designated pursuant to Section 251(b)(2) of BBEDCA.

6 The 2017 Budget includes placeholder amounts of nearly $11 billion per year for Government-wide OCO funding from 2018 to 2021. The placeholder amounts continue to reflect a total OCO budget authority cap from 2013 to 2021 of $450 billion, in line with previous years' policy, but do not reflect any specific decisions or assumptions about OCO funding in any particular year.

7 For 2018 through 2026, the cap adjustment levels are a placeholder that increase at the policy growth rates in the President's Budget. The existing disaster relief cap adjustment ceiling (which is determined one year at a time) would be reduced by the amount provided for wildfire suppression activities under the cap adjustment for the preceding fiscal year. Those amounts will be refined in subsequent Budgets as data on the average costs for wildfire suppression are updated annually.

Table S–12. Economic Assumptions [1]

(Calendar years)

	Actual 2014	2015	2016	2017	2018	2019	Projections 2020	2021	2022	2023	2024	2025	2026
Gross Domestic Product (GDP):													
Nominal level, billions of dollars	17,348	17,948	18,669	19,510	20,345	21,237	22,155	23,121	24,128	25,179	26,272	27,413	28,603
Percent change, nominal GDP, year/year	4.1	3.5	4.0	4.5	4.3	4.4	4.4	4.4	4.4	4.4	4.3	4.3	4.3
Real GDP, percent change, year/year	2.4	2.4	2.6	2.6	2.4	2.3	2.3	2.3	2.3	2.3	2.3	2.3	2.3
Real GDP, percent change, Q4/Q4	2.5	2.2	2.7	2.5	2.4	2.3	2.3	2.3	2.3	2.3	2.3	2.3	2.3
GDP chained price index, percent change, year/year	1.6	1.0	1.4	1.9	1.8	2.0	2.0	2.0	2.0	2.0	2.0	2.0	2.0
Consumer Price Index,[2] percent change, year/year	1.6	0.1	1.5	2.1	2.1	2.3	2.2	2.3	2.3	2.3	2.3	2.3	2.3
Interest rates, percent:[3]													
91-day Treasury bills [4]	*	*	0.7	1.8	2.6	3.1	3.3	3.4	3.4	3.3	3.3	3.2	3.2
10-year Treasury notes	2.5	2.1	2.9	3.5	3.9	4.1	4.2	4.2	4.2	4.2	4.2	4.2	4.2
Unemployment rate, civilian, percent [3]	6.2	5.3	4.7	4.5	4.6	4.6	4.7	4.7	4.8	4.9	4.9	4.9	4.9

* 0.05 percent or less.

Note: A more detailed table of economic assumptions appears in Chapter 2, "Economic Assumptions and Interactions with the Budget," in the *Analytical Perspectives* volume of the Budget.

[1] Based on information available as of mid-November 2015.
[2] Seasonally adjusted CPI for all urban consumers.
[3] Annual average.
[4] Average rate, secondary market (bank discount basis).

Table S–13. Federal Government Financing and Debt

(Dollar amounts in billions)

	Actual 2015	Estimate										
		2016	2017	2018	2019	2020	2021	2022	2023	2024	2025	2026
Financing:												
Unified budget deficit:												
Primary deficit (+)/surplus (−)	215	376	201	69	90	11	−22	39	9	−56	−3	6
Net interest	223	240	303	385	460	523	574	621	668	706	744	787
Unified budget deficit	438	616	503	454	549	534	552	660	677	650	741	793
As a percent of GDP	2.5%	3.3%	2.6%	2.3%	2.6%	2.4%	2.4%	2.8%	2.7%	2.5%	2.7%	2.8%
Other transactions affecting borrowing from the public:												
Changes in financial assets and liabilities:[1]												
Change in Treasury operating cash balance	40	76	......	......	......	......	......	......	......	......	......	......
Net disbursements of credit financing accounts:												
Direct loan accounts	79	104	129	109	112	103	103	102	104	108	110	110
Guaranteed loan accounts	9	13	3	−1	−2	−4	−6	−7	−3	−2	−2	4
Troubled Asset Relief Program (TARP) equity purchase accounts	−1	*	−*	−*	−*	−*	−*	−*	−*	−*	−*	−*
Net purchases of non-Federal securities by the National Railroad Retirement Investment Trust (NRRIT)	−1	*	−1	−1	−1	−1	−1	−1	−*	−*	−*	−*
Net change in other financial assets and liabilities[2]	−228	203	......	......	......	......	......	......	......	......	......	......
Subtotal, changes in financial assets and liabilities	−101	397	131	107	110	99	97	94	101	105	107	114
Seigniorage on coins	−1	−*	−*	−*	−*	−*	−*	−*	−*	−*	−*	−*
Total, other transactions affecting borrowing from the public	−102	396	131	107	109	99	96	93	100	104	107	113
Total, requirement to borrow from the public (equals change in debt held by the public)	337	1,012	634	560	659	633	649	753	777	755	848	906
Changes in Debt Subject to Statutory Limitation:												
Change in debt held by the public	337	1,012	634	560	659	633	649	753	777	755	848	906
Change in debt held by Government accounts	−11	301	82	175	152	119	103	48	56	84	13	−11
Change in other factors	6	−1	2	2	3	3	2	2	2	2	1	2
Total, change in debt subject to statutory limitation	332	1,313	718	736	814	754	754	803	835	840	862	897
Debt Subject to Statutory Limitation, End of Year:												
Debt issued by Treasury	18,094	19,407	20,123	20,858	21,671	22,423	23,175	23,977	24,811	25,651	26,512	27,408
Adjustment for discount, premium, and coverage[3]	19	19	21	22	23	25	26	27	28	29	29	30
Total, debt subject to statutory limitation[4]	18,113	19,426	20,143	20,880	21,694	22,448	23,201	24,004	24,839	25,680	26,542	27,438

Table S–13. Federal Government Financing and Debt—Continued

(Dollar amounts in billions)

	Actual 2015	Estimate										
		2016	2017	2018	2019	2020	2021	2022	2023	2024	2025	2026
Debt Outstanding, End of Year:												
Gross Federal debt:[5]												
Debt issued by Treasury	18,094	19,407	20,123	20,858	21,671	22,423	23,175	23,977	24,811	25,651	26,512	27,408
Debt issued by other agencies	26	27	27	26	25	24	23	22	21	20	19	17
Total, gross Federal debt	18,120	19,433	20,149	20,884	21,695	22,447	23,199	23,999	24,832	25,671	26,531	27,426
Held by:												
Debt held by Government accounts	5,003	5,305	5,386	5,561	5,713	5,832	5,935	5,983	6,039	6,123	6,136	6,124
Debt held by the public[6]	13,117	14,129	14,763	15,324	15,982	16,615	17,264	18,016	18,793	19,548	20,396	21,302
As a percent of GDP	73.7%	76.5%	76.5%	76.1%	76.1%	75.8%	75.5%	75.5%	75.4%	75.2%	75.2%	75.3%
Debt Held by the Public Net of Financial Assets:												
Debt held by the public	13,117	14,129	14,763	15,324	15,982	16,615	17,264	18,016	18,793	19,548	20,396	21,302
Less financial assets net of liabilities:												
Treasury operating cash balance	199	275	275	275	275	275	275	275	275	275	275	275
Credit financing account balances:												
Direct loan accounts	1,144	1,248	1,377	1,486	1,598	1,701	1,805	1,906	2,011	2,119	2,229	2,339
Guaranteed loan accounts	11	25	28	27	25	21	16	8	5	3	*	4
TARP equity purchase accounts	*	*	*	*	*	*	*	*	*	*	*	*
Government-sponsored enterprise preferred stock	106	106	106	106	106	106	106	106	106	106	106	106
Non-Federal securities held by NRRIT	24	24	23	22	22	21	20	20	19	19	18	18
Other assets net of liabilities	–250	–47	–47	–47	–47	–47	–47	–47	–47	–47	–47	–47
Total, financial assets net of liabilities	1,234	1,631	1,762	1,869	1,979	2,078	2,175	2,269	2,369	2,474	2,581	2,695
Debt held by the public net of financial assets	11,882	12,498	13,001	13,454	14,003	14,537	15,089	15,748	16,424	17,074	17,814	18,607
As a percent of GDP	66.7%	67.7%	67.4%	66.8%	66.6%	66.3%	66.0%	66.0%	65.9%	65.7%	65.7%	65.7%

* $500 million or less.

[1] A decrease in the Treasury operating cash balance (which is an asset) is a means of financing a deficit and therefore has a negative sign. An increase in checks outstanding (which is a liability) is also a means of financing a deficit and therefore also has a negative sign.

[2] Includes checks outstanding, accrued interest payable on Treasury debt, uninvested deposit fund balances, allocations of special drawing rights, and other liability accounts; and, as an offset, cash and monetary assets (other than the Treasury operating cash balance), other asset accounts, and profit on sale of gold.

[3] Consists mainly of debt issued by the Federal Financing Bank (which is not subject to limit), Treasury securities held by the Federal Financing Bank, the unamortized discount (less premium) on public issues of Treasury notes and bonds (other than zero-coupon bonds), and the unrealized discount on Government account series securities.

[4] Legislation enacted November 2, 2015 (P.L. 114–74), temporarily suspends the debt limit through March 15, 2017.

[5] Treasury securities held by the public and zero-coupon bonds held by Government accounts are almost all measured at sales price plus amortized discount or less amortized premium. Agency debt securities are almost all measured at face value. Treasury securities in the Government account series are otherwise measured at face value less unrealized discount (if any).

[6] At the end of 2015, the Federal Reserve Banks held $2,461.9 billion of Federal securities and the rest of the public held $10,654.8 billion. Debt held by the Federal Reserve Banks is not estimated for future years.

OMB CONTRIBUTORS TO THE 2017 BUDGET

The following personnel contributed to the preparation of this publication. Hundreds, perhaps thousands, of others throughout the Government also deserve credit for their valuable contributions.

A

Andrew Abrams
Chandana L. Achanta
Brenda Aguilar
Shagufta Ahmed
Steven Aitken
David W. Alekson
Victoria L. Allred
Melanie R. Althaus
Lois E. Altoft
Jessica A. Andreasen
Benton T. Arnett
Aviva R. Aron-Dine
Anna R. Arroyo
Emily Schultz Askew
Lisa L. August
Karen Augustin
Renee Austin
Kristin B. Aveille
Sara Aviel
Anjam Aziz

B

Michelle B. Bacon
Jessie W. Bailey
Paul W. Baker
Carol A. Bales
Pratik S. Banjade
Avital Bar-Shalom
Amy C. Barker
Taylor J. Barnard-
  Hawkins
Bethanne Barnes
Jonathan Barnett
Patti A. Barnett
Jody M. Barringer
Mary Barth
Sarah O. Bashadi
Amy Batchelor
Jennifer Wagner Bell
Kheira Z. Benkreira
Joseph J. Berger
Benjamin Bergersen
Elizabeth A. Bernhard
Jamie Berryhill

Kyle Bibby
Emily R. Bilbao
Christopher Biolsi
Danielle Blanks
Mathew C. Blum
James Boden
Erin Boeke Burke
Cassie L. Boles
Melissa B. Bomberger
Cole A. Borders
Ariel V. Boyarsky
William J. Boyd
Mollie H. Bradlee
Joshua Brammer
Michael Branson
Alex M. Brant
Joseph F. Breighner
Eric J. Bremen
Andrea M. Brian
Erik G. Brine
Candice M. Bronack
Jonathan M. Brooks
Jayson Browder
Dustin S. Brown
Jamal T. Brown
Michael T. Brunetto
Robert W. Buccigrosso
Shannon Spillane
  Buckingham
Kathryn Buckler
Pearl Buenvenida
Paul Bugg
Tom D. Bullers
Scott H. Burgess
Ben Burnett
Ryan M. Burnette
John D. Burnim
John C. Burton
Nicholas S. Burton
Mark Bussow
Dylan W. Byrd

C

Steven Cahill
Emily E. Cain
Gregory J. Callanan

Erin L. Campbell
Eric Cardoza
Matthew B. Carney
J. Kevin Carroll
William S. S. Carroll
Scott D. Carson
Sean C. Casey
Mary Cassell
Daniel E. Chandler
Maureen M. Charan-
  Danzot
James Chase
Nida Chaudhary
Michael Chelen
Anita Chellaraj
Yungchih Chen
Gezime Christian
Deidre A. Ciliento
Michael Clark
Peter Clunie
Ilona Cohen
Angela Colamaria
William P. Cole
Victoria W. Collin
Debra M. Collins
Kelly T. Colyar
Karen M. Conaway
Jose A. Conde
Margot Conrad
Sarah Haile Coombs
Shavonnia Corbin-
  Johnson
Justin P. Cormier
Jessie Crabb
Catherine E. Crato
Joseph Crilley
Rose Crow
Juliana Crump
Craig Crutchfield
David M. Cruz-
  Glaudemans
C. Tyler Curtis
William Curtis
Charles R. Cutshall

D

Nadir Dalal
D. Michael Daly
Rody Damis
Neil B. Danberg
Lisa E. Danzig
Alexander J. Daumit
Joanne Chow
  Davenport
Kenneth L. Davis
Margaret B. Davis-
  Christian
Chad J. Day
Carolyn M. Dee
Michael Deich
Tasha M. Demps
Paul J. Denaro
Chris J. DeRusha
John H. Dick
Darbi S. Dillon
Julie Allen Dingley
Derek M. Donahoo
Angela M. Donatelli
Paul S. Donohue
Shaun L. S. Donovan
Bridget C. Dooling
Vladik Dorjets
Lisa Cash Driskill
Laura G. Drummond
Laura E. Duke
Matthew S. Dunn

E

Matthew C. Eanes
Jacqueline A. Easley
Jeanette Edwards
Emily M. Eelman
Claire Ehmann
Anthony Eleftherion
Christopher J. Elliott
Tonya L. Ellison-Mays
Thomas H. Elwell
Adaeze B. Enekwechi
Noah Engelberg
Michelle A. Enger

Mark T. Erwin
Edward V. Etzkorn

F

Chris Fairhall
Robert Fairweather
Edna Falk Curtin
Michael C. Falkenheim
Hunter Fang
Shao W. Fang
Kara L. Farley-Cahill
Christine E.
   Farquharson
Kira R. Fatherree
Andrew R. Feldman
Patricia A. Ferrell
Russell Ficken
Lesley A. Field
Mary Fischietto
E Holly Fitter
John J. Fitzpatrick
Josephine M. Fleet
Darlene B. Fleming
Tera L. Fong
Nicholas A. Fraser
Elizabeth A. Frederick
Farrah B. Freis
Nathan J. Frey
Tamara L. Fucile

G

Arianne J. Gallagher
Elizabeth Garlow
Andrew Garrett
Marc Garufi
Thomas O. Gates
Jeremy J. Gelb
Roy J. Gelfand
Emily R. Gentile
James Ghiloni
Tony Gilbert
Brian Gillis
Janelle R. Gingold
Joshua S. Glazer
Porter O. Glock
Andrea L. Goel
Ja'Cia D. Goins
Jeffrey D. Goldstein
Oscar Gonzalez
Charles H. Grant
Kathleen A. Gravelle
Richard E. Green

Aron Greenberg
Brandon H. Greene
Elyse Greenwald
Justin M. Grimes
Hester C. Grippando
Marc Groman
Stephanie Grosser
Andrea L. Grossman
Locher M. Grove

H

Michael B. Hagan
Tia Hall
Jaelith Hall-Rivera
William F. Hamele
John Theodore
   Hammer
Jennifer L. Hanson
Linda W. Hardin
Derek M. Hardison
Dionne Hardy
Melanie Harris
Patsy W. Harris
Holly R. Harrison
Nicholas R. Hart
Paul Harvey
Ryan Bensussan
   Harvey
Abdullah Hasan
Alyson M. Hatchett
Kyle W. Hathaway
Laurel S. Havas
Nora K. Hawkins
Mark Hazelgren
Jeffrey K. Hendrickson
John David Henson
Kevin W. Herms
Alexander G.
   Hettinger
Peter N. Hewitt
Gretchen T. Hickey
Michael J. Hickey
Cortney J. Higgins
Mary Lou Hildreth
Amanda M. Hill
Andrew D. Hire
Thomas E. Hitter
Jennifer E. Hoef
Adam Hoffberg
Stuart Hoffman
James S. Holm
Michele Holt
Lynette Hornung-Kobes

Brian M. Hoxie
Grace Hu
Jamie W. Huang
Rhea A. Hubbard
Kathy M. Hudgins
Jeremy D. Hulick
Alexander T. Hunt
Lorraine D. Hunt
James C. Hurban
Jaki Mayer Hurwitz

I

Adrian B. Ilagan
Tae H. Im
Mason C. Ingram
Anthony C. Irish
Janet E. Irwin
Paul Iwugo

J

Antoine L. Jackson
Crystal E. Jackson
Keisha Jackson
Brian M. Jacob
Manish Jain
Varun M. Jain
Carol Jenkins
Nate Jenkins
Will Jenkins
Carol S. Johnson
Katherine B. Johnson
Kim I. Johnson
Michael D. Johnson
Bryant A. Jones
Danielle Y. Jones
Denise Bray Jones
Lisa M. Jones
Othni A. Jones
Shannon Maire Joyce
Hee Jun

K

Paul A. Kagan
Daniel S. Kaneshiro
Jacob H. Kaplan
Michele D. Kaplan
Jenifer Liechty
   Karwoski
Regina L. Kearney
Douglas (Doug) E.
   Keeler

Daniel J. Keenaghan
Matthew J. Keeneth
Ioanna Kefalas
Hunter S. Kellett
Cliff Kellogg
Timothy J. Kelly
Nancy B. Kenly
Amanda R. Kepko
Alper A. Kerman
Saha Khaterzai
Paul E. Kilbride
James H. Kim
Rachael Y. Kim
Barry King
Emily C. King
Kelly Kinneen
David E. Kirkpatrick
Benjamin W. Klay
Greg Knollman
Kevin E. Kobee
Elizabeth B.
   Kolmstetter
Chloe Kontos
Andrea G. Korovesis
Lori A. Krauss
Joydip Kundu

L

Christopher D. LaBaw
Jonathan S. Lachman
Leonard L. Lainhart
James A. Laity
Chad A. Lallemand
Lawrence L. Lambert
Alexandra Langley
Daniel LaPlaca
Anthony Larkins
Derek B. Larson
Eric P. Lauer
Jessie L. LaVine
Suzette Lawson
Mary A. Lazzeri
Karen F. Lee
Sarah S. Lee
Susan E. Leetmaa
Annika N. Lescott
Stuart Levenbach
Malissa C. Levesque
Matthew I. Levine
John C. Levock
Sheila Lewis
Bryan León
Jeremy L. León

Wendy L. Liberante
Richard Alan
　Lichtenberger
Sara Rose Lichtenstein
Kristina E. Lilac
Erika Liliedahl
Jennifer M. Lipiew
Adam Lipton
Joseph M. Liss
Thomas Liu
Tsitsi Liywalii
Rayden Llano
Patrick Locke
Sara R. López
Alexander W. Louie
Adrienne Lucas
Gideon F. Lukens

M

Chi T. Mac
Deborah L. Macaulay
Ryan J. MacMaster
David A. Mader
Natalia Mahmud
Claire A. Mahoney
Chad Maisel
Dominic J. Mancini
Noah S. Mann
Robert Mann
Iulia Z. Manolache
Sharon Mar
Harrison D. Marks
Celinda A. Marsh
Daniel Marti
Brendan A. Martin
Rochelle W. Martinez
Nicole M. Martinez
　Moore
Richard K. Mattick
Andrew Mayock
Shelly McAllister
George H. McArdle
Scott J. McCaughey
Alexander J.
　McClelland
James McCoy
Connor G. McCrone
Timothy D. McCrosson
Anthony W. McDonald
Christine A. McDonald
Katrina A. McDonald
Renford A. McDonald
Kevin E. McGinnis

Luther McGinty
Tara McGuinness
Kevin J. McKernin
Christopher McLaren
Robin J. McLaughry
Megan B. McPhaden
William J. McQuaid
William J. Mea
Melissa R. Medeiros
Aalok S. Mehta
Inna L. Melamed
Patrick J. Mellon
Barbara A. Menard
Flavio Menasce
Jose A. Mendez
Jessica Nielsen Menter
Justin R. Meservie
P. Thaddeus
　Messenger
Todd Messer
Jordan Metoyer
William L. Metzger
Daniel J. Michelson-
　Horowitz
Ashley E. Miller
Julie L. Miller
Kimberly Miller
Susan M. Minson
Asma Mirza
Mia Mitchell
Rehana I. Mohammed
Shara Mohtadi
Emily Mok
Stephanie Mok
Claire Monteiro
Joe Montoni
Cindy H. Moon
Johanna L. Mora
Zachary Morgan
Kelly Morrison
Joshua A. Moses
Kelsey Mowatt-
　Larssen
James S. Mulligan
Taylor Mulligan
Niyat Mulugheta
Tecla A. Murphy
Christian G. Music
Hayley W. Myers
Kimberley L Myers

N

Jennifer M. Nading
Jeptha E. Nafziger
Larry J. Nagl
Anna M. Naimark
Barry Napear
Robert Nassif
Scott Nathan
Ashley M. Nathanson
Allie R. Neill
Kimberly P. Nelson
Melissa K. Neuman
Joanie F. Newhart
John D. Newman
Kimberly Armstrong
　Newman
Teresa O. Nguyen
Brian A. Nichols
John T. Nichols
Tige Nishimoto
Douglas E. Nivens, II
Ross Nodurft
Tim H. Nusraty
Joseph B. Nye

O

Erin O'Brien
Devin L. O'Connor
Matthew J. O'Kane
Brendan J. O'Meara
Justin M. Oliveira
Paul D. Oliver
Brandon J. Ona
Farouk Ophaso
Allison B. Orris
Edgar Ortega
Jared Ostermiller
Tyler J. Overstreet
D. Brooke Owens
Adeniran Oyebade

P

Benjamin J. Page
Heather C. Pajak
Jake Paris
Jennifer E. Park
Sangkyun Park
Sharon Parrott
John C. Pasquantino
Angeli Patel
Arati N. Patel

Terri B. Payne
Christopher V. Pece
Falisa L. Peoples-Tittle
Michael A. Perz
Andrea M. Petro
Stephen P. Petzinger
Stacey Que-Chi Pham
Carolyn R. Phelps
Karen A. Pica
Brian K. Pipa
Joseph Pipan
Kimberly A. Pohland
Aaron W. Pollon
Mark J. Pomponio
Ruxandra Pond
Ally G. Pregulman
Celestine Michelle
　Pressley
Larrimer S. Prestosa
Jamie M. Price
Daniel Proctor
Robert Purdy

R

Lucas R. Radzinschi
Latonda Glass Raft
John Rahaghi
Moshiur Rahman
Maria S. Raphael
Aaron D. Ray
Jeffrey Reczek
Meagan Reed
Mark A. Reger
Rudolph G. Regner
Paul B. Rehmus
Sean C. Reilly
Thomas M. Reilly
Richard J. Renomeron
Keri A. Rice
Shannon A. Richter
Kyle S. Riggs
Fermaint Rios, Jr.
Emma K. Roach
Beth Higa Roberts
Daniel C. Roberts
Donovan Robinson
Marshall J. Rodgers
Meredith B. Romley
Dan T. Rosenbaum
Eric Rosenfield
Jefferson Rosman
Caroline K. Ross
David J. Rowe

Mario Roy
Danielle R. Royal
Brian Rozental
Joshua Rubin
Jacqueline Rudas
Trevor H. Rudolph
Anne E. Rung
Erika H. Ryan

S

Fouad P. Saad
Preeya Saikia
John Asa Saldivar
Alvand A. Salehi
Mark S. Sandy
Subu Sangameswar
Katherin Monica
    Santoro
Joel J. Savary
Philippa Scarlett
Lisa Schlosser
Tricia Schmitt
Kyle Benjamin
    Schneps
Andrew M. Schoenbach
Daniel K. Schory
Jack L. Schreibman
Margo Schwab
Nancy E. Schwartz
Mariarosaria
    Sciannameo
Tony Scott
Jasmeet K. Seehra
Robert B. Seidner
Max C. Sgro
Kala Shah
Shahid N. Shah
Shabnam
    Sharbatoghlie
Tanzia Sharmin
Dianne Shaughnessy
Jessica Shaver-Lee
Paul Shawcross
Howard A. Shelanski
Melissa Shih
Gary F. Shortencarrier
Sara R. Sills
Samantha E.
    Silverberg
Benjamin R. Simms
Brandon A. Simons
Whitney O. Singletary

Robert Sivinski
Benjamin J. Skidmore
Jack Smalligan
Craig M. Smith
Curtina O. Smith
Stannis M. Smith
Erica Socker
Silvana Solano
Roderic A. Solomon
Raquel Spencer
David A. Spett
John H. Spittell
Kathryn B. Stack
Travis C. Stalcup
Scott R. Stambaugh
Nora Stein
Lamar R. Stewart
Gary R. Stofko
Carla B. Stone
Terry W. Stratton
Joseph G. Stuntz
Frank Sturges
Thomas J. Suarez
Kevin J. Sullivan
Sarah Sullivan
Jessica L. Sun
Erin Sutton
Yasaman Sutton
Jennifer A. Swartz
Christine Sweeney
Ben Sweezy
Christina Swoope
Aaron L. Szabo

T

Jamie R. Taber
Robert D. Talcovitz
Teresa A. Tancre
Naomi S. Taransky
Stephanie Tatham
Benjamin K. Taylor
Myra L. Taylor
Ruben Tejeda
Randy Tharp
Amanda L. Thomas
Judith F. Thomas
Payton A. Thomas
Will Thomas
Courtney B.
    Timberlake
Philip Tizzani
Thomas Tobasko

Rosanna Torres
    Pizarro
Mariel E. Townsend
Gil M. Tran
Natalie Trochimiuk
S. Lorén Trull
Lily C. Tsao
Donald L. Tuck
Austin Turner
Melissa H. Turner
Benjamin J. Turpen

U

Nicolas Ufier
Carolyn T. Ugolino
Troy A. Uhlman
Shraddha Upadhyaya
Darrell J. Upshaw
JoEllen Urban
Taylor J. Urbanski

V

Matthew J. Vaeth
Ofelia M. Valeriano
Amanda L. Valerio
Cynthia Vallina
Haley Van Dyck
Sarita Vanka
David W. Varvel
Areletha L. Venson
Alexandra Ventura
Patricia A. Vinkenes
Dean R. Vonk
Ann M. Vrabel

W

James A. Wade
Rana Wahdan
Katherine K. Wallman
Heather V. Walsh
Kan Wang
Tim Wang
Sharon A. Warner
Michael Watts
Gary Waxman
Mark A. Weatherly
Bess Weaver
Jeffrey A. Weinberg
Sharon K. Weiner
David Weisshaar

Philip R. Wenger
Max W. West
Michael S. Wetklow
Steve Wetzel
Arnette C. White
Catherine E. White
Kamela White
Kim S. White
Sherron R. White
Chad S. Whiteman
Katie Whitman
Brian Widuch
Mary Ellen Wiggins
Shimika Wilder
Calvin L. Williams
Debra (Debbie) L.
    Williams
Rebecca Williams
Jamie Wilson
Paul A. Winters
Julia B. Wise
Julie Wise
Elizabeth D. Wolkomir
Raymond J.M. Wong
Charles E.
    Worthington
Lauren E. Wright
Sophia M. Wright
William Wu
Bert Wyman
Steven N. Wynands

X

Mohao Xi

Y

Abra S. Yeh
Melany N. Yeung
David Y. Yi
Elliot Y. Yoon
Carl H. Young, III

Z

Ali A. Zaidi
Thomas P. Ziehnert
Bill Zielinski
Gail S Zimmerman